Case Studies in
Computer Aided Learning

Case Studies in
Computer Aided Learning

Edited by

Robert L. Blomeyer, Jr.
and
C. Dianne Martin

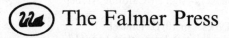 The Falmer Press

(A member of the Taylor & Francis Group)

London · New York · Philadelphia

UK   The Falmer Press, 4 John Street, London, WC1N 2ET

USA   The Falmer Press, Taylor & Francis Inc., 1900 Frost Road, Suite 101, Bristol, PA 19007

First published 1991

Library of Congress Cataloging-in-Publication Data
Case studies of computer aided learning/edited by Robert L.
   Blomeyer and C. Dianne Martin.
      p.   cm.
    Includes bibliographical references and index.
    ISBN 1–85000–646–6 — ISBN 1–85000–647–4 (pbk.)
    1.   Education — United States — Data processing — Case
studies.   2.   Education — Great Britain — Data processing
— Case studies.   3.   Educational innovations — Case
studies.   I. Blomeyer, Robert L.
II.   Martin, C. Dianne.
LB1028. 43. C37   1991
370′.285—dc20   90–42903
                                               CIP

British Library Cataloguing-in-Publication Data
Case studies of computer aided learning.
   1.   Schools. Teaching. Applications of computer systems
   I.   Blomeyer, Robert L. II. Martin, C. Dianne
   371.334

   ISBN 1-85000-646-6
   ISBN 1-85000-647-4 pbk

Jacket design by Caroline Archer

Typeset in 10/12 Times by
Graphicraft Typesetters Ltd. H.K.

Printed in Great Britain by Burgess Science Press, Basingstoke on paper which has a specified pH value on final paper manufacture of not less than 7.5 and is therefore 'acid free'.

Contents

Contents

Introduction

Computers, Clay Pots, and Case Studies

Ray C. Rist

Had I the opportunity to write the introduction to a volume such as this ten years ago, I am sure I would have begun with an emphasis on how tenuous were our understandings of and approaches to the study of educational innovation. The research literature on change was fragmented and its applications to education were uneven. The work on studying the adoptions of innovations at the different levels of a school system was just off the ground. And finally, the emphasis on the process and dynamics of implementation as a key dimension in the innovation effort was recognized by but a scant number of researchers. In short the situation in educational research was such that clear pronouncements and thoughtful assessments of what we had come to learn about educational innovation were few and far between.

The irony is that ten years later, the introduction to this volume can begin the same way. The study of innovation as a source of change has been progressing at a noticeably slow pace; we are not much removed from our understandings of a decade ago. Unfortunately, this coincides with the United States undertaking a large, costly, and broadly supported effort at educational innovation — the introduction of computer technology into the classroom. That this innovation has been attempted without much serious research as to how it might be successfully implemented bespeaks the vulnerability to a 'rediscover the wheel' approach in city after city across the nation.

Indeed, school district after school district has been using scarce monies to equip their schools with computers and the associated paraphernalia, be it software, furniture, specially ventilated rooms, or in-service training for the teachers, to name but four. Amidst this financial and organizational commitment to a high profile innovation, the educational research community has not kept pace. Basic questions remain unanswered, for example, on:

1   the cognitive impacts that computers have on students;
2   the ways that computers have changed the style and content of teaching;

3   how such an innovation finds its way successfully into some schools
     and not into others;
4   the impacts differential distribution of computers among school dis-
     tricts will have on children from different racial, regional, or language
     backgrounds; and
5   how computers might change the basic logic of 'one classroom and
     one teacher' which has so dominated the American approach to
     organizing the learning experience.

Six of the papers in this volume are by American authors. They describe
various efforts to introduce and institutionalize computers within schools. As
such, the papers provide a window on how this particular innovation is faring
in American schools. The seventh paper comes from England and describes
how such studies are not yet happening there.

All six of the US papers have employed a qualitative case study approach, deliberately bypassing efforts at quantification, documenting 'input-
output' measures, or amassing time series data on minutes and hours that the
computers were in use. Two of the papers are now themselves more than ten
years old and serve as a critical benchmark from which to assess changes
in how the research community has come to understand this massive educational innovation. That the latter four papers have clearly built upon some
of the insights and approaches of the earlier two papers is encouraging.
Further, the later papers have also been able to make use of some recent
theoretical developments that strengthens their own work. This is most notable in these papers with respect to implementation.

What remains disconcerting (but not the fault of these authors) is the *ad
hoc* nature of these studies, each done in a different place, asking somewhat
different questions, and each emphasizing different findings. It is simply too
soon in this area to find much theoretical or policy convergence. But having
said this, the papers do share a concern with one key question, 'What is going
on here?' And it is because of the importance in trying to find an answer to
that question that this book is unique and welcomed. It deserves the careful
attention of all who are concerned with educational innovations in general
and computer applications in particular.

Computers and Case Studies

While the current collection of case studies addresses different aspects of the
innovation at the respective sites, it is important to note that each of these
papers has also sought out for study a most elusive concept — organizational
change. As noted above, this is an area of inquiry where there remains much
to do to understand how technological change is introduced, modified, and
eventually absorbed into an organization. That the present authors have tried
while so many others have only settled for developing measures of student

performance or new software applications, for example, is entirely to their credit.

What these six case studies do offer is a means to learn about a complex instance of educational innovation. Indeed, their choice of the case study approach is entirely appropriate when considering the methodological options as well as the intended uses of their research. Taken together they provide a more comprehensive understanding of the relation of computer technology and schooling than if each were taken alone. Each case is concerned with extensive description and analysis of their individual instance, trying to tease out the relation of the innovation to the context in which it was introduced. That such papers are both needed and only rarely available suggests just how little systematic study this particular area of organizational change has received.

The distance the work in this area still has to travel can be put into perspective by referring to a recent publication of the United States General Accounting Office. In a 1987 paper entitled *Case Study Evaluations,* the GAO described at least six different applications of the case study method (GAO, 1987). These six applications ranged from the most basic ('illustrative') to the most complex ('cumulative'). The criteria for each of these six applications can be applied to the papers in this present volume. When doing so, it is readily apparent that current case study approaches to the introduction of computers into schools as an educational innovation is at the low end of the continuum, if one accepts these papers as good representatives of present efforts. The six papers here can be individually described as 'illustrative' or 'exploratory'. They cannot be described in terms that are associated with the other end of the continuum, i.e., as assessment of 'program effects' or as being 'cumulative' in nature. Collectively, however, these case studies invite comparisons that evoke naturalistic generalization.

The present status of case study work for this particular educational innovation may be explained in several ways. First, the innovation itself is relatively young and has not been a part of the educational scene for nearly as long as have other innovations such as desegregation or Headstart, for example. Thus one might argue that there simply has not been the time to develop the same level of understanding or sophistication.

A second possible reason for the current state of case study research is that the innovation itself has been entirely decentralized. The decision to place computers in classrooms has been made at the local level, period. There have been no federal incentives nor have there been federal mandates to do so. Consequently, decisions are made at the local level as to when, why, and how computers will be introduced into the schools. Developing a research agenda when confronted with these thousand points of light — all generated at the local level and uncoordinated from one district to another — is not possible for other than a well-funded and sizeable research organization. Such an effort, to date, has not occurred. The individual researcher is necessarily left with the option for studying a single instance, or perhaps several instances, hoping thereby to be able to generate at least some basic site-specific data.

A third plausible explanation for the current state of case study research on computers as an educational innovation is that it may be simply too soon to determine what effects can be attributed to the computers per se. Establishing causality is never easy, and in this instance it may be more difficult than normal. Determining the contribution of the computer in contrast to so many competing explanations for why student performance did or did not rise, for example, is simply not assessed with an off-the-shelf evaluation strategy. Thus, the researcher is left to provide descriptive data on the events and perceptions surrounding the introduction of the innovation. Doing more at present, developing a case study approach that would assess causality, is not possible.

A fourth (and here last) possible explanation for the present situation with regard to case study research on computers as an educational innovation is that qualitative researchers have a hard time conceptualizing and then studying technology. The case of computers in the schools is but a particular and most recent instance of a more general situation. Qualitative researchers do not gravitate towards the study of physics in schools, typing classes, or strategies being employed to teach calculus. Rather, they move towards the study of social interaction, patterns of organization, and the relation of the individual to the setting. More on this shortly.

The six case studies in this volume do represent an important contribution, as noted above, to our understanding of the various changes that come about in schools as a result of the introduction of computers. Indeed, these cases document that the change has taken place within the schools on at least two levels and that both levels are important to address so far as the institution is concerned. Succinctly, this particular educational innovation has to be studied on both the organizational and the cultural levels. Organizational changes include the introduction of new curriculum materials, a re-arranging of activities during the school day for students, the introduction of a new cadre of 'experts' into the school, new maintenance personnel to attend to the machines, re-arranging the physical space in the individual classrooms, a new area of budget concern for the principal and central administrators, and the multiple aspects of dealing with computers and software security, to name but several. These papers make clear that bringing computers into schools has the very real potential to fundamentally change the 'business as usual' assumptions educators might have about how they ought to go through their day. The organizations simply do not remain static once computers are introduced.

But having said that the organizations are not static is not the same as saying that the changes are all positive. Introducing computers produced resentment, hostility, and skepticism among some teachers and administrators.

Not everyone saw the computer as a positive addition to the school or to the individual classroom. Organizationally, this effort at innovation was not without some costs just as it was not without some benefits. But how these are distributed says much about who and where in educational organizations one might find those receptive to innovation and change, as well as where one might find resistors.

The second area where these papers make clear that this innovation needs to be carefully studied is in the cultural ethos of the school. While documenting changes here is difficult, evidence is nonetheless available. Specifically, these papers show that the switch from thinking of what should go on in school as being primarily the interaction of teacher and student to also including the student-machine relationship has been vital to the impact of the innovation. It is only with this change in perspective that the dissonance decreased, for example, on the lessening reliance on books, on using time that had been used for going to the library for now going to the computer room, or the diminished time for reading aloud. Legitimizing sources of information for the student which were not conventional, e.g., teacher or librarian, changed some traditional cultural perspectives in the school.

There were also cultural changes of another general type that impacted the school. The introduction of computers meant that by the time the students were in the middle school (or high school at the latest), many of them knew as much as or more about the computers than did their teachers. This shift in expertise and familiarity with the innovation caused some clear changes in the previous relations of teachers and students vis-à-vis decisions over curriculum content and the pace of the presentations. In the instance of this innovation, traditional differences of status and role responsibilities between teachers and students diminished, but did not disappear.

Another level of cultural impact was the high level of expectations that the parents had for their children becoming computer literate. This emphasis came concurrently with the teachers themselves learning about computers and their applications. Consequently, the teachers were often on the defensive about their own level of knowledge. The computers became a challenge to their traditional areas of expertise as well as their views of themselves as professionals. They as teachers were students in this area and it was a position many did not like — especially when the parents were constantly pressing for still more applications. The teachers were confronting an innovation that moved at a fast pace and with an ever expanding knowledge base that was outside the realm of expertise for many of them. It had been one thing to learn a new textbook in every five to eight years whenever new book adoptions took place. Computers and their ever changing software were something else.

Introducing computers into the schools has changed the contour of the learning field. How the system worked in the past has not held up to the pressures of this innovation. Administrators, teachers, students and parents alike have all had to cope with an innovation that is a moving target — either in its technical dimensions or in its implications for the culture and organization of the school.

Computers and Clay Pots:
Some Final Comments on Methodology

As I prepared to write this Introduction, I reviewed a considerable corpus of qualitative research on schools. I looked in particular for those instances where the focus was on the role or impact that technology had on an individual school or even an individual classroom. I found little to no qualitative work in this area. There were multiple studies of gender socialization, race relations, classroom interaction patterns, high school peer cultures, the roles and responsibilities of administrators, to name several. But when I tried to find studies on the impacts of technology, e.g., television, tape recorders, and, indeed, computers, there was very little to be found. The issue of why this is so is beyond the scope of these remarks. But it is apparent that those doing qualitative research in schools are both more comfortable with and interested in the interactions and relationships among organizations or individuals than in the presence of technology.

This is no small omission, given that technology has been such a dominant concern and emphasis of the innovations in American education for more than several decades. Little has been done qualitatively to address the relation of education and technology. Not attending to the question, 'What is going on here?' speaks of a serious gap in our understandings of American schooling. The British paper included here makes explicit that the gap exists there as well. Given that the tradition in England on the use of qualitative research in schools is at least as strong as one can find in the States, the question persists as to why qualitative researchers have studiously avoided the area.

While the traditional roots of qualitative work come from anthropology and sociology, there is nothing there that should either preclude or deter researchers from studying current applications of technology. Just as it was acceptable to study the uses of clay pots in agrarian societies, so it is appropriate that attention should be given to technology in our own society.

There is this curious blind side to much of the work on our schools. Technology is bringing major change into the schools — and presumably has been for some time now — and the research community responds with the sounds of silence. There are whole clusters of questions related to the innovation that pose challenges for the qualitative researcher. The questions are related to the levels and directions of change that the innovation has brought about, its acceptance in different sectors of the educational system, impacts on formal and informal status systems, consequences for the curriculum, and on and on. I understand that it is an empirical question as to how much change, at what speed and in what sectors of education computers are having the greatest impact. But that there is so little work that even asks the minimal questions about technology and its impacts suggests whole areas of work open to fruitful inquiry.

If I am correct that there is a dearth of work on the introduction of computers and their instructional as well as organizational impacts, then the contribution of the present volume becomes even more important. These papers represent a unique collection of research efforts to systematically examine the place of computers in the schools. The individual authors do not offer us global understandings nor do they generate macro theoretical frameworks for the study of technology in education. What they do contribute are carefully crafted case studies on the introduction, diffusion, and uneven adoption of a highly popular (and costly) educational innovation.

This small collection of cases, spread out over time and done in different parts of the country by different researchers, represents a leap forward that has been badly needed in our study of education. What they suggest is that managing change is not easy, the adoption of innovation takes time, and the final cost-benefit ratio may look nothing like the one that initially guided the policy makers in their deliberations. These papers are a first foray into an area where many other researchers have feared to tread. Making sense, both in pedagogical and cultural terms, of the changes that computers have brought to the American classroom is a challenge that can no longer be ignored.

I doubt that there was equal resistance among early anthropologists to study clay pots or among early sociologists to study juvenile gangs as there seems to be at present to the qualitative study of technology. That technology shapes our lives in dramatic ways day in and day out is a given truth. That it shapes key aspects of how we structure the educational experience for students may also be taken as given. But that we know so little of the process or of the consequences of this innovation drops a pressing research challenge into our laps. The present authors are to be commended for taking up that challenge. They have prised open for all of us a window on the relation of technology and schooling that has been too long shut.

Reference

GENERAL ACCOUNTING OFFICE (1987) *Case study evaluations,* Washington DC: US General Accounting Office.

1

Micro Views of Computers in Education

Introduction

Over the past twenty to twenty-five years there has been much discussion about the advantages and disadvantages of using computers with children in the classroom setting. Educators have divided themselves into two camps — the computer enthusiasts and the skeptics. Armed with glowing anecdotal evidence of great intellectual strides made by children with computers, the enthusiasts have lobbied for the allocation of more and more resources for computer-related instruction and management in education. The skeptics, on the other hand continue to demand hard evidence to show that putting children on computers can increase the literacy rate, raise test scores, improve student retention, and indeed, give the overall boost to our ailing educational institutions that is being hyped by the vendors of the new instructional technologies.

Attempts to carry out quantitative research have produced meagre, and often conflicting, results of the effects of technology in the classroom. It is interesting to note that when reading the findings of such research, the researchers themselves often state that the results do not seem to reflect all of the gains that the particular treatment has produced. The studies in this book are illustrative of an emerging body of research in the United States and England that uses the qualitative lens to examine the dynamics of people interacting with computer technology in educational settings from a holistic, naturalistic point of view. Each study illustrates the richness of the qualitative paradigm in achieving a fuller picture of particular environments or 'microworlds' (Papert, 1980) in which children, teachers and administrators are interacting with computers.

These studies were chosen based upon two criteria. First, each one exemplifies the use of case study research techniques in examining the effects of computers in education. The discussions of methodology and the use of a variety of approaches to qualitative data in the respective studies show how the qualitative paradigm can be adapted to illustrate the relationship of technological innovation to education. Secondly, each case study presents data and findings that should be helpful to educators who are trying to make decisions now about the appropriate uses of new technologies in education. The power of such research is found not in sweeping generalizations, but rather, in the presentation of thick data that allows decision-makers to find similarities to their own situations. Such naturalistic generalizations can provide a way of 'knowing how things are' to guide future actions in similar cases (Stake, 1978). Bass (1978) stated this in her landmark study of alternative schools:

> In understanding this study ... we were primarily concerned with accurately describing the ... process in a few districts. We felt that by providing a qualitative sense of the factors that are important ... these case studies could help educational policymakers interested in developing educational options in other settings and suggest hypotheses for future research. (p. 17)

In the first section we present two studies that look at the effects of mainframe computer-assisted mathematics instruction (CAI) in two different classroom cultures. Both these studies were conducted during the late 1960s and are presented here both for their historical contribution to methodology and their relevance for contemporary policymaking. The Smith-Pohland article, 'Education, Technology and the Rural Highlands', is a reprint of a classic multiple-site case study of mainframe-based mathematics CAI implemented with teletypes as workstations. Its practical lessons about CAL remain valid and relevant fifteen years after its initial publication in *AERA Monograph Series on Curriculum Evaluation*, Number 7 (Stake, 1974).

In their anthropologically-oriented case study, Smith and Pohland provide a culturally sensitive analysis showing the introduction of a technology-based delivery system into an underdeveloped rural area of the United States. Data collected during the study were field notes produced from the on the-spot observation of children at the teletype terminals, summary observations and interpretations produced from informal interviews and discussions, and documents such as computer print-outs and formal records. Theirs is one of the first and certainly one of the methodologically significant studies of the genre.

The second study by Bernadine Evans Stake, 'PLATO and Fourth Grade Mathematics', was conducted in the late 1970s for the Electronic Testing Service (ETS). Like the Smith-Pohland study, it examines the use of mainframe-based mathematics CAI, but in a single fourth grade classroom. In this case, the computer-based math lessons are delivered by the PLATO[1] instructional system. The study also shows how use of an electronic mail facility on the system (p-notes) had consequences for instructional management and the development of functional literacy skills by participating students. This linkage between math instruction and language learning suggests that with some computer-aided learning systems, interactive instruction in all subject matter areas may have important consequences for language learning and development of literacy skills.

Stake's highly sensitive study takes place during the mid-1970s in a single classroom where PLATO mathematics materials were in use by fourth grade students. It contains one of the most detailed written accounts available describing the ecology of changes in the teacher's role that are necessary for students to successfully use CAI as a supplement to classroom learning. The data collection technique used in the study was the 'responsive case-study approach' in which ordinary people (teachers and students) tell the story through an independent account of their actions and words. According to Guba and Lincoln (1981), 'Events are documented and thoughts recorded in order to provide the readers with a vicarious experience' (p. xx). The experiences of the teacher and students detailed in this study may be typical of the initial fears, frustrations and rewards still experienced by teachers and students when CAI is integrated with classroom teaching and learning.

The observations and interpretations from these two important pioneering case studies of computer aided learning raise important questions about the overall effectiveness of and definition of an optimal role for computer aided instruction as an instructional tool. The continuing relevance of their findings illustrates the need for additional naturalistic research documenting the ways that teachers and students use instructional technologies in educational environments.

Note

1   The PLATO[R] computer-based instructional system (Programmed Logic for Automated Teaching Operation) was first invented by Dr. Donald Bitzer at the University of Illinois in the 1960s. Its successor (the NovaNET[SM] system) is the oldest and the largest computer-based instructional system in the world with over 12,000 hours of instructional materials in over 100 subject areas. PLATO[R] is a registered trademark of Control Data Corporation and NovaNET[SM] is a registered service Mark of University Communications Inc. at the University of Illinois.

References

BASS, G.V. (1978) 'District policies and the implementation of change', *A study of alternatives in American education, Vol. I* (Rand Report R-2170/1-NIE). Santa Monica, CA: Rand Corporation.

GUBA, E. and LINCOLN, Y. (1981) *Effective evaluation,* San Francisco: Jossey-Bass.

PAPERT, S. (1980) *Mindstorms,* New York: Basic Books.

STAKE, R.E. (1978) 'The case study method in social inquiry', *Educational Researcher,* 7, pp. 5–8.

STAKE, R.E. (Ed.) (1974) *Four evaluation examples: Anthropological, economic, narrative, and portrayal,* AERA monograph series on curriculum evaluation no. 7. Chicago: Rand McNallay.

Chapter 1

Education, Technology, and the Rural Highlands[1]

Louis M. Smith and Paul A. Pohland

A **full** evaluation results in a story, supported perhaps by statistics and profiles. It tells what happened. It reveals perceptions and judgments that different groups and individuals hold-obtained, I hope, by objective means. It tells of merit and shortcoming. As a bonus, it may offer generalizations ('The moral of the story is...'.) for the guidance of subsequent educational programs. (Stake, 1967, p. 5)

Consider the following. In a remodeled broom closet of a school located in a remote and all-but-forgotten 'hollow' of the Rural Highlands, a child is seated in front of a standard teletype. Oblivious to his surroundings, including another child watching intently over his shoulder, he depresses the 'start' button on the right of the keyboard. Almost instantaneously the teletype chatters into life and, through the wonders of twentieth-century technology, a message appears on the roll of paper in front of him: 'Please type your number and name'. Carefully the child types his number — each child has his own — strikes the space bar, spells his first name, and spaces again. Without breaking the rhythm the teletype prints the last name, drops down a line, prints a coded drill number, and after briefly identifying the kind of arithmetic drill to be presented (for example, addition, subtraction, mixed drill), presents the first problem (for example, $4 + \_\_ = 9$). The typewheel repositions itself for the answer and with an air of expectancy waits for the child to type in the answer. If the answer is correct and completed within ten seconds, the teletype prints out the next problem. If an incorrect response is given, the message appears: 'No, try again'. After a predetermined series of problems has been presented, the child is given the total number of problems worked, the percent correct, and the number of seconds taken to complete the drill. The drill is concluded as the teletype prints out a final message: 'Goodbye, *(name)* Please tear off on the dotted line'. Grasping the corner of his print-out, the child tears it off the roll, and rolling it up into a cylinder returns to his classroom as the child who has been watching impatiently begins the cycle anew.

Such was one of our images of the Computer Assisted Instruction (CAI) program as it existed in the Rural Highlands during the 1968 – 69 school year. Yet it was not the sole image; it does not represent the 'full' story of CAI. In some fundamental sense it represents too small a slice of the totality of CAI. As Malinowski (1935) says of the Trobriand Islander in another but analogous context:

> If you want to know him, you must meet him in his yam gardens, among his palm groves or in his taro fields. You must see him digging his black or brown soil among the white outcrops of dead coral and building the fence, which surrounds his garden with a 'magical wall' of prismatic structures and triangular supports. You must follow him when, in the cool of the day, he watches the seed rise and develop within the precincts of the 'magical wall,' which at first gleams like gold among the green of the new growth and then shows bronzed or grey under the rich garland of yam foliage. (p. xix)

So it was with CAI. Our Melanesia was the Rural Mountains; the school children of the region our Trobrianders. Our yam gardens were the classrooms, and our palm groves and taro fields the broom closets, special rooms, and odd corners that housed the teletype terminals. We, too, noted the 'magical wall of prismatic structures and triangular supports' that enclosed CAI. In the broadest sense that 'wall' was the culture of the region itself. At another level it was a complex of organizations — state and federal agencies, universities, school districts, regional laboratories — that planned, supported, and administered the program. At yet another level, it was a blend of issues related to curriculum innovation, diffusion of technology, and improvement of instructional processes. A 'full story' would of necessity take all of these issues into account. Our task, however, was more limited: we were to contribute to an evaluation of the CAI program.

CAI as a Complex Social and Technical System: The First Major Finding

The System Is Up, Is Down, Is Up....

The major finding of this study was that the Computer Assisted Instruction (CAI) program neither ran smoothly nor consistently throughout most of the school year. Not until the middle of March did the program operate with some degree of reliability. April 1 was the first time the number of drills reached the 1,000 mark; however, not until the middle of April did the program consistently reach that level.[2] As late as April 3, teachers reported to us, 'We have had nothing since February 17 ... not a single day (all year) that was error free.... The kids don't talk about it much any more' (Field Notes, 4/3).

Problems with the ABC-4 computer at Leestown and the ABC-6 at the Northeast Institute for Research in the Behavioral Sciences (NIRBS) almost totally disrupted the program for about four months. This situation combined with the problems of malfunctioning teletypes and data sets made for erratic performance. In the long run, the 1968–69 experiences may well prove to be invaluable for program developers; however, for the individuals engaged in the program it was an unending stream of frustration. Perhaps that mood was best captured by one little girl whose print-out contained a misprinted message, 'Cry again'. And, as the child reported to her teacher, 'Oh, Mrs. Martin, I could just cry again and again' (5/29).

As a result of this almost total breakdown of the system during the period of our observation, we rephrased our initial guiding question to: 'What difficulties arise when one brings the most sophisticated educational technology into a rural, economically deprived, and still relatively isolated region of the country?'

Analysis and Interpretation of the Social and Technical Systems

The cultural milieu of the Rural Highlands

Human activity, as Sindell (1969) observes, does not take place in a 'social and cultural vacuum'. Rather, it is embedded in a complex configuration of beliefs and attitudes, culturally prescribed roles, statuses, and social identities, economics, politics, and geography. So it was with CAI. As the CAI system struggled to attain operational status we found ourselves drawn more and more into an analysis of the culture of the Rural Mountains. It seemed to us that an anthropological approach was appropriate if the 'full story' of CAI was to be told and if the dynamics of CAI as an innovative educational program were to be revealed.

We were not insensitive to the possibility that outsiders may misread norms and values of a culture different in some respects from one's own. We hoped, however, to avoid the dangers of the casual visitor who deprecates the people as unmotivated, uncaring, and unconcerned. We spent too much time in the region and came to know intimately a small number of the people, particularly among the students, teachers, and administrators, to take that narrow view. Additionally, we have seen the hostility engendered by outsiders who moved in and out of the region quickly with programs of one kind or another and who failed to get to know the people, their needs, desires, and aspirations. However, as cultural elements impinged upon us they became integral parts of the overall study. As we observed and participated in the cultural life of the Rural Mountains certain aspects of life appeared as recurrent phenomena. We came to identify these facets by terms and phrases such as 'present-time orientation', 'simple hedonism', 'folk-hero imagery', 'stoicism', 'political orientation', 'kinship and nepotism', 'localism', 'conversationalism', and the like. All of these were closely interwoven into the life fabric of the region.

One does not live long in the Rural Highlands without sensing the localist orientation of the people. No doubt the topography of the region, its hills and valleys, and until recently the general lack of good transportation and communication facilities contributed to a restricted view of the world. Place locations were given in terms of 'up the creek' and 'down the hollow'. The common unit of identity was not the town, state, region, or country, but the county. Early in the field work we noted:

> One other item regarding the county as the unit came up as we were
> watching the *Today Show* on TV. When the program phased into
> the local accounts, even weather reports were phrased in terms of
> county units. More generally, local news was county news. (5/68)

Clearly, the localist outlook of the people posed problems for a program such as CAI which, at a minimum, required a regional perspective.

Time also had a different quality. The more frantic pace of the metropolitan community was strangely absent. There seemed to be little or no concern for deadlines, in getting things done today. For the successful operation of the CAI program this had dysfunctional consequences. As cases in point we would note the long delays in gathering, transmitting, and processing the names of children included in the program and the responses of telephone company personnel who, on being informed of problems one day, would postpone contacts and resolutions until another. Time seemed to have a present rather than future orientation. Perhaps the very immutability of the hills engendered this. Perhaps, too, the economic impoverishment of the region made the concerns of the day preeminent. Unfortunately for CAI, more long-range concerns — for example, the installation and testing of equipment — demanded future time considerations.

An additional aspect of the culture was that the population seemed to have generalist rather than specialist orientation. The people seemed to have experienced a broad general background and tended to engage in several kinds of jobs or roles simultaneously and equally well. It was common to find teachers who farmed, farmers who did semiskilled factory work, and so forth. Such an orientation seemed to blend with a higher tolerance or zone of indifference regarding anticipated levels of performance.

A sense of stoicism pervaded the region. We sensed resignation and acceptance of the way things are rather than a driving urge to change the world. One has visions of the difficulties of wresting a livelihood from the hills and hollows. We did not see the farther reaches of this continuum — despair and hopelessness — in the school people we met. Many accounts picture the Rural Highlands region this way. Yet the traces of that resigned acceptance were there. If the CAI system broke down, as it frequently did, that was the way the world went.

The combination of isolation, stoicism, and general poverty seemed to result in a conversational rather than an activity-oriented culture. Occasions for 'passing the time of day' occurred regularly and were maximized. The world of technical reports, research monographs, and intensive and lengthy analyses seemed foreign. Subphenomena were the 'folk hero' images that sprang up and became dominant themes in the conversational lifestyle. Among educators, the group with whom we were most intimately acquainted, idiosyncratic behavior was nurtured and elaborated into reputations. Stories were told and retold with humor, affection, and respect. For instance, outside of the domain of tales surrounding local educators, a prevailing topic of interest was basketball. Success in basketball quickly qualified individuals both for the hero role and for providing a sure ladder to success. The code was simple: winning is the name of the game; sportsmanship is for the cheerleaders. More significantly, the local basketball team provided the cohesive basis of the community. During tournament time all else was secondary — including CAI on several days.

Tying these various strands of the culture together is what we referred to among ourselves as a simple hedonism. Pleasure is where you find it, and the more complex striving for status was, except in a few rare and notable exceptions, conspicuously absent.

Kinship ties in the region were quite strong. Even the massive out-migration has not appreciably weakened the bonds. Families socialized in the 3 R's ('reading, writing, and the road to Dayton') go to little Highlands communities in the large metropolitan cities and return with considerable frequency and in large numbers.

A subphenomenon is what we called the 'professional education subculture'. Strong family relationships represented in the school systems were not at all unusual. Mothers and daughters, fathers and sons, and kin several steps removed populated the professional teaching and administrative ranks extending backward in time for several generations. What might be called nepotism elsewhere is an accepted part of the way of life in the Rural Highlands.

Nepotism raises the issue of politics, and politicking is the cultural lifeblood of the region. By politics we mean the exercise of influence, the giving and receiving of favors. Usually such favors were small and within a wide and tolerant zone of legal indifference. Occasionally they became excessive, and thus the source of major conflicts, for example, bus buying, coal buying, vote buying, as even a casual reading of the local newspapers indicated. Everyone was expected to play the game, even outsiders like ourselves. At this point we recorded in the Field Notes:

> As an aside, the third grade teacher was telling us to use our 'political influence' [and that was her phrase] to make CAI work a little better. She wants us to use that 'influence' to activate a second teletype stored but not in use at the school. She further talked about how they were going to 'perish' at Majors Crossing since the

positions of State Auditor and State Highway Commissioner, or jobs very close to that, were no longer held by local people. (4/69)

Within this context it was highly unlikely that CAI would remain apolitical. Consequently, later in the year as CAI became enmeshed in the larger concern for regional data processing, it was not altogether surprising to hear one highly placed educator state bluntly, 'CAI is not so much an educational or social issue as a political issue' (1/69).

Perhaps because of our own latent needs and dispositions, we found the cultural milieu one we responded to positively, one we were able to enter into and become part of even though we were outsiders, and one with which our methodological stance seemed compatible. Beyond this more personal reaction, the cultural milieu was significant in multiple ways in the functioning of the CAI program.

Funding: cuts, delays, and changes
If one were to select the most important single event responsible for much of the difficulty incurred during the year, the several aspects of funding would rank near or at the top. The initial proposal submitted by the local Title III agency, the Rural Highlands Educational Improvement Organization (RHEIO), approximated $417,000. This was reduced to about $258,000. This cut had a multitude of consequences that were disastrous for the CAI operation. It had immediate and negative impact on NIRBS where the program originated, on RHEIO, and on the individual schools and school districts of the region.

The impact of the cut in funds was felt strongly by NIRBS. The Institute's CAI program operated almost exclusively on 'soft money'. The reduction in funds necessitated a severe cutback in personnel. As a member of the Institute staff said, 'We went from a six-page directory to a three-page directory'. Forty to fifty people were dismissed. The reduced funding meant that the program became operational about six weeks after school started. The reduced financing placed a tremendous burden upon the remaining staff in terms of research and development as well as maintaining viable service on a day-to-day basis. This was particularly acute in periods of breakdowns and hardware change.

Related to the budget cut was the delay in funding. By midsummer of 1968 no assurances of continued funding had been made. Funding was not firmly committed until early fall. As a consequence, none of the preparations for implementing the program could be made, for example, ordering terminals, contracting with the telephone companies, and installing data sets. As a direct result, CAI in some schools was not fully operational until late winter — several months behind schedule.

A related issue was the United States Congress' passage of the 1968 (Green) Amendment to ESEA which funneled Title III funds through the State Department of Education. This further reduced available funds, generated considerable competition among the various organizations within the state, and consumed scarce time and energy resources of the administrators of the CAI program.[3]

The dispersal decision

One of the most significant and culturally determined actions taken by RHEIO's Board of Directors was to disperse the available teletypes throughout the 10,000 square miles of the region. Briefly, the situation was as follows. Prior to the 1968–69 school year, CAI had been introduced to the Rural Highlands on a limited experimental basis largely under the control of 'outside' and cosmopolitan agencies. Plans for the 1968–69 school year, contingent upon full Title III funding, projected an increase in the number of teletypes from twenty to sixty distributed over twenty-nine school districts. Two events, however, significantly altered the situation. The first was the drastic reduction in Title III funds. The number of terminals available for the program in 1968–69 was reduced from sixty to thirty. The second change was in the locus of control. As a 'continuation project' control was centered in the hands of RHEIO as the responsible local Title III agency, an agency whose board of directors was composed almost entirely of local school superintendents. Since the superintendents had pledged their support for the program on the basis that each school district would share in its benefits, the decision was made to disperse the available teletypes over all school districts in the region.

Retrospectively, one might argue that the future of CAI in the Rural Highlands was determined by this decision.[4] The wide dispersal of the terminals over the twenty school districts and the region's 10,000 square miles of rugged terrain had several major consequences. Clearly, it provided an occasion for the local superintendents to demonstrate that they had the best interests of 'the boys and girls of the county' at heart. Second, it legitimated their power as a decision-making body within RHEIO. Third, since the program was transmitted via telephone lines some efforts were made to improve the quality of local telephone communications systems. All of these consequences were peripheral to the CAI program qua program.

Viewed programmatically, however, the dispersal decision was on balance dysfunctional for CAI. Fewer teletypes per school necessarily limited the number of children any school could schedule and the intensity of exposure. Thus the impact of the program on any given child or class was weakened.

The decision to limit each school to one teletype made the hiring of supervisory personnel economically unfeasible. Consequently, either teachers had to do double duty as teachers and monitors or the program ran unattended. Neither condition was satisfactory. As operational difficulties increased, more and more teacher time was consumed by supervisory demands, and by and large, teachers reacted negatively. One commented, 'CAI interrupts me unbelievably. It has been nothing but a headache'. She went on to recall that a few days ago, 'I got absolutely nothing done. I was in and out with the computer teletype all morning long' (12/5).

The alternative — to leave the terminals unattended — was equally untenable. Our Field Notes contain numerous references to the fact that the system was operable, but no one had informed the teachers that it was. Furthermore, much of the frustration that children experienced at the teletypes and much of the competitive behavior observed was a result of the absence of supervisory personnel.

The decision to disperse the teletypes throughout the region exacerbated the existing maintenance problems. During much of the year maintenance was the responsibility of one man. Maintaining service in an area covering 10,000 square miles would have been difficult even with no personnel change-overs, well-trained personnel, and good transportation networks. As it was, none of these conditions prevailed, and short breakdowns turned into long ones. In April our Field Notes read:

> The issues of service and communication continuously comingled as
> she (the teacher) talked. She reported that RHEIO's CAI coordinator
> has been down twice, but that she hasn't seen a serviceman since late
> last fall. No one since then has been down to take a look at the
> malfunctioning teletype in her room. (4/69)

A fourth consequence of the dispersal decision was the magnification of coordination problems with the local telephone companies. Ultimately seven independent phone companies were involved, five of them located in the Rural Highlands. Clearly, introducing relatively sophisticated electronic components into these systems posed many problems.

Service problems related to the dispersal decision were magnified by RHEIO's later decision to establish dual operations centers. Originally all activity was centered in Leestown. Later, the administrative services were relocated in Midland, the largest city in the region. Calls for service were consequently routed to both centers with predictable time lag and confusion. Still later, a decision was made to establish service facilities at both locations. However, since RHEIO had only one serviceman for the greater part of the year, this did little to alleviate the problems.

Technical problems

In any innovative project certain technical difficulties may be anticipated. When one moves into a program as technically sophisticated as CAI, the universe of possible malfunctions increases enormously. Such was the experience of the CAI program in the Rural Highlands.

The initial problem encountered as a result of the reduction in funds was the inability of the Northeast Institute to develop the necessary program material (software). This meant that the 'spiral' program scheduled for operation in the fall of 1968 was unavailable and the 'unit' program developed earlier was substituted for it. The chief problem here was that teachers trained in the spiral program in the 1968 summer workshop at Leestown were largely unfamiliar with the unit program.

More serious than the 'software' problems were those involving 'hardware': the ABG-4 and ABG-6 computers, the data sets, the telephone lines, and the ubiquitous teletypes. During late October and early November, the ABC-4 computer at Leestown was inoperable for intermittent periods. A combination of factors including the lack of technically trained personnel, remodeling of the facilities, the laying of rugs in the computer area, lack of temperature and humidity controls, a long period of disuse, and noncompatibility with the equipment at Northeast University all contributed to the problem, which was magnified by well-meaning but ineffective attempts by nontrained personnel to service the equipment via long distance instructions from Northeast Institute.

A similar but even more critical condition prevailed for about a three-month period (late December to mid-March) when the Northeast lab shifted from an ABC-2 to an ABG-6 computer. The difficulties encountered in 'getting the 6 up' and making it compatible with the Leestown '4' resulted in a three months' loss of service and a noticeable decrease in teacher enthusiasm for the program.

The telephone lines caused major difficulties. In addition to coordinating the activities of seven separate companies, there were problems unique to the region and to the personnel responsible for installing and maintaining the necessary equipment. By and large, most of the local telephone companies were illequipped to assume a major role in this experiment. Their facilities were inadequate and their personnel largely untrained in installing and servicing sophisticated data transmission equipment. Antiquated equipment, rural roads, bridge building, strikes, random signals generated by branches rubbing across the telephone lines, and the migration of more adequately trained personnel, all compounded the difficulties. Additionally, it was frequently hard to determine whether a specific breakdown was a result of line trouble, teletype trouble, or computer problems either at Leestown or Northeast Institute. This inability to pinpoint the source of trouble lengthened the breakdown periods with their attendant dysfunctional consequences.

Another set of hardware problems involved the teletype machines themselves. These ranged from broken switches to severe malfunctions. Error-free print-outs were the exception rather than the rule for most of the year. Isolating the specific component of the system that was responsible for the trouble was a major problem. The lack of available trained personnel was felt keenly when difficulties were encountered. Teachers rarely attempted to service the teletypes even in a minimal way. A workshop session on 'the care and feeding of the teletype' bore little fruit.

Related to all the above were internal organizational problems, both between schools and within a particular building. These centered on the communication linkages between the Leestown facility and the outlying stations. Since the system was undependable, the individual schools became increasingly dependent on Leestown for information about the status of the system. However, since the system could be 'up' one minute and 'down' the next, even the reliability of this communications source became suspect.

Personnel
Repeated references have been made thus far to personnel problems, both qualitatively and quantitatively. This was largely a culturally determined phenomenon. The CAI program was embedded in a region almost totally within one of the 'poverty zones' of the country. Occupational opportunity is limited, and we were repeatedly informed of the outmigration from the region. A substantial percentage of the ambitious and trained people leave the region to find more rewarding employment elsewhere. Furthermore, since there is a minimum of industry within the region, the influx of well-trained technical, professional, and administrative personnel is limited. The combination of heavy outmigration and subsequent turnover plus the limited influx of 'outside' personnel posed serious problems for the Rural Highlands' organizations. Although in-service training programs were instituted as part of a larger effort to 'upgrade the region', the personnel problems they experienced had a negative impact on CAI.

The nature of curriculum development
A qualitatively different set of problems and issues was presented when we focused on CAI as an innovative program in the process of development. Supposedly, we, as observers, were part of a group executing a summative evaluation of a presumably stabilized program. Yet within the totality of a particular curriculum development project, CAI was indeed in the 'formative' stage. Clearly, the Northeast Institute's decision to abandon the 'unit' concept in its curriculum in favor of the spiral curriculum organization was indicative of the unfinished nature of the CAI program.

Basic, perhaps, is the nature of the innovative, creative personnel assembled at Northeast to develop CAI. Our impression was that the group was primarily oriented to research and development (R & D) rather than to commercial service. This was expressed both verbally and in practice. Changes in the subroutines were constantly being made. For example, the automatic printing of a daily summary was discontinued and made an option available on call from any specific teletype station. Procedures to converse via teletype between stations were built into the program. These changes were creative and increased the flexibility of the system. However, the changes often were not communicated to the teachers. Consequently, the teachers not only did not know how to avail themselves of the additional services, but became distressed when anticipated services, for example, the daily report, were not forthcoming. The lack of communication between the several organizations consistently emerged as a critical element in our observation and analysis.

The major issue, however, concerns the number and kinds of changes to be made in an innovative program while it is in process. Benefits as perceived by innovators may be perceived differently by people who have limited resources to carry out the administrative duties in communication, in training, and in reorganizing systems necessary to attain the benefits. And the 'benefits' may be perceived drastically differently by the ultimate users — the teachers and pupils who find themselves as pawns in a system that changes in surprising and unanticipated ways and independently of their control. When the machine does not work as it is supposed to, a 'benefit' cannot be discriminated from a 'breakdown'. We think a distinction between the R & D stance and the commercial service stance is important conceptually and practically.

The set of problems associated with high staff creativity was magnified by the general cut in federal funding. For NIRBS, such cuts made securing 'hard money' clients — essentially school districts — mandatory. Perversely, its success in attracting new clients elsewhere in the country was dysfunctional for the Rural Highlands program. An increase in clients required an increase in computer capacity. The subsequent changeover from the ABC-2 to the ABC-4 was fraught with unanticipated difficulties in making the computers compatible, which, when combined with staff shortages at the Northeast Institute, resulted in the loss of approximately three months' time.

The multiple organizational structure
One of the features of the CAI program that clearly identified it as a mid-twentieth century phenomenon was the complex interorganizational structure erected to implement it. At a minimum, that structure included the US Office of Education; the State Department of Education; various State and local Title III agencies; a state university; a regional educational laboratory; a powerful superintendents' group; seven telephone companies; several school boards; and a number of schools, classes, teachers, and children. Obviously, communication and coordination problems were massive and, in our opinion, were never satisfactorily resolved. In part, this was due to the lack of an authoritative administrative structure. More important, however, from our perspective, were the goal-oriented interorganizational conflicts that prevailed. In a real sense the CAI program became a pawn in the jockeying for power, prestige, and control of the educational destinies of the Rural Highlands.

Conclusion

Given this set of cultural, fiscal, political, programmatic, and organizational factors, it was no surprise that the program fared badly. To ourselves we phrased it as 'the system is up, is down, is up, is down'. For most of the intimately involved participants in the CAI program, the 1968-69 school year was one of frustration and disappointment.

Louis M. Smith and Paul A. Pohland

Rithmetic in the Rural Highlands: The Second Major Finding

Teacher Utilization of CAI

Initially we had hoped to make the major focus of our study the utilization of CAI by classroom teachers. The limited operationality of the system largely frustrated this intent. However, we did garner a number of observations and impressions that suggest possible directions for future investigation. Throughout this discussion, it should be kept in mind that the CAI program was conceived as a drill and practice exercise designed to complement and reinforce concepts previously taught.

Two general impressions of arithmetic teaching and teacher utilization of CAI stand out in bold relief: the dominance of textbook-centered teaching and the wide variability in CAI utilization. Most of the mathematics instruction we observed was the traditional textbook-bound, rote passage through the text. Consequently, in many classrooms, the teachers engaged in a considerable amount of classroom drill in spite of the availability of the drill and practice routines available through CAI. Savings of classroom time for concept development and individual instruction were not realized. In this respect, one of the major potential contributions of CAI was minimized. However, we saw several highly creative, original teachers who approached mathematics as the process of discovery.

As an adjunct to the regular classroom program, CAI was utilized in diverse ways. On a gross level, significant differences among teachers were observed with regard to the integration of CAI and the regular classroom programs. Such differences ranged from no observable attempt at integration to constructing the entire year's mathematics program around it. Quite naturally, but most unfortunately, the teacher with the most sophisticated plan for utilizing CAI suffered the greatest disappointments and frustrations during the course of the year.

Another facet of the integration of CAI with classroom work was the relationship between the drills taken by the children at the terminals and the regular classroom work. As a whole, the general observation was that relationships were minimal. Early in November we recorded the following:

> I made a specific point of checking with two of the (first grade) girls about where they were currently in their math lessons. I wondered how closely the drills that they were taking corresponded to what they were doing in class. Apparently it is not very close. Ruth told me that the day's classroom lesson was on 'writing mathematical sentences'. The drills, however, were all simple addition and subtraction problems. (11/7)

Later in the school year this issue was examined again. Excerpts from the Field Notes catch the flavor of our conversations with some of the children on this point.

I also asked Edith about the relationship between the materials she had on the teletype and what they were doing in class. The conversation ran as follows: *Obs*: 'Are you doing multiplication in class?' *Edith*: 'We're doing fractions'. I also asked Dick: 'Is it (the drill) anything like what you're doing in class?' His answer was a very emphatic 'No!'. (4/2)

Several factors seemed to be involved in creating this situation: (1) the approximately six-week delay in starting the CAI program; (2) frequent system breakdowns; and (3) the fact that few teachers appeared to be aware of or chose to exercise the option of reassigning 'units' to the children once they were placed in the program.[5]

Considerable variability was also observed in the use of print-outs. Some teachers used them as subject material for the entire class recitations. Others insisted that all errors on the print-outs ascribable to children be corrected before the papers went home. In at least one instance a manual containing all the drills was made available to the children as 'workbook exercises' prior to their 'taking a drill'.

Variability also existed in recording the results. Some teachers kept accurate daily records; others did not. Similar variations existed regarding the regular checking by the teachers of the students' print-outs.

One of the most encouraging features of utilization was the generally high priority assigned to the CAI program by teachers and administrators. The most extreme example of that was recorded in mid-spring.

> Related to the newness and the fact that the program is finally running is the fact that Mr. Davies [the principal] has declared that the CAI program shall take precedence over all other activities in the school at the present time. I had asked him whether a definite schedule of time had been assigned for each of the several teachers to send their children to the terminal area. In brief, there has not been, and the children are simply called out by the aide whenever there is time for them to come or whenever their name appears on the list. (4/4)

More typically, classes were assigned specific times during the day to work at the terminals. Students were dismissed from class, either singly or in groups ranging from two to twenty, to 'take a drill'. This movement in and out of the classrooms did not seem to be a particularly disturbing feature either to the teacher or the other members of the class, once routines were established.

In addition to teacher preference, much of the variability in utilization appeared to be the result of three factors.

1   A general breakdown in communication resulted in considerable confusion about the precise nature of the program. Programmatic decisions made at the administrative level were not always communicated to the teachers. For example, immediately prior to the opening of school a decision was made to use the older 'units' rather

than the newer 'spiral' program. It was not communicated to the teachers. Subsequently, one of the teachers visited during early spring was under the impression that the 'spiral' program was in fact operating and that the drills his children were taking were merely a series of pretests;

2 Not all schools and teachers utilizing CAI participated in the summer CAI teacher-training workshop;

3 Where the teletypes were placed in reasonably close proximity to the classrooms, usage as well as teacher supervision was facilitated. Where the location was more remote, problems of pupil movement, maximum utilization, and supervision were increased. Teletype placement in the classroom was not satisfactory. While it would appear to be the logical location, the noise level and attention-directing properties of teletype activities proved a great distraction from on-going instructional programs.

Tales From the Teletypes

Initially the CAI drill and practice routine appeared to be simple and straightforward. Only after we were well into the observation period did we begin to see that this was not the case. A wide and complex range of physical, emotional, cognitive, and social behaviors was involved. The following data and its interpretation will shed some light on the CAI operation as a whole and will suggest some lines for future research.

Enthusiasm, attention, and concentration
One of our major concerns during the observational year was the behavior of the children at the teletypes. Our experience with other published accounts of educational innovations left us skeptical of the 'hold' the terminals were supposed to have on the children in terms of eagerness to 'sign on', attention, intensity of concentration, and so on. However, our initial observation of the children working at the teletypes reduced that skepticism markedly. In the Field Notes we summarized our reactions thus:

> One of the striking things here was the fact that once the kids got into the cage[6] they attended mightily to the stimulus conditions as though no one else were about. Both of us were struck by the fact that the kids got quite caught up in the exercises and attend to the machine and interact with it with great vigor as though no one else were outside or no one was sitting in the chair immediately behind them waiting to get on the machine as soon as they had finished. We noticed that the seat never was allowed to cool off. Hardly had one kid slipped out than another kid was in. Although we did not time it,

it could not have been more than five to ten seconds in between as the kids moved in and out of it. (5/28, Pre-experimental year)

One of our concerns was to what degree this enthusiasm might wane over the course of a school year. In general, the data suggest that it did not. For example, the Field Notes for 11/7 read:

Some observations on the fourth grade as they work on the terminals. First, the kids have no trouble signing on the program at all. They were extremely business-like, getting to work immediately. In fact, some of them pressed the start button before they even sat down. (Later in the day I was to notice that as the kids came in they would press the start buttons of the teletypes serially as they moved across the room. Four of the machines were in operation today.[7] So you can imagine the youngster coming in, pressing the start button on teletype 1, moving over to number 2, pressing the start button, moving over to number 3, pressing the start button, and if either 1 or 2 began chattering away quickly dashing back to either 1 or 2 and sliding into the seat quickly before someone else could.)

The children's enthusiasm for CAI, the general absence of supervisory personnel, and the practice of sending groups of children to the teletype at one time combined to provide additional insights into the dynamics of the program. Early in the year we noted:

One final note from this afternoon's observation: When more than three youngsters are up here [in the terminal area] they tend to stand and watch their classmates work. Very few of them can actually sit on the chairs provided and patiently wait their turn. Patience is not one of the great virtues one observes among grade-school children.
During this last half-hour period one little girl who tried to wait fairly for 'her turn' found herself being consistently and literally shoved to the rear of the line by others who were more aggressive. Finally, she became a bit aggressive herself and stood at the shoulder of the girl who was working at the terminal waiting for her to finish. As soon as the girl finished, she plunked herself down in the vacated seat without giving anyone else a chance to beat her to it. (10/10)

Somewhat later we observed:

2:40 p.m.
There was practically a fight for the terminals by three boys. (11/7)

This type of total concentration appears to be a general phenomenon extending over all age groups and locales. Not only was this observable in the schools visited in the Rural Highlands, but in our brief observations in other widely dispersed sections of the country as well. Elementary-school children, high schoolers, teachers, and the observers quickly became 'hooked on the machine'. During our initial visit we noted that 'the teachers are caught up in it (CAI) almost as much or more so than the kids. It reminds us of the "kid with a new toy" kind of phenomenon' (5/28).

The reason or reasons for the attractiveness of the CAI program are more difficult to ferret out. To the best of our knowledge, no one has seriously addressed this question. It has been suggested that the individualized nature of the program, its uniqueness and newness, the period of time required to do a drill, the immediate feedback, the short amount of time (ten seconds) allowed to make a response to the stimulus item, and the concomitant challenge of 'beating the machine' are all contributory factors. The children were not articulate about the phenomenon; to them it was simply 'fun'. As one first grader put it, 'It's more fun than arithmetic' (10/10), or as another said, 'I would be happy if all we had was this (pointing to the teletype) and math and lunch' (10/11). Somewhat more rational was Mark's comment to the effect that he liked working on the teletypes because 'all you have to do is push buttons' (5/16). But by and large, the reaction was typically phrased as in this brief dialogue between Ricky and Ellen:

Ricky: You and me go crazy on these computers.
Ellen: I love to do these.
Ricky: I love this, Ellen.
Ellen: Me too. (11/19)

'The exception proves the rule.' So it was with CAI. Not all children were enthusiastic about it. One child bluntly stated, 'I hate the machine. I intend to goof off as often as I can' (10/9). Other less extreme instances were also noted. One child observed that 'the machine scares me'. Occasionally class activities were of such interest that students preferred to remain in the classroom — rather than take a teletype drill. This became a particularly acute problem toward the end of the school year and posed a classic value dilemma. And one small boy simply preferred his teacher's company to that of a teletype.

Similar but limited exceptions to the attention and concentration phenomena also occurred. Our notes carry several instances of students being acutely aware of what was going on around them. For example:

9:50
Miss Jane is changing the ribbon on a teletype. The boy working on the adjoining teletype is completely ignoring his own work to watch her. He pays attention to the drill before him only after she chides him, saying, 'Watch your own paper'.

Gay was quite a bit annoyed at the noise around her. Her annoyance was primarily directed to the group of four children seated in the chairs behind her who were engaged in a conversation. It didn't seem to me that they were talking very loudly at all, but shortly after she had gotten started she turned around and in a rather sharp voice said, 'Be quiet'. I note parenthetically that she scored 100 percent in 122 seconds. (10/10)

Not only were the students aware of general background noise, but were, on occasion, very aware of the students waiting in line. Typically, the student next in line would station himself directly behind the child working. This created tensions of its own. We recorded one such episode as follows:

Student working at teletype to student waiting: 'Don't stand behind my back like you did yesterday. I can't work'. (10/23)

We raise these issues to emphasize three points: (1) The enthusiasm, attention, and concentration phenomena while widespread are not universal; (2) scheduling and supervision are critical aspects of the program; and (3) there is a clear need to examine carefully the interaction between personality variables, study skills, and learning devices such as CAI. More generally we would argue that the dynamics of CAI are not well worked out and that a series of carefully planned laboratory type experiments in which key variables can be manipulated is in order.[8]

Emotionality, anxiety, and exhaustion
At times the emotional behavior was more noticeable than the mathematical behavior. Instances of extreme nervousness were observed. For example:

Carole had the nervous habit of banging on the side of the teletype with her right hand as the problem was typed out. This nervousness also showed up in the fact that she constantly drummed her fingers and periodically would shake the teletype with both hands. (12/7)

Self-consciousness was also exhibited by some. Gail was an extreme case. After observing her on one occasion we recorded:

Gail was extremely conscious also about other people seeing her work. She waited until there was only one person in the room before she sat down at the terminal. [Typically, in this class, children were sent up in groups.] At that, she covered the print-out with her hand and forearm so that no one else could see it. When she caught my glance, she immediately spread her fingers apart so that I could not see it either. (10/22)

Some of the youngsters — typically those who had the greatest difficulty with the drills — found the work genuinely exhausting. Robert's experience in that regard was not atypical. The Field Notes contain such an episode.

Robert had the longest print-out I had ever seen for one lesson. It took him 614 seconds to complete it. He did not do particularly well. After he had finished he looked at me and in a 'Whooo, am I bushed' voice said, 'I wish I were as good in arithmetic as I am in spelling'. When I asked, 'Why, do you have trouble with math?' he responded with a very emphatic 'Yes!' (12/7)

Our records do not contain enough written classroom data on individual children to determine the degree to which these reactions were basic to the children's personality, to classroom learning in general, or more situationally specific to CAI.

Animism: The verbal interaction

One of the more interesting behaviors observed was the verbal interaction between the child and the teletype. In a very real sense an animistic quality of the teletypes engaged the students totally. In that respect, the program seemed to move from a drill-and-practice routine to a higher level tutorial program. Our Field Notes consistently refer to the verbalization that took place. Excerpts read:

One of the girls whom I watched particularly was engaged in direct conversation with the terminal all the way through the drill. Some of her comments included: 'You're crazy. How would I know that? Oh, let's see. How would I know? Oh, that's easy'. In between statements she was scratching her head rather violently. (10/22)

Jean talks to machine: 'Oh, no! It's gotta be … oh, darn! Oh, wait a minute. Oh, … oh God!' (4/29)

Much of the verbalizing had to do with computing answers to the problems. Marcia was a case in point. The Field Notes record the episode thus:

On first seeing problems like $3 + 6 = 1 + \underline{\hspace{1em}}$, Marcia reacted by saying, 'Oh, no, I can't do this'. Nonetheless, she tried, verbalizing the problem as '3 + 6 is 9 take away 1 is 8'. On the next problem, $6 + 2 = \underline{\hspace{1em}} + 3$, she counted out the problem on her fingers, verbalizing as follows, '6 and 2 is 8, take away 3 is 5'. (11/9)

At other times, the verbalizing took the form of self-criticism. After mis-reading a 65 as 55, Craig blurted out, 'Oh gosh!' and later, 'I didn't think about that' (5/14).

Social dimensions: CAI as a group activity

An additional development that appears also to be at variance with the notion of an individualized program of instruction was the amount of group activity at the teletypes. Typically it involved either a group of two or more children working jointly on a drill or some authorized person (child or adult) assisting the child at the terminal. In either case, the assistance may or may not have been solicited.[9] An example of this occurring early in the year involving Sara and Susan was recorded as follows:

Sara had never worked on the terminals before, and was consequently totally unfamiliar with it. Her friend, Susan, stood right at her shoulder and showed her how to do it step by step. Not only was Sara unfamiliar with the terminal, but she also had a great deal of difficulty with simple mathematics. She tended to count out everything on her fingers and rarely was able to complete a problem before the 'Time is up. Try again' message or the answer was given. I mention this at this point because as Susan was standing right next to her she was constantly helping her out. There was nothing individualized about this at all in terms of its being simply a game between the machine and Sara. Susan was mediating constantly throughout the drill.... About midway through the drill, Sara simply let Susan take over almost totally. Susan not only verbalized each problem for Sara and took it apart mathematically for her, but also suggested answers. Finally, at the end, she also typed in the answers. (10/10)

Joint working could be considered both authorized and necessary. Frequently this occurred when children were first introduced to the teletypes. The situation became intensified when, as in the first grade drills, a certain degree of reading ability was also required. Our notes record:

One of the real problems that first graders face is their inability to read. The reading itself is minimal but even in something as simple as 'How many y's are there?' a certain amount of reading is required. Some of them simply could not do it. As a result, both Miss Jane and I occasionally stood by and read the questions to the kids. They were able to count the x's, y's, o's, equal signs or whatever, but they became rather badly confused on the greater than and less than signs. To a rather large degree, at least with first graders, CAI is as much a reading exercise as it is a math exercise. (10/10)

If these were examples of help both solicited and necessary, other situations developed where one or the other or both were missing. For example:

Jennie is on the TTY. Two boys are helping her. Jennie: 'Timmy, come here and help me'. She pushes buttons as he calls the numbers. (1/22)

Occasionally an aide became heavily involved in working a particular drill. For example:

I watch her [Karen's] lesson.... It is an interesting triad of child, aide, and machine. Mrs. Clay helps considerably, especially on horizontal addition and which number to write first. Karen checks out her answer first with Mrs. Clay [before typing it in]. She looked pleased with her 90 percent. (12/11)

Later, we were to comment, as we had done previously, about the validity of the scores obtained in this fashion. Typically, they were erroneously high since computational errors were corrected before they were typed in. Insofar as many of the children were working the same or equivalent drills, the validity of the scores was questionable. Where a consciously competitive atmosphere was maintained this situation was particularly acute.

As we noted earlier, a social variable was associated with the CAI program. Conversations were frequently carried on during the course of a drill that were not of a 'helping' nature. For example:

> Dan is standing next to Michael as Michael works out his problems. The two boys carry out a running conversation during the entire drill. There was a great deal of laughter and a great many comments similar to 'Oh, that's a hard one,' or 'Oh, I think I can do this one'. (12/7)

From all of this, several issues emerge rather clearly. First, it accents the importance of having an aide available both to monitor the behavior of the children in the terminal area and thus cut down or eliminate gross group behavior, and to provide legitimate assistance where needed. Second, it accents the social dimensions of a presumably individualized program. Third, it suggests that pupil scores be viewed with caution, particularly if they are obtained in a nonsupervised setting. Our experiences tend to make us skeptical of the validity of print-out scores on a number of bases.

Competition

An unanticipated development regarding CAI social activity was the degree of competition generated by the program. At the outset, it should be stated that this appeared to vary across particular schools, particular classrooms within buildings, and individuals within subgroups. Why that should be we do not know; however, it was quite clear that competition did exist.[10]

The competition took several forms: (1) completing the greatest number of drills on a given day, (2) completing a drill in the shortest time, (3) achieving the highest score on a given drill, (4) a combination of time and score. We observed examples of all of these.

The competition to see who would complete the greatest number of drills was concentrated in one particular second grade classroom and illustrated another facet of the variability in usage among teachers. Here the teacher had chosen to maximize the utilization of the terminals. Children from her room were permitted usage of the equipment any time either they or the terminal were free. This was a generally unique pattern since our data indicate that most teachers were under the assumption that children were to be limited to one drill per day. In any event, multiple drills were the norm in this particular instance. The Field Notes record several instances of this.

> Ellen worked out six lessons on the teletype, one right after the other.
> ... Apparently she and Eric are trying to beat Barbara's record. Prior

to their coming up [to the terminals] Barbara had worked more drills than anyone else. (11/9)

Much later in the year similar notes were taken.

Glenn had just finished drill #7 for the day. He plans to do '9 or 10 today'. He went on to say, 'I'm going to do some after school, too'. Currently, according to Glenn, Amy has the record since 'yesterday she did nine'. (5/19)

While time and scores were not significant elements of competition in this class, in other classes and schools they were. This was heightened by the practice of one teacher of posting the 100's on the tackboard. This public recognition had a variety of consequences that seemed inappropriate for an 'individualized' instructional program. In any event, the competition existed. The Field Notes record:

I overheard Tom and Dwight, two of the boys who were among the first to 'sign on' the terminals, comparing scores. Tom finished first and asked Dwight, 'What did you get?' (11/7)

Even more dramatic was the following episode:

Midway through the morning I happened to notice three boys working on the terminals. They made an effort to start together, and it was a real contest. It should be noted that the three boys were not on the same lesson. Nevertheless, there was a great deal of competition to see (1) who would finish first, and (2) who would get the highest percentage. The boy who finally did finish first raised his arms above his head like a boxer's and crowed rather exaltedly, 'I won, I won'. The sweet smell of success was even greater when he found out that he had achieved a higher percentage score on his test than either of his two buddies. Both of them looked a little bit crestfallen, particularly the boy who ended up last. (10/24)

In one particular school, the class 'record' was a matter of common knowledge. 'Beating the record' was a definite goal. Our Field Notes captured the flavor of this type of competition also.

David, 100 percent, fifty-eight seconds. 'If I'd gotten that I would have tied the class record'. He pointed to where he had typed in a too rapid ten and the machine hadn't recorded it and he had to retype. The class record is fifty-six seconds. (4/30)

The self-competition, the banter that went along with the competition, the emotional reactions of delight and despair — all were observed. Excerpts from the Field Notes of an extended observation summarize these dimensions and, in a sense, the human qualities of CAL.

9:50

Benny: 'Darn, I pushed the wrong button'. He shows me his twelve instead of 132.

Walt laughed at him during the process. (*Obs*: The boys in this bunch are all highly competitive with each other and with how they do.) This is his eighth or ninth 100 in a row. Sixty-eight seconds is his best. Class best is in the fifties.

Becky is in. Comments they get to go again because the 8th graders are elsewhere. Claps hands, 'I got a 100'. 'Sixty-six seconds, — good ... best time I've gotten'.

Eddie — a fast punching lefty. He talks problems out loud also, 'Ninety-three. I got the same as Fred but he was seventeen seconds better'. Eddie had a ninety-seven second time.

John says Martin has a fifty-eight. Guy, 100 in sixty-two seconds. He talks to Karl about his time and indicates 'You gotta beat it'. Karl groans with his first error.

Joy comes running down the hall followed by one of the boys. He watches her very attentively. She grimaces, slaps her face lightly as she makes a mistake, 'Ah, I got 93 percent'. 'I beat my answer by one second, seventy-two instead of seventy-three'.

10:18

Burt observed her very carefully as she took the lesson, even to the point of holding the paper up. 100 in sixty-four seconds — his best time, but still behind the fifty-six of Martin's as he reported it. (5/29)

The preceding excerpts suggest some latent dimensions of CAI that do not typically show up in the literature. There is, for example, a gamelike quality that includes players, spectators, rules, winning and losing, spatial restrictions, and the like. There is also a social dimension. Typically those waiting to be next take an avid and sometimes active part in the drill exercise. The affective involvement is also very high. Emotional outbursts were not uncommon. The visibility of performance, whether by word of mouth or by public display, was unexpectedly high and suggests a further variable that is largely ignored in the published accounts of CAI.[11]

Roger's tale

We have somewhat facetiously labeled this broad section of the paper 'Tales from the Teletype'. It seems appropriate on several counts to conclude this section with one more complete 'tale'. It illustrated for us the positive values of CAI in a dramatic and human way that we have not emphasized to this point. One of the virtues of CAI as with any innovative program is its potential for 'making a difference in a child's life'. Roger was one such child. This is his story as we recorded it in the Field Notes:

Roger was an exceptional child. According to the teachers, his reputation at the school was that of a mentally handicapped child mixed with a large dose of cantankerousness and laziness. His teacher reported that they had had him tested regularly and frequently by experts but that none of the tests was able to pinpoint his trouble. Roger was one of the youngest of a large family and all of the children of that family had the reputation of being troublemakers and dullards. None of the family had ever gone past grade school, and several of the older brothers and sisters had dropped out of school before finishing the eighth grade. Roger also had an artificial hand as a result of a hunting accident. After the teachers left, Mr. Corey, the principal, in a rather disgusted voice said, 'There's absolutely nothing wrong with Roger. The trouble is with the teachers'. He went on to say that one of the major problems with 'our profession' was that teachers tend to categorize children and to put them into slots from which there is no escape. He felt there was absolutely nothing whatsoever wrong with Roger but that the teachers felt that coming from that particular family he was lazy and stupid and simply would not learn even if he had the ability to do so. As a case in point he mentioned that Roger was the only youngster in the school who had been able to figure out independently that the top row of numbers on the teletype keyboard could be used as a number line. Consequently, he did addition in the following fashion: If the problem was 3 + 5, put your finger on the 3 and then count over 5 and you end up on the 8, press the 8 and you have your answer. It takes a certain amount of intelligence to do this, and Mr. Corey used this as an example that Roger was not mentally retarded or anything else. As the evidence began to unfold later, I found myself agreeing with Mr. Corey.

The story, at any rate, is that rather than doing just one lesson on the terminals, Roger stayed at the terminals until he had completed four of them. He was bound and determined to sit there until he had gotten 100 percent on one of the drills and on the fourth try he did. He ended up with a print-out about five feet long that he displayed very proudly. The teachers refused to believe that he had done it all by himself. Mr. Corey's interpretation was that it was as though Roger was trying to show the teachers — as well as to prove to himself — that he really could produce and achieve as well as anyone else. At that point, the principal turned to me and said, 'Maybe you'd like to talk to Roger yourself. If you would, I can go and get him for you'. [*Obs*: That may not be verbatim, but it is awfully close.] He did so, and a few moments later a very freshly scrubbed and cheerful looking boy of about nine was brought into the office. Mr. Corey left the office and allowed me to talk to Roger privately. Part of the conversation revolved strictly around the CAI program. Roger 'likes the hard ones best,' and, in general, the CAI program is 'a whole lot of fun'. Since Mr. Corey's reference to computation by number line was in the back of my mind, I asked Roger how he figured out problems on the teletype. I didn't get a repeat of the number line business at all; rather, 'I just think it out'. I gave him a few examples of simple addition of the nature of $4 - 3$ and then $14 + 7$ and he thought for a moment and came up with the right answers. When I referred to the four drills that he had done in one day he really perked up. Almost immediately, however, his face fell and he remarked that from now on he was only supposed to do one at a time. (12/5)

Perhaps the thing that makes this tale a most encouraging one to us is that we have had a long-standing commitment to the educational process, a psychology of teaching if you will, that will 'turn kids on' and make learning an exciting and stimulating adventure. CAI was such an experience for Roger. From what we could infer, Roger was a potential dropout who was 'saved' in the best sense of the word. For Roger, and for others like him, CAI was an important part of the curriculum.

Summary

In this section, 'Rithmetic in the Rural Highlands, we have focused on two broad sets of issues. The first dealt with teacher utilization of CAI as a supplementary mathematics program. The second set concentrated on pupil behaviors at the teletype.

The major finding with regard to teacher utilization was the wide variability observed. Such variance included the degree of integration with classroom activities, the use of print-outs, recording results, routines for dismissing children to the terminals, priorities assigned to the program, understanding of the nature of CAI, frequency of usage, and the like. As we noted previously, much of this variance can be attributed to the frequency of down time and poorly articulated communications networks.

The second set of interests focused on pupil behaviors at the terminals. As we observed the children, engaged in dialogue with them, and thought about what we saw and heard, we constantly found ourselves asking: What are the latent variables that are operating? In a sense, we were questioning the formal doctrine of CAI, seeking to discover the stimulus configurations which in a complex way were responsible for the concentration, enthusiasm, attention, and anxiety we observed. In short, we began looking at the emotional as well as cognitive aspects of CAI.

A major concern with regard to pupil behaviors was that CAI had considerable social significance. Overt manifestations of this were in the group rather than individual activities frequently observed at the teletypes and the varying forms of competition that developed. These issues became interwoven with the problems of teacher assistance and supervision. Ultimately, we began to see CAI not as a simple and straightforward drill routine, but as a complex of physical, social, emotional, and cognitive behaviors inextricably intertwined and shaped both by administrative routines and norms of the particular schools and classrooms. For us, all of these elements were combined in a unique yet general way in Roger's tale.

Conclusion

In the prefatory remarks of our discussion we heard a plea for evaluators to 'tell the full story' of programmatic and curricular efforts. In abbreviated fashion we have tried to do this for one instance of curriculum reform. Although a secondary admonishment called for 'statistics and profiles', we elected Malinowski's (1922) alternative, the pursuit of the 'imponderabilia of actual life' in the Rural Highlands.[12] We have tried to describe something of the region and its culture, the program, the schools, and the children. We hope our account has a relevance for a number of quite diverse groups: government bodies such as the Congress and the Office of Education who are involved in the timing and routing of funds, educational administrators who make key decisions regarding the ratio of program size to resources, curriculum developers and innovators whose program creativity and service responsibilities pull them in opposing directions, and classroom teachers who continually seek aid in solving the fascinating but difficult problems of pupil learning and development. Each of these groups is faced with a continuous series of dilemmas, difficult decisions. The alternatives, their manifold consequences, and the mixed and uneven subsequent utilities represent the excitement and frustration in the human condition in education. Finally, and most importantly, we hope our description and analysis continues the trend of reevaluation of educational evaluation.

Methodology

Methodological discussions tend to fit more awkwardly in participant observer accounts than they do in reports of more classical experimental studies. Consequently, we have collected several items in this supplement so as not to destroy the continuity of the data and interpretations presented earlier. Our content is threefold: (1) the general context of evaluation in which this present report was generated; (2) a brief descriptive presentation of how we, as observers, went about studying the Computer Assisted Instruction (CAI) program; and (3) a discussion of several important issues in methodological theory that will link the participant observer approach to more classical stances of evaluation and research.

The General Context of the Evaluation

The most general statement of CEMREL's overall approach to the evaluation of the CAI program appears in Russell (1969). A brief recounting of that position helps establish a context into which the present work falls. Earlier, we phrased it as a 'three-legged' evaluation model. The point of view abstracted three broad classes of research methodology; three specialized staff groups; and three clusters of attendant purposes, foci, problems, and data into three operational approaches to an interrelated evaluation. The 'first leg' of the model was the experimental design — a fairly standard but careful attempt to measure academic achievement gains with standardized instruments, pre- and post-tests, and appropriate control groups — in short, a summative evaluation of learning outcomes. The 'second leg' of the evaluation retained the quantitative focus but attacked the affective-attitudinal domain with survey research technology and carefully focused questionnaires and interviews of relevant groups: pupils, parents, and teachers. The 'third leg' was the participant observation or field work component. This approach accented a careful description recorded in daily in situ field notes and developed a more analytical and theoretical conception of the program than the other two approaches.

The 'three-legged' formulation was rationalized into basic dimensions by Russell (1969). Discriminations were made among (1) roles — formative and summative; (2) foci — students, materials, and mediators; and (3) data — scale measures, questionnaires, and participant observation. For our purposes we present Table 1.1 which develops the 'three-legged model' a step further in terms of analyses by Stake (1967) and Scriven (1967). The model suggests our conception of the broader context of evaluation and the specific contribution of anthropological-type field work to educational evaluation.[13]

CAI Field Work Procedures

One of the aspirations we have in this supplement is a brief but careful account of the procedural aspects of the evaluation. In part, we hope to make clear the steps we took in generating the data and interpretations of the report. In addition, we hope our procedural account will be a specific statement useful as an object lesson regarding more general usage of participant observation in the evaluation of school programs.

Table 1.1: A reinterpretation of the Cemrel evaluation model

| Technological and Theoretical Basis | Analysis of the Evaluation Model | | | |
	Inquiry Process	Instruments	Roles	Focus
1 Psychological	Experimental design, randomly assigned experimental and control groups within classes, pre- and post-tests of achievement	Standardized achievement tests	Summative	Students
2 Sociological	Panel surveys, construction of 'favorability' indexes	Structured teacher and student attitude questionnaires, parent interviews	Summative	Students and mediators
3 Anthropological	Participant observation field work	Observers: field notes, informal interviews, documents	Summative and formative	Students, mediators, materials, goals

The initial focus: foreshadowed problems

Persons engaged in qualitative research strategies disagree regarding the degree to which there should be *a* problem, *some* problem, or *no* problem that initially guides the observer. Our position has come to be strongly in accord with Malinowski's (1922) 'foreshadowed problem' conception. In June, before beginning systematic observation of the July teacher workshop but after making preliminary arrangements regarding entry, we wrote the following three paragraphs indicating our initial definition of the problem.

> During the 1968–69 school year, we will engage in intensive observation, description, and conceptualization of the Computer Assisted Instruction program. At the descriptive level, our intent is to gather careful, valid data regarding the day-to-day utilization of CAI by pupils, teachers, and schools. The mundane ways the equipment is used and its impact on the school will provide the data for the conceptualizing and theorizing. Hopefully, the research will result in a number of useful implications for teachers, administrators, and researchers in education.

> The foci for analysis cannot be indicated finally at this stage; participant observational research does not lend itself to this kind of initial conceptual clarity. In this sense, it contrasts sharply with hypothesis testing in more usual verificational research. Several tentative 'foreshadowed problems' from the Psychology of Teaching project do exist, however, and will guide the initial observations: first, the impact of CAI on teacher decision-making will be considered. In *The Complexities of an Urban Classroom* (Smith and Geoffrey, 1968), and

later in *Teacher Plans and Classroom Interaction* (Smith and Brock, 1970), we developed initial ideas we hope to elaborate in the context of CAI. Second, dimensions of teacher-pupil relationships, for example, teacher awareness, ringmastership, control, and so forth, were raised in the earlier monographs and will be built upon here. Third, concepts of classroom social structure and process, for example, pupil roles, activities, and interactions, will be analyzed in terms of the descriptive data from CAI classrooms. Fourth, the personality and behavior of children in the rural poverty setting of the Rural Highlands will be compared and contrasted with that found in poor urban children who had come from rural areas and who had roots in similar settings.

The organizational and innovative aspects of CAI will be focused upon also. We think these are a most understudied aspect of a psychology of teaching and should contribute greatly to enhanced understanding of CAI. Specifically, we hope to build upon the kinds of analyses begun in *Anatomy of Educational Innovation* (Smith and Keith, 1971). In that volume we were concerned with team teaching, nongradedness, individualized instruction, and so forth. CAI represents another important innovation. The problem of changes in school organization wrought by innovative practices are largely unknown. Our attempt will be to focus on anticipated-unanticipated consequences.

The reader will note that the final product is only partially a result of the initial problem statement. The problem evolved as events in the real world played themselves out.[14]

The degree of involvement

The rules regarding the nature of a field worker's involvement and the amount of time spent in the field are not clear. Anthropologists studying primitive communities often argue for a minimum of a calendar year because much of the community life is cyclical and is determined by the changing seasons. Insofar as schools have such a rhythm or insofar as curriculum projects have annual funding, a similar argument might be made.

Our degree of involvement was not quite that intensive; yet in the course of the CAI evaluation we spent, in total, ninety-four man-days in field observation. We think that that degree of involvement, while perhaps inadequate by anthropological standards, gave us a comprehensive picture of the innovative program. We were able to participate in some of the joys and the disappointments, the usual and unusual, the trivial and the important aspects of CAI and school life when they occurred. From these experiences, captured and incorporated in our field notes, we built the detailed description and analysis discussed earlier. In this manner we hoped to understand better the implications of CAI.

More specifically, we were in Rural Highlands through several main periods. During the spring of 1968 we made initial contacts with the staff of Rural Highlands Educational Improvement Organization (RHEIO), Leestown State University (LSU), and the superintendents of the cooperating districts. In July we spent a week in the teacher training workshop at LSU. From September through May 1968–69 we visited each of the schools at least twice and in several of the schools we observed intensively. We were in the Rural Highlands at least once during each month.

During January we spent three days at the Northeast Institute for Research in the Behavioral Sciences' (NIRBS) CAI Laboratory and also observed their settings in the local public schools. In May we spent two days observing the CAI operation in a third setting, Carpenterville, a small city in another part of the country. Concomitant with the above visits, we were in regular communication by telephone and letter with various people connected with the program.

The kind of records we kept are also characteristic of our use of participant observational techniques. They are of three broad varieties: (1) field notes — on-the-spot records of observations, for example, of children at the terminals; (2) summary observations and interpretations — dictated summaries of observations, informal interviews and discussions; (3) documents — formal records, such as computer print-outs. In the vernacular, we have 'several file drawers' of data. By specific count, we have more than 900 pages of single-spaced typed notes. These raw data are the basic materials upon which we draw for our description, analysis, and interpretations. The final report is a distillation of those data.

Strategy and tactics in observation

Throughout the evaluation, the 'particular circumstances'[15] surrounding the CAI project modified the direction of our inquiry. Initially, they included the following: (1) geographical dispersion of the CAI program over 10,000 square miles (ultimately thirty schools and twenty school districts); (2) considerable distance between the field setting and the researcher's base of operation; and (3) multiple teams of researchers which permitted a concentration on collecting certain types of data. The first and most important of these may be used to speak to the selection-of-setting issue in any wide-scale curriculum evaluation study. Simply stated the problem is: given limited resources, does one (1) focus the investigation upon a limited number of settings for intensive observations; (2) attempt to cover all settings equally intensively; or (3) arrive at some combination of intensive/moderate observation? Ultimately we resolved this problem on the basis of 'theoretical purpose and relevance' (Glaser and Strauss, 1967).

Our procedures were essentially the following. During the late spring of the preevaluation year we toured the region with a staff member of RHEIO, the local Title III agency.[16] This gave us the opportunity to become acquainted initially with the region, the schools, and the personnel. Of the settings available, one was a university laboratory school. Our prior interests in the broad aspects of teacher training, the possibility of seeing a variety of models of arithmetic instruction, and the utilization of CAI in an undergraduate curriculum suggested that the laboratory school would be an appropriate setting. Furthermore, the computer was located on campus and by observing there we would gain the added advantage of being at the center of the communications network. A further advantage was that it was reasonably close to several outlying rural schools that were also utilizing CAI. Hence, we would be in a position to observe similarities and differences on a number of dimensions, for example, variance in socioeconomic status, aspiration level, rural vs. small town, localism vs. cosmopolitanism, and so forth. Given that decision, we searched for other settings that would further serve to maximize similarities and differences and thus generate comparative groups for analytic purposes. Ultimately we discovered one where all the math was taught by one teacher with the teletype located in the classroom. It was also in a small town setting and, fortunately, in close proximity to a rural school, thus maintaining the rural/small town referent. We selected a private school as a third site. This added a public/nonpublic dimension to our investigations. This school was located in the same community as the local Title III agency, thus providing ease of access to other information sources. These three settings (five schools) became the foci for intensive observation. The remaining schools were visited occasionally and briefly for comparative purposes.[17]

A further dimension was involved in the selection of comparison groups. We wanted to compare the differences between systems as well as the differences within systems. Consequently, during the course of the year we visited very briefly other CAI settings in widely dispersed parts of the country. This gave us the opportunity to compare particular phenomena — for example, the incidence of competitive behavior — observed in the Rural Highlands with other settings. Once the settings problem was resolved it became necessary to determine how best to utilize time and personnel resources. Our plan called for intensive observation in the fall, moderate to light observation during the winter, and intensive observation toward the close of the school year. To accomplish this we engaged in joint field work in the spring of the pre-experimental year, during the week-long summer workshop, and during the opening week of school. Thereafter we adopted an alternating schedule — one observer at a time in the field. While we typically concentrated our individual efforts in a particular setting, we occasionally switched vantage points. This served multiple purposes. By identifying ourselves individually in discrete settings we maximized the opportunities to become part of the respective social systems and thus became privy to information typically unavailable to 'outsiders'. Switching settings provided a constant check on the validity of the data collected. Deliberately building such flexibility into the basic strategy enhances the credibility of the final product.

In brief, that was our initial focus, our degree of involvement, and our strategical decisions. They seemed relevant to the circumstances and problems in which we found ourselves.

Aspects of a Theory of Fieldwork Methodology[18]

Standard participant observation

At one time or another we have described our procedures as being in the tradition of 'standard participant observation'. More recently, as we have tried to clarify our work in relation to what is done by other field workers, we have come to believe that there is no such reality as 'standard participant observation' or 'standard field work procedures'. Our position now is that the particular intent of the researcher, as well as the particular circumstances, determine the specific procedures utilized. To a considerable degree, such intents also determine the form and content of the published account of the research.

A cursory inspection of a half-dozen examples of participant observation studies suggests at least four dimensions along which the research styles vary (Table 1.2). For our purposes we have labeled these emphases as: (1) descriptive narrative, (2) generation of theory, (3) verification of theory, and (4) quantification of data. For illustrative purposes we compare and contrast our efforts with those of field workers from anthropological, sociological, and social psychological traditions: Glaser and Strauss (1967), general analysis; Becker and his colleagues (1961), study of a medical school; Festinger *et al.* (1956), study of a group predicting the end of the world; Blau (1955), study of two government agencies; and Wolcott (1967), educational anthropological study of an Indian village and school.

The emphasis on the descriptive narrative refers to the importance placed on a clear 'full story', of the program, group, organization, or culture under study. Only Glaser and Strauss deemphasize the narrative. The generation of theory, that is, the invention of concepts, hypotheses, and models distributes the research styles. Festinger *et al.*, come to the field with an intensively developed theory; traditional educational anthropology is less interested in theory generation. In contrast, Glaser and Strauss, as well as ourselves, strongly accent such efforts. The verification of theory is minimized by us, while Festinger *et al.* see it as their principal target. Wolcott's general atheoretical position minimizes verificational as well as generative aspects of theory. The others are more moderate in this regard.[19] Quantification is minimized by us, Wolcott, and Festinger *et al.* Glaser and Strauss are more moderate. Becker and Blau quantify in different ways: Becker quantifies field notes while Blau quantifies interactional data.[20]

It seems imperative that field workers describe carefully the methods used in each study and that codification of procedures continues.

Table 1.2: Variations in fieldwork

Dimensions of Field Work	Low	Dimensional Emphasis Moderate	High
Descriptive Narrative	2		13456
Generation of Theory	45	3	126
Verification of Theory	15	236	4
Quantification of Data	145	2	36

Exemplars of Varying Field Work Traditions
1. Smith and Pohland   *CAI*
2. Glaser and Strauss   *Grounded Theory*
3. Becker *et al.*   *Boys in White*
4. Festinger *et al.*   *When Prophecy Fails*
5. Wolcott   *A Kwakiutl Village and School*
6. Blau   *Dynamtics of Bureaucracy*

Valid data: The sine qua non of evaluation

Malinowski, in discussing the 'imponderabilia of actual life,' comments:

> Living in the village with no other business but to follow native life, one sees the customs, ceremonies and transactions over and over again, one has examples of their beliefs as they are actually lived through, and the full body and blood of actual native life fills out soon the skeleton of abstract construction. (1922, p. 15)

We would urge the reader to consider the implications of this kind of observation for what a test maker might call the validity of his measures. In our study we observed teachers, pupils, machines, and a variety of lessons. We talked with teachers and pupils informally about their problems, plans, activities, and reactions. We talked informally with the members of multiple organizations: school principals and supervisors, telephone repairmen, computer experts, and so forth. In most instances we got along very well. In some instances we were interested strangers who were out of the authority structure, who knew what was going on, who would listen, and who would empathize. The method has a potency that we came to appreciate only gradually, and we believe we obtained a valid picture of the CAI program.

In pursuing the logic of the validity of our data, we found considerable help in the technical test development literature, for example, *Technical Recommendations for Psychological Tests and Diagnostic Techniques* (American Psychological Association, 1954) and a paper especially relevant to our purposes entitled 'Convergent and discriminant validation by the multitrait-multimethod matrix' (Campbell and Fiske, 1959). The essence of the latter is that investigations of personality traits should be analyzed by measuring a number of traits with a number of methods. For instance, one might be interested in variables such as ascendancy, hostility, and activity level. One might measure these through methods such as objective personality tests, projective devices, and sociometric nominations. Campbell and Fiske argue that the pattern of intercorrelations indicates reliabilities, validities, and method or instrument errors.

Their major conclusion was that many analyses of test data on personality traits contain large components of method variance. Only as one approaches the problem with multiple kinds of measures of multiple dimensions can one locate these method errors. As some correlations converge at high levels and as others diverge they gather data relevant to an expanded conception of construct validity. As we have thought about our use of participant observation technique, we felt that the style of our approach had fundamental logical commonalities with that of Campbell and Fiske (1959).

We have expanded their scheme into a multimethod, multivariable, multiperson, and multisituation matrix. A glance at Table 1.3 indicates that our methods included observation, informal interviewing, and collection of documents. Rather than investigating personality traits alone, we were concerned with classroom group variables and organizational variables as well. In addition to the teachers, pupils, and CAI curriculum which were our focal interests, we were involved with other teachers, principals, and individuals in diverse positions in multiple organizations. Finally, the situations in which we found ourselves were multiple. Within the classrooms we were involved in several areas of the curriculum. We arrived unannounced as well as announced. We were in the classrooms in different schools and in varied organizations, all of which contributed to the program.

While our approach was qualitative rather than quantitative and while we did not get 'complete' data from each cell in the matrix, we obtained a valid picture of our phenomenon: the case study of an innovative educational program. While we have not glorified our procedures with a term such as construct validity, we think our approach captures the best of that point of view. When we say in the vernacular 'that's the way it was', we have few doubts about our description and analysis.

Emphasis on the descriptive narrative

Most field workers place some emphasis on the descriptive account or narrative. Our own preference as nonparticipant observers, in contrast to Glaser and Strauss (1967), is to emphasize the narrative strongly. There are a number of reasons for this. (1) A careful, thorough-going descriptive account seems to be a prerequisite for grounded theory. Stated somewhat differently, the presence of a carefully documented narrative seems to correlate closely with credibility. For instance, we developed some of the descriptive material in *The Complexities of an Urban Classroom* (Smith and Geoffrey, 1968) explicitly for this purpose. (2) We have strong feelings and beliefs that the utilization of theory for the solution of practical problems in education is very important. This requires a fairly intensive descriptive account, particularly since teachers and educational administrators tend to think in situationally specific terms. One needs to know the context out of which the concepts came and to which they will be referred back. (3) The kind of theory

Table 1.3: Validity of Participant Observation: A Multimethod, Multiperson, Multisituation, and Multivariable Matrix.

1 *Methods*
   1.1 Observation
   1.2 Informal interviews
   1.3 Documents: lesson materials, computer print-outs, etc.
2 *Persons*
   2.1 Pupils
   2.2 Cooperating teachers
   2.3 Principals
   2.4 Other teachers
   2.5 Multiple incumbents of multiple positions in multiple organizations
3 *Situations*
   3.1 Pupils at terminals
   3.2 Classroom teaching: announced and unannounced visits
   3.3 Multiple parts of the curriculum — in addition to arithmetic
   3.4 Multiple schools
   3.5 Multiple organizations
   3.6 Multiple parts of the country
4 *Variables*
   4.1 Individual: schemas, traits, motives
   4.2 Group: classroom interaction, activity, sentiments
   4.3 Organizational: schools, universities, R & D, Title III

that we have been generating is what Glaser and Strauss would call a substantive rather than a formal theory. In this sense it is more closely tied to a particular setting and the requisite description of that setting. (4) We take the position that when an investigator begins his work, he does not know the full range of theoretically relevant concepts. In a study such as our CAI project the dynamics of the innovation changed over time, and a concept of theoretic relevance might be only dimly perceived or perceived not at all at the beginning. Again, this suggests the necessity for a detailed descriptive account. Given the choice of an overabundance of data containing much chaff but a potentially dense data base or little chaff but a potentially thin data base, we opted for the former. (5) Related to the preceding is the possibility of integrating data obtained from one study with that of other studies. We would simply maintain that the richer the descriptive account of each study, the easier and potentially more fruitful this cumulative effort can become. (6) Most of the teaching in which we have been involved has been of an applied sort, and the people who finish the training programs go into the kinds of settings that we have been studying. Once again, this provokes a need for a careful view and descriptive account. (7) In working with a number of students and others who have used or wanted to learn the method, we have often seen a good bit of anxiety about the way the method works. The descriptive or narrative job, while difficult to write in an interesting and lucid style, is at least initially an easy place to begin. Only after one has struggled a bit with the description and begins to see the possibilities of organizing and abstracting from such concrete materials the broader ideas, concepts, hypotheses and models, can one move freely and well.

We have a strong conviction that ultimately all hypotheses and models must be put to careful verification. The usual strategy here becomes the correlational analysis, field study, or even better, the laboratory or field experiment. Additionally, however, the building of a series of interrelated participant observer field studies in which one is basically generating a theory also has, as a side result, the gradual accumulation of propositions that have more than a bit of credibility and that approach the form of principles.

Emphasis on theory generation
In our earlier account of the CAI program we have accented the descriptive narrative, the CAI story. The theoretical orientation is implicit rather than self-conscious. In agreement with Glaser and Strauss (1967), our general position argues that participant observation is ideally suited to the generation of grounded theory. We present one brief illustration of such a thrust.[21] The descriptive material presented earlier on the 'dispersal decision' might be conceptualized in accordance with Figure 1.1. The key concept becomes the ratio of program magnitude to available resources. The primary antecedent is the localist and political content of group norms. The major consequences are political, technological, and programmatic.

Beyond being a summary statement, pictorial models such as Figure 1.1 have considerable heuristic value. Essentially, Figure 1.1 is a miniature theory, a chain-like series of propositions regarding educational innovation. Each one-step postulate and two-step theorem is an hypothesis susceptible to proof in other settings. For example, following only one major strand of the model, we can develop the following nine hypotheses:

1   The more localist and political the norm content, the greater the probability of dispersing scarce resources widely.
2   If scarce resources are widely dispersed, maintenance problems increase.
3   If maintenance problems increase, longer and more frequent periods of interrupted service occur.
4, 5, 6   As interrupted service increases, utilization decreases (4), teacher frustration increases (5), and pupil frustration increases (6).
7, 8, 9   As utilization decreases and teacher and pupil frustration increase, pupil achievement is minimized (7, 8, 9).

In retrospect, all of this appears very obvious, logical, and perhaps even simple-minded. Yet prior to the actual observations in the field setting, the 'obvious' was not so obvious, and issues that seriously affected the CAI program were perceived only 'through a glass darkly'. Being 'face to face', the field work shed some light on the interlocking conceptual framework on the CAI program.

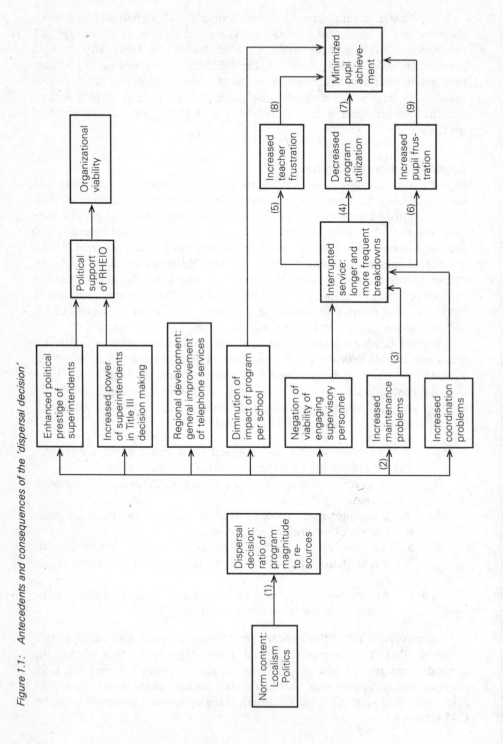

Figure 1.1: Antecedents and consequences of the 'dispersal decision'

Summary

Space limitations prohibit raising further issues, such as team relationships in participant observation, descriptive versus theoretical sampling, and theoretic sensitivity which Glaser and Strauss (1967), among others, have explored. Our intent has been to place our approach to field work in a more general model of curriculum evaluation, to clarify some of the specific procedural decisions and the reasons for making them, and to raise briefly some of the more interesting general issues in a theory of field methodology. Finally, our hope has been to develop some interest in and legitimation for participant observation within the growing technology of evaluation.

Notes

1   This research was supported by the Central Midwestern Regional Educational Laboratory, Inc. (CEMREL), a private nonprofit corporation supported in part as a regional educational laboratory by funds from the United States Office of Education, Department of Health, Education and Welfare. The opinions expressed in this publication do not necessarily reflect the position or policy of the Office of Education, and no official endorsement by the Office of Education should be inferred.

2   Overall there were thirty terminals in the schools. The hope was that approximately fifty children (two classes) might each have a computer drill lesson each day. On occasion some schools ran as high as ninety lessons in one day.

3   This intensified the political dimension of the innovative educational program, a significant but little analyzed phenomenon.

4   This suggests that evaluation models might well include social scientists skilled in the analysis of decision making.

5   It seemed to us that over and above the general unfamiliarity with the system, teachers as a whole were most reluctant to make any adjustments in the system for fear of tampering with the integrity of the experimental design aspect of the evaluation. While this fear was ungrounded, it nevertheless existed.

6   One of the settings for the teletype was a wire enclosed book storage closet located in the main hall of the school. To the observers it looked like a 'cage'.

7   Early in the school year this school had four teletypes. As the 'dispersal decision' took effect, the number was reduced.

8   The educational theorist immediately will want to synthesize the literature from Harlow (1950), Berlyne (1960), and White (1959).

9   This, too, is apparently a common element of the program as we observed identical situations in other CAI settings.

10   Parenthetically, we would note that the concepts of 'individualized instruction' and competitive behavior are incompatible.

11   It might be argued that the behaviors observed were a function of some small but intrinsic features of the CAI program and thus beyond the control of outside influence. Again, we would agree in part and not only admit the possibility but hypothesize, for example, that the competitiveness observed was enhanced by such features of the program as the printing of percent correct and the time taken to complete the drill, the ten-second response time allowed, the directiveness of the program, and the like. On another occasion we hope to move toward an analysis of these small but potentially significant aspects of the stimulus confi-

guration known as the CAI program. These latent variables may account for more outcome variance than the manifest variables, for example, individualization in level and pace, brevity of practice, and feedback, which are part of the formal doctrine of the program's creators. Phrased alternatively, these latent stimulus dimensions may engender what Stephens (1956, 1960, 1968) has called for a long time 'nondeliberative factors in learning and spontaneous schooling' and which Rothkopf (1965, 1968) has noted and labeled more recently as 'mathemagenic behaviors'. CAI in its varying formats offers a potent operational vehicle for clarification of such important theoretical ideas.

12 In the methodological supplement, we entertain some arguments relative to the validity of such data.

13 Among the model's several weaknesses, we are concerned mostly with (1) the unresolved nature of educational theory; (2) the sequencing of evaluation efforts among the three modes; and (3) the classes of people who use or make decisions based upon the results.

14 In training students for field work we now emphasize strongly the initial problem statement and the expected evolution and redefinition of the problem. Our experience with the 'no initial focus' stance is that many beginning field workers are left apprehensive and confused. In retrospect, we always had to write such statements because we were seeking funds or justifying our activities for our organizational superiors who needed such a statement in their files. We had not appreciated the latent function of such organizational demands for an initial clarity in the problem under study.

15 Our reference here is to Homans' (1949) delightful phrasing of a significant methodological issue: 'People who write about methodology often forget that it is a matter of strategy, not of morals. There are neither good nor bad methods, but only methods that are more or less effective under particular circumstances in reaching objectives on the way to a distant goal' (p. 330).

16 It is important to realize, as the several citations of notes made during the 'preevaluation period' attest, that field work begins as soon as one enters the field, regardless of the initial reasons for being there.

17 In addition the five intensive observation schools were all in a subset of nine schools which were part of the 'experimental design' leg of the overall evaluation.

18 In part, this analysis was generated through several attempts to come to grips with the position taken by Glaser and Strauss (1967).

19 Our personal preference is to move toward verification in settings where careful controls can be instituted, careful measures developed for significant concepts, and large enough samples of subjects can be obtained. The concept of teacher awareness, generated in Smith and Geoffrey (1968), has received this attention in Smith and Kleine (1969).

20 Our analysis of the quantification issue is presented in *Go, Bug, Go!' Methodological Issues in Classroom Observational Research* (Smith and Brock, 1970).

21 More intensive arguments, attempts, and illustrations in other settings appear in Smith and Geoffrey (1968), and Smith and Keith (1971). Pohland (1970) extends the CAI analysis to interorganizational theory.

References

AMERICAN PSYCHOLOGICAL ASSOCIATION, COMMITTEE ON PSYCHOLOGICAL TESTS (1954) *Technical recommendations for psychological tests and diagnostic techniques*, Washington, DC: APA.

BECKER, H.S. (1958) 'Problems of inference and proof in participant observation', *American Sociological Review, 28*, pp. 652–60.

BECKER, H.S., GREER, B., HUGHES, E. and STRAUSS, A. (1961) *Boys in white: Student culture in a medical school*, Chicago: University of Chicago Press.

BERLYNE, D.E. (1960) *Conflict, arousal, and curiosity*, New York: McGraw-Hill.

BLAU, P.M. (1955) *The dynamics of bureaucracy*, Chicago: University of Chicago Press.

CAMPBELL, D.T. and FISKE, D.W. (1959) 'Convergent and discriminant validation by the multitrait-multimethod matrix', *Psychological Bulletin 56*, pp. 81–105.

FESTINGER, L., RIECKEN, H. and SCHACHTER, S. (1956) *When prophecy fails*, New York: Harper Torchbook.

GLASER, B.G. and STRAUSS, A.L. (1967) *The discovery of grounded theory: Strategies for qualitative research*, Chicago: Aldine.

HARLOW, H.F. *et al.* (1950) 'Learning motivated by a manipulation drive', *Journal of Experimental Psychology 40*, pp. 228–34.

HOMANS, G.C. (1949) 'The strategy of industrial sociology', *American Journal of Sociology 54*, pp. 330–37.

MALINOWSKI, B. (1922) *The argonauts of the western pacific*, London: Routledge.

MALINOWSKI, B. (1965) *Coral gardens and their magic. Volume I, Soil-tilling and agricultural rites in the Trobriand Islands*, Bloomington: Indiana University Press.

MERTON, R.K. (1957) *Social theory and social structure*, (Rev. ed.) Glencoe, Illinois: Free Press.

POHLAND, P.A. (1970) *An interorganizational analysis of an innovative educational program.* (Unpublished doctoral dissertation) St. Louis, MO.: Washington University.

ROTHKOPF, E.Z. (1965) 'Some theoretical and experimental approaches to problems in written instruction', in KRUMBOLTZ, J.D. (Ed.), *Learning and the Educational Process* Chicago: Rand McNally & Co (pp. 193–221).

ROTHKOPF, E.Z. (1968) 'Two scientific approaches to the management of instruction', in GAGNE, R. and GEPHART, W. (Eds), *Learning Research and School Subjects*, Itaska, Illinois: Peacock pp. 107–132.

RUSSELL, H. (Ed.) (1969) *Evaluation of Computer Assisted Instruction Program*, St. Ann, Missouri: CEMREL.

SCRIVEN, M. (1967) 'The methodology of evaluation', in TYLER, R.W. GAGNE, R.M. and SCRIVEN, M. (Eds), *Perspectives of curriculum evaluation*, Chicago: Rand McNally (pp. 39–83).

SINDELL, P.S. (1969) 'Anthropological approaches to the study of education. *Review of Educational Research 39*, pp. 593–95.

SMITH, L.M. and BROCK J.A.M. (1970) *Go, bug, go!: Methodological issues in classroom observational research* (Occasional Paper Series #5), St. Ann, Missouri: CEMREL.

SMITH, L.M. and BROCK, J.A.M. (1975) *Teacher plans and classroom interaction*, St. Ann, Missouri: CEMREL.

SMITH, L.M. and GEOFFREY, W. (1968) *The complexities of an urban classroom*, New York: Holt, Rinehart and Winston.

SMITH, L.M. and KEITH, P.M. (1971) *Anatomy of educational innovation*, New York: Wiley.

SMITH, L.M. and KLEINE, P.F. (1969) 'Teacher awareness: Social cognition in the classroom', *School Review 77*, pp. 245–56.

STAKE, R.E. (1967) 'Toward a technology for the evaluation of educational programs', in TYLER, R.W. GAGNE, R.M. and SCRIVEN, M. (Eds), *Perspectives of curriculum evaluation*, Chicago: Rand McNally (pp. 1–12).

STEPHENS, J.M. (1956) 'Nondeliberative factors underlying the phenomenon of schooling', *Educational Theory 6*, pp. 26–34.

Louis M. Smith and Paul A. Pohland

STEPHENS, J.M. (1960) 'Spontaneous schooling and success in teaching', *School Review* *68*, pp. 152–63.

STEPHENS, J.M. (1968) *The process of schooling*, New York: Holt, Rinehart and Winston.

WHITE, R.W. (1959) 'Motivation reconsidered: The concept of competence', *Psychological Review 66*, pp. 297–333.

WOLCOTT, H.A. (1967) *Kwakiutl village and school*, New York: Holt, Rinehart and Winston.

WHYTE, W.F. (1955) *Street corner society* (Rev. ed.), Chicago: University of Chicago Press.

Chapter 2

PLATO Mathematics: The Teacher and Fourth Grade Students Respond

Bernadine Evans Stake

Methodology for the Study of the Utilization of PLATO[1]

This case study of the evaluation of PLATO and Fourth Grade Mathematics was designed and carried out to gain an in-depth understanding of the use of PLATO in the classroom. As part of the Educational Testing Service (ETS) Evaluation Team studying the National Science Foundation's funded research on PLATO mathematics, I became curious about what was happening with individual children and teachers over time as they worked and played with PLATO. The ETS evaluation, directed by Ernest Anastasio, concentrated on statistical data from many observations and tests to examine the worth of the innovation. The Champaign-Urbana elementary school data were intended to be a part of the whole, originally not intended to describe a single classroom. According to plan, the aggregated data alone were to tell the story.

Gradually it became clear that a self-sustaining case study would be of value. The resulting report was, 'PLATO and Fourth Grade Mathematics' (Stake, B.E., 1977).

At the beginning of the second year of the ETS work a decision was made to study one classroom in depth and to produce case studies of a few children in that room. Ms. Hamilton's[2] room was chosen, perhaps because she had kept the best logs the first year and because the implementation of PLATO in her room was exemplary. The children chosen to be observed were not the mathematics 'winners'. Two children who appeared to have average mathematics ability turned out to have more ability than expected. Another child whose work at school was usually graded as 'failing' experienced some success with PLATO math.

The study was designed to provide an in-depth look at the children and Sheila Hamilton, the teacher. It was decided to use what Guba and Lincoln (1981) have called a naturalistic-responsive approach. This approach is naturalistic in that ordinary people tell the story by their actions and words. Events are documented and thoughts recorded in order to provide readers with a vicarious experience. The children's and their teacher's experiences with

PLATO, it is hoped, will give the reader insight into how PLATO in one classroom was utilized to teach mathematics to these twenty-four children.

Ideas for the design of this case study come mainly from the educational research approach of Robert E. Stake (1975, 1977) and his writings about responsive evaluation and case study. The methodology was also influenced by Sylvia Scribner's (1976) anthropological research. A 'bounded system', the classroom, was designated as the focus of the study for collection of data. Observations, interviews and document review (mainly the teacher's log) provided the bulk of the 'thick data' collected over a two year period. With these data PLATO was described in context to assist readers in drawing their own conclusions and revising their own generalizations. Such observations have been compared to naturalistic studies of animals, where close observations of their actions and sounds are made in order to describe their habits (Tinbergen, 1971). The focus of this study was to gather data on the culture of the fourth grade classroom and the micro-culture of the space around the PLATO terminals as PLATO was being implemented.

This is the story of Ms. Hamilton's first two years of teaching with PLATO. The story of the first year, 1974–75, was drawn from Ms. Hamilton's teacher's log, classroom observations, teacher interviews and random observations of students at the terminals. Sixty-minute observations were made regularly twice a month in the first school term. During the first half of the hour the classroom was observed and the remaining half hour was spent observing individual children at the terminal. On the same visit brief informal comments from the teacher were solicited.

Additional information was collected the second year. Observations in the classroom were more frequent. The teacher's log and interviews with the teacher and the children added a second and third dimension. To detail their progress on PLATO, three particular children were observed over two semesters: Sara, Ted and Kate. Formal interviews were conducted twice a year with a few selected students and the teacher. In the second school year regular visits to the classroom were made weekly, and in addition to those visits, observations were made during different times of the day over a one week period to get a picture of a day with PLATO. At the beginning of each school year, two observers observed the classroom at the same time in order to compare and corroborate data. In response to the teacher requests and to special events, random visits were made as well. These observations, informal talks with the teacher, teacher and child interviews and the teacher's log provided the data of the study.

The following case study is drawn from the longer version, 'PLATO and Fourth Grade Mathematics' (Stake, B.E., 1977). In the present version, Sara, 'a student described as average' and her teacher were chosen as the main informants and their experiences are reported here. A quarter of the vignettes of the classroom activities are included in this report in order to detail the culture around the terminals and to describe the teacher's and Sara's experience with PLATO. In the original two hundred page study the observations tell the story of more children.

An attempt was made to examine both the activites around the terminal and activities in other parts of the room and to see if there were differences between the 'cultures' in the two parts of the room. Also effort was made to determine if the children were 'governed by the terminal' or if the children controlled the terminal. This abbreviated report tells less of the context of the room and more of PLATO, Ms. Hamilton and Sara. Sara's progress in mathematics is detailed over the school year.

Ms. Hamilton, Sara and the other children in the classroom are discussed in relation to the PLATO terminals and learning in mathematics. Descriptions of the teacher working with children, planning their curriculum and implementing PLATO are presented in detail to provide the reader with insight into this particular curriculum innovation in classroom instruction. It is hoped that the reader will be able to visualize the culture of the PLATO classroom from the descriptions of children interacting with the terminals, their classmates and their teacher and come to know what it was like to spend two years with PLATO and Ms. Hamilton. With these data the reader is urged to triangulate and draw inferences from your own experience.

Ninety Nine, One Hundred, One Thousand Rationale
For PLATO Mathematics

PLATO is a computer based teaching system individualizing student instruction. Its lessons were designed to allow students to work at their own pace.[3] Lesson performance was recorded and 'evaluated' by the computer located at the Computer-Based Education Research Laboratory (CERL). Children sat at a terminal with a typewriter keyboard and 'touch panel'. Each child responded to directives and questions on the screen by touching it or by typing a message onto the screen. PLATO responded to the child's directives and prescribed work in accordance with the child's previous performance. Children learned mathematics as they interacted with the terminal to work the lessons presented on the screen. Animated graphics helped keep attention on the screen.

Certain curricular materials were programmed for the teaching of mathematics. At the time (1977) these were designed for fourth, fifth, and sixth grade children in American classrooms. The curriculum was developed in three areas of mathematics: graphs, whole numbers, and fractions. These materials were the result of development and field trials at the University of Illinois. The work was sponsored in large part by the National Science Foundation and was evaluated by the Educational Testing Service.

Introduction of PLATO into the classroom created a considerably different way of bringing children and materials together for instruction in mathematics. PLATO occupied a fixed space in a corner of the classroom where children came to interact with it. The space around the terminals became the locus for highly purposive work in an uncommon classroom sub-culture.

Ours is a society that honors numbers as well as the written word. Many people who cannot use either numbers or words effectively are out of the mainstream of communication. In numbers and words there is a power which almost everyone yearns to share. Numbers are particularly powerful. They are used to predict the outcome of elections and to justify expenditure of funds. Numbers in research are used to support claims for different theories. Economic health is measured by gross numbers. Higher numbers represent more wealth, more power, or, on the other hand, more heart attacks, more pollution. School policies are often determined by statistics showing costs and benefits. When numbers possess such apparent power they can intimidate people and exclude people from privilege. Complex statistical reports and high scores on tests can manipulate people's decisions. The claims made by such reports and tests are often accepted even when the statistics and tests are not understandable.

The computer is a tool that can be used to simplify and restructure numerical information to make it more easily understood. At times, however, the use of the computer does not simplify, but complicates and confuses. Computers can be used capriciously, merely to impress people with the complexity of technology. Since numbers and computers are not always used effectively, it is important to show young people how numbers and computers can be used for their benefit.

CERL ... Three Areas Of Mathematics Lessons

CERL is the acronym for the Computer-based Education Research Laboratory at the University of Illinois. In the early 1960s Donald Bitzer developed the plasma display panel — the single most unique feature of PLATO — permitting replacement of the irregular patterning cathode ray tube. Bitzer was responsible for the creation of PLATO, but more than that, his genius and optimism were often forces that allowed a seemingly anarchical operation to continue to make progress.

Robert B. Davis, a widely respected mathematics curriculum developer, was principally in charge of the PLATO mathematics curriculum. He put together a team of six authors to work on three areas of mathematics: graph lessons, whole numbers and fractions lessons. Gerald Glynn and Don Cohen created the graph lessons. Bonnie Anderson Seiler and Charles Weaver conceptualized whole numbers and the fractions lessons were designed by Sharon Dugdale and David Kibbey.[4]

From the beginning PLATO mathematics was a multifaceted operation. In 1974 PLATO was implemented in twelve classrooms in the Champaign-

Urbana area. The authors wrote lessons, discussed routing procedures and curriculum problems, evaluated lessons, talked to teachers, oriented teachers and observers and wrote more lessons. Others developed additional hardware, routed lessons, talked to the authors and maintained the system. It was difficult even for the staff to keep up with all that was happening. There were teacher meetings; staff meetings; visits from experts in curriculum and experts in hardware. There were visitors from Japan, from Germany, from Sweden and many other countries. There were calls for help from teachers: 'Touch panels aren't working.' 'The system is down.' 'The lessons are all mixed up.' 'The air conditioner isn't working.' 'Sally can't access her lessons.' 'The keyset won't type.'

When a call came in, typically an author would take it, discuss the problem with the teacher and sometimes rush out to the school. Teachers and authors usually felt that they couldn't wait for Tony, the general repairman. Ties between the authors and the teachers were close — no doubt at a cost to the production quota.

The operation was fluid. If a problem arose in the curriculum, something was changed. If authors didn't like the way a lesson was working for children, they changed it. If teachers pointed out that children needed more help, the authors went back and developed more assistance. If the patches had shown it would have been the craziest of crazy quilts.

Utilization of PLATO: the Teacher's Response

The Fourth Grade Classroom — Year One

The teacher's role in the classroom is a major determining factor of the climate of the classroom. Ms. Sheila Hamilton structured and controlled the environment to allow children some freedom to work independently and to be creative, but that freedom was dependent upon the children's acceptance of responsibility in making choices. Ms. Hamilton organized lessons and activities so that the children had limited freedom of movement and socialization, stressing concern for the rights of others. Children were given more and more freedom as they accepted responsibility. Usually they were not responsible for determining the content of their lessons. They could select when they wished to work on required lessons and their privileges were determined by their ability to finish work.

Sheila Hamilton's teaching of fourth grade children reflected an adventurous and creative spirit. Sheila had traveled in many countries, bringing back slides and cultural artifacts which she shared with the children. She took the children on educational excursions including a visit to the State Capital. These trips provided a special opportunity for Ms. Hamilton to teach concern for others and responsibility while they were learning about the tools and customs of other times and places.

On her own time Ms. Hamilton studied history and portrait drawing. In school she helped children build Egyptian tombs, sew pioneer quilts and model Indian artifacts of clay. She had a well-developed sense of history and culture and tried to impart it to the children.

Ms. Hamilton was committed to the teaching profession. She said, 'The only trouble with teaching is that it consumes all my time.' It consumed her time because she was always doing extra projects and taking trips with the children. She was interested in new ideas and wanted to try out those ideas to help children learn. Sheila seemed to be able to make innovative changes and at the same time protect the classroom atmosphere and herself from great disruption. She protected the old while trying out the new.

Sheila Hamilton was introduced to PLATO at the same time that she was introduced to a new school. In the fall of 1974 when she began teaching she was dismayed by the behavior of the children at this school.

September, 1974

Teacher's Log: I am not one of the original volunteers. I was assigned to Johnson School in August and moved to the community a few days prior to new teacher orientation. I had heard of PLATO through friends who were greatly impressed with it and excited by it. After first using PLATO my feelings were mixed. I was impressed and excited but also frustrated. I knew that some of the children had used PLATO and would be more at ease with it than I. Also, I learned, teachers were to have spent forty hours on PLATO during the summer. New teacher orientation had been overwhelming. This district is 'super organized'. There seems to be too many things to remember, too many materials with which to become familiar. In addition came the question, 'What is expected at Johnson School?' The latter was probably the most frustrating. Resolving it left little time for concern about PLATO.

The first week of school was a nightmare. I felt the children were generally self-centered, lacking self-discipline, unable to function in group situations and disrespectful to each other as well as to adults. From the cumulative folders, I learned all but three of the twenty-two should be able to work at or above grade level. Six of the twenty-two had previously been scheduled with the social worker. I recommended an additional two. Six had been in other supportive programs. This year Debbie has Title I assistance in reading; Nancy works daily with the learning disabilities teacher; Barry, Sally, Frank, Kent, and Larry are seeing the social worker. Larry, Sean and Sandra have shown immature outbursts of temper. Peter, Larry, Nancy and Sean have refused to work with our Title III instructional aide. There are other, more subtle problems with the class. I have cited these to indicate special problems and hint at the atmosphere they tend to create.

I am not a novice. This is my fourteenth year of teaching elementary children. Child behavior has *not* been a problem for me in the past. With this class freedom leads directly and immediately to confusion and disorder. The children are difficult and responsibly immature. Currently my impressions are as follows:

> Barry — easily distracted, clownish, bright with very poor study habits. Adrift — possibly due to problems at home, lacks concentration, works only in one-to-one situation. *Very poor* work habits, poor work.

> Sandra — does not interact well with other children, wants to do well, works hard, gets angry when she doesn't understand something, cries when teased by other children, tends to feel others don't care about her — may result from home problems.

> Anika — conscientious, works hard and usually well.

> Gary — bright, well-adjusted, happy, alert, polite, does work quickly and well, above grade level in all areas, popular....

I have taught in traditional schools. Johnson is considered a school open to new ideas and methods, tending toward the open classroom. Although I have read about and visited some open schools, I have had no formal training for this approach to education. During the first month of school, I found myself constantly revising the organization of my teaching. PLATO was not yet in operation. I knew it must be integrated into this organization. I soon discovered that children were willing to work only on the assignments that were 'R&R' (required for recess).

Having talked with more experienced 'lab school' teachers, we switched from daily to weekly goals. The first day of the week assignments were given in math, spelling, language arts, and science. The assignments were posted on the board. The children were expected to plan their daily schedule, reading being the only daily requirement.

Weekly Goals — Math September 16–20
1   Math progress check — Monday
2   Practice x's facts at least 15 min. each day
3   Be ready for x's challenge
4   Groups:

I	II
SRA[5] p. 24–30 (self check)	MIA p. 43–49 (self check)
MIA[6] p. 52–60 (self check)	SRA p. 15–17 (self check)
2 worksheets	3 worksheets

September 16, 1974

Ms. Hamilton considered teaching whole numbers the main objective in fourth grade math. On the long bulletin board above the cloak closet a space game illustrated the children's progress on addition, subtraction, multiplication and division facts. Children were given five seconds to look at a flash card and write the answer to the whole number fact.

Teacher's Log: A 'challenge' system was set up for basic facts. The planets and sun were displayed and 'rockets' labeled with each child's name — orange for addition, green for subtraction, yellow for multiplication, blue for division. On the basis of the diagnostic testing each child's name was placed under a planet for addition and subtraction. Since no one did well on multiplication or division no rockets were placed in this area.

Individual flash card challenges were given each day — oral responses. If they were successful on their planet, they moved their rocket to the next planet toward the sun and had one chance that day to move again. They could continue taking challenges and moving until a fact was missed. When + or – 9s were passed the entire set of cards were given. If this was passed the rocket was placed on the sun. After two weeks, half the class had passed addition, about one-quarter subtraction. We started to concentrate on multiplication about the third week of school.

Skills of carrying and renaming were also tested. Almost everyone needed reteaching and lots of review with renaming in subtraction. Addition results were good, but I was aware that many children were finger counting.

By the third week, most children were not handing in daily plans and could not remember their assignments. Therefore, an individual copy of assignments with a check-off list was started. The children seemed to find this easier to handle and more assignments were being completed. Papers and the check sheets were put in folders with the child's name and I go through each folder every night.

Each day I meet with small groups to discuss new concepts or problem areas. I also meet with each of the reading groups. Individual conferences are used to discuss work, give special help or special assignments. I find that these children are attentive in small groups, but even the better students lack attentiveness when the entire class is addressed. Several times a week we have twenty to thirty minutes of quiet reading – material of their choice. Most of the children look forward to this time and become very engrossed in their reading.

Since there had been several dates given for starting PLATO and several delays, I decided not to give my class a date of operation until that day arrived. They waited patiently — after the initial questions when the terminals were placed in the rooms.

Sheila Hamilton's log shows repeated concern for organization and structure in the room.[7] She tried to create something of an optimum learning environment for the children. She kept records of children's progress in all subject areas and the children's folders of work were carefully checked and sent home for inspection. PLATO terminals were arranged to fit into the classroom and a schedule for use was set up, all subject to revision regularly.

September 16–20, 1974

> *Teacher's Log: Graphing Lessons.* Don Cohen came to the room to sign each child onto the terminals giving them the procedure and getting their sign-on and passwords. This was done individually and took a couple of days. At this time the terminals were arranged so that each unit faced a different direction. This proved unsatisfactory as it was difficult to observe the terminals, get to them quickly and make sure that the right person (or anyone) was on a terminal. The terminals were then placed in a line, facing the same direction. This has been much better for monitoring and children are often able to discuss differences or ideas and help each other. At Don's suggestion a two inch board was placed under each terminal at the back. This reduced glare from our lights on the terminal display.
>
> It was necessary to set up some type of schedule for use of the terminals. At first a card was placed on each terminal. Names and check off boxes were on each card. Children were asked to put an X or fill in the box when they had completed their turn. Later they were asked to tell how many minutes they were on. There was a great range, sometimes from sixteen to forty-three minutes. If a child was 'knocked off', when they went back in they had a new set of thirty minutes. This caused many social problems.
>
> This method of record keeping was used for only a short time. It was difficult for me to know whose turn it was because no one carried a pencil to the terminal to put a check behind their name. We were always asking who had had a turn.
>
> A vertical row of library book pockets was placed on the chalkboard for each terminal. A number was placed on the terminal at the top of the vertical column. Cards with each child's name were placed in the pockets with the name showing. As a child finished his turn, he took a couple of steps to the board, turned his name card over so that no name showed and went to get the next person below. It is easy to check terminal use from the opposite side of the room. Also, if a child forgets to tell the next user, someone else usually notices and acts as a reminder. The ones who haven't been on can see how soon their turn will come and if an empty terminal is spotted, it isn't necessary for me to call off names. Instead of a specified time block (Mary 9–9.30), we start at the top and just advance until all are finished. If someone is out of the room or meeting with a special group or teacher when their time comes that person is skipped. Also if those on one terminal complete their lessons early (due to absences or

other reasons) it is easy to spot and transfer a child from one terminal to another.

Since PLATO was a scarce resource Ms. Hamilton organized the use of it to give everyone a turn. Other teachers had more difficulty organizing the classroom for implementation of PLATO or they didn't worry about it. Some considered PLATO an add-on and others set aside a specific time each day for a child to work at the terminal. Ms. Hamilton seemed to be thinking more than most about ways to facilitate the details of structuring the classroom for optimum learning. She also discovered on the first day of using the terminals that PLATO had a potentiality for motivation and control of behavior. Several unruly youngsters were intrigued with PLATO. It served from there on (in part, of course) as a reward for good behavior in the classroom.

Teacher's Log: The children were all eager to begin using PLATO. A few had had limited exposure at the end of third grade; a few had older brothers or sisters who were signed onto PLATO and let them on once and awhile. For most children it was the first time. They picked around a little with the keys, but soon learned which ones were most needed and before long they were hardly looking at the keyset.

Two children made great impressions the first day of terminal use. Larry had been a problem since he put his foot through the door. He was obviously in need of a great deal of attention — not from classmates — from the teacher. Anytime he did not receive 'instant attention' he laid on the floor, making loud noises, kicking his legs. This was not a new behavior for him. I learned that he *enjoyed* verbal battles with previous teachers. Larry had had some experience with PLATO. He was at once at home with the terminal. This was to date the only task that he tackled 'on his own' — the first non-one-to-one achievement. From the first day he was staying after school for an extra turn. This became an important factor in control. He could stay for an extra turn only when he had been cooperative during the day. This motivated him and slowly he began to correct his behavior. He often stays an hour after school.

Barry had no previous experience on PLATO. Although his behavior was not as unusual as Larry's he had also been referred to the social worker. He accomplishes nothing and seems to remember very little of practiced skills. He missed almost all addition and subtraction facts and doesn't remember borrowing in subtraction. I teach him renaming every day. The next day — or even the same afternoon — he has forgotten and we must go through all of it again.

I watched Barry as he first signed on and started to work on the terminal. I couldn't believe this was the same boy. He was at last catching on quickly and performing well. This was his first success in over a month of school. PLATO is the one thing he is ready and anxious to do. He watches for his turn and is happiest when he is using the terminal — gladly gives up recess for his turn.

As with Barry and Larry, PLATO seemed to provide a special private space for some children. They could be engaged in learning new skills in a non-threatening atmosphere and at the same time be rewarded by instant feedback. Children somehow felt accepted and satisfied to the extent that they did not need or want to protest. Instead they enjoyed the challenge of the lessons. Sheila Hamilton was grateful to have found a way to reach children who seemed to find most of their school day an unrewarding experience. Ms. Hamilton's record keeping of the children's progress on PLATO and the regular mathematics curriculum were important to her. She started early to integrate PLATO and the school mathematics curriculum.

October 28, 1974

This morning Ms. Hamilton settled the children down to a quiet working atmosphere. As an observer I noted, 'There was a low buzz of conversation and kids were allowed to move about the room as they pleased. I have a feeling that there are underlying rules about this. The room is less tense.' Another observer noted: 'Children work quietly alone, occasionally a couple of children interact. Otherwise interaction is with the teacher.'

Four children worked on PLATO terminals and the other children worked at their seats on worksheets. Ms. Hamilton supplemented PLATO mathematics with her regular mathematics lessons. GRAPHS were the only lessons 'running' on PLATO in October, and GUESS MY RULE (Graphs, 4b) was one of the main lessons. Ms. Hamilton prepared GUESS MY RULE worksheets to accompany the lessons on PLATO. Children worked on the worksheets and referred to examples of GUESS MY RULE on the chalkboard.

It is interesting to note that Ms. Hamilton as a new teacher with many demands on her time worked especially hard to relate PLATO mathematics to her curriculum. Many of the other teachers in the ETS study used PLATO as supplementary mathematics and didn't try to coordinate it with the school mathematics curriculum.

October 29, 1974

GUESS MY RULE[8] problems were written on the black board with examples of possible solutions. Obviously Ms. Hamilton was helping the children with this PLATO lesson. She was integrating the PLATO graph lessons with the whole number lessons she was teaching.

Children were working on individual lessons. Ms. Hamilton was sitting at her desk and individual children came up to her to talk about the lessons. The room was decorated for Halloween. Children's writing and other work was displayed. A chart for the Halloween Committee meeting listed activities

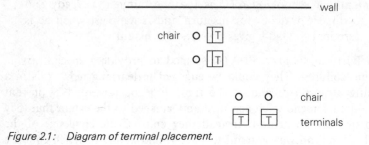

Figure 2.1: Diagram of terminal placement.

for the party. On one bulletin board was 'A Packet of Puzzles at the Blue Kangaroo' (puzzles for children to work at their leisure).

Two of the terminals were situated so the pupils were visible from other parts of the room. The other two were placed at right angles so the terminals separated the pupil operators from the rest of the class, as seen in Figure 2.1.

Harry was at the terminal. He had finished TODAY'S DATE (Whole Numbers, Fl) and talked to PLATO as he continued with BATTLESHIP (Graphs, lb). 'Look how PLATO is moving.' 'Who hit him?' 'I've got him cornered.' Harry kept choosing correct responses. Then he talked to the child next to him. 'You beat me so much.' 'Golly I'm havin' a hard time.' When Harry chose TOWER OF HANOI (Graphs, 4m) Don Cohen, developer of the graph lessons, told him how to move. Harry said, 'I know how to play.' Harry worked at TOWER OF HANOI. After many moves PLATO showed Harry how to play.

November 10, 1974

> *Teacher's Log*: As I said, I have been concentrating on their learning basic facts. At the same time, I feel that it is important to correlate classroom and PLATO. Therefore, the children have had 'PLATO worksheets'. Sometimes this is done as a part of the weekly progress check.
>
> Most children had discovered the procedure for plotting points on the graph and especially enjoy BATTLESHIP. They were able to make the transfer to paper easily. There were, however, a few children who were guessing at points and needed further instruction in locating them.
>
> Many children were stumbling through GUESS MY RULE, some watching the terminal of a friend for a solution. We discussed patterns in numbers as a group and worked many GUESS MY RULES together. I put a number of card games on the board which they were encouraged to work *with* their friends. After a couple of days — sometimes a week — we would go over the patterns and rules together (see Figure 2.2 for examples of GUESS MY RULE problems).

GUESS MY RULE		GUESS MY RULE		GUESS MY RULE		GUESS MY RULE		GUESS MY RULE		GUESS MY RULE	
□											
0	0	0	2	1	2	2	7	2	5	3	27
1	7	1	7	2	15	3	9	3	9	4	35
2	10	2	12	3	22	4	11	4	13	5	43
3	13	3	17	4	29	5	13	5	17	6	51
4	16	4	22	5	36	6	15	6	21	7	59

Figure 2.2: Examples of GUESS MY RULE problems.

At first, the children found these very difficult. Then they began to see patterns and form rules. PLATO began to use minus numbers (see Figure 2.3 for examples of GUESS MY RULE using minus numbers).

0	2	1	−1	0	3	0	0
1	7	2	−4	1	1	1	1
2	12	3	−7	2	−1	2	8
3	17	4	−10	3	−3	3	27
4	22	5	−13	4	−5	4	64

0	0	0	1	1	−2	0	3
1	−1	1	−2	2	0	1	−1
2	−4	2	−5	3	2	2	−5
3	−9	3	−8	4	4	3	−9
4	−16	4	−11	5	6	4	−13

Figure 2.3: Examples of GUESS MY RULE problems using minus numbers.

Minus numbers were confusing, especially when they started minus and changed to plus. Again, I feel that more regular sessions would have helped get the idea across more quickly. A few did quite well — Gary, Harry, Kent and Sandy. After two or three weeks of reinforcement, the major portion of the class was doing fairly well.

The class also did the booklet on GUESS MY RULE prepared by PLATO authors. Some of these were quite difficult. They were given a week to do what they could before we discussed rules.

Some took them home and discussed the problems with their parents. By the end of the week, all problems had a rule — except one, which did not have a pattern or rule.

In addition to the GUESS MY RULES given here, the numbers were sometimes given out of order so that it was necesary to organize them before beginning to work on the rule (see Figure 2.4 for examples of GUESS MY RULE problems using unordered numbers).

3	17	0	2
0	2	1	7
4	22	2	12
2	12	3	17
1	7	4	22

Figure 2.4: Examples of GUESS MY RULE problems using unordered numbers.

November 4, 1974

Ms Hamilton reviewed and evaluated lessons as she monitored children at the terminal. She also spent time working at the terminal after school to review the lessons.

Sheila found NAMES FOR TODAY'S DATE (Whole Numbers, Fl) a source of frustration for her and the children. When a child signed onto PLATO he/she was required to write a new NAME FOR TODAY'S DATE (Whole Numbers, Fl) such as 8–2 for the 6th of November. Each day required a different name and each child was expected to find a name different from those used earlier in the day. Children who signed on early used easy names and others who signed on later in the day were challenged to find something else. Sometimes the requirements would be beyond the child's experience or take too much of the child's time to find a NAME FOR TODAY'S DATE and leave little time for other activities on PLATO. Children were encouraged to use division and multiplication, but addition (and occasionally subtraction) was most often used. Some children learned to use a series of 0's or brackets to satisfy a new solution: $5 + (0) + (0) + (0) + (1) + (0) = 6$. In using brackets they learned that a bracket on one side required a bracket on the other side also or PLATO would not accept their solution.

When Sheila told Don and Jerry about the problems, they visited the room and worked with the children at the chalkboard to prod their creativities. They tried to make the business of composing more interesting. The children did well after Don and Jerry's help. Ms. Hamilton kept a 'Dates' board where children could record their NAME FOR TODAY'S DATE for the day opposite their own names to reinforce what PLATO was doing and to emphasize the many solutions. Certain children acted as 'checkers' to determine which names were correct names for the day's date.

December 3, 1974

The children were working on learning the multiplication facts and multiplying with one and two place multipliers. The previous week Ms. Hamilton had worked with groups to teach two place multiplication. This week she worked with individual children who were in the middle (those between one place multiplication and two place multiplication). In helping one child with two place multipliers, she wrote on the chalkboard 42×13 and 13×42 and asked him what the difference in the problems was. Then she asked him why he got the same answer.

Ms. Hamilton gave a progress check the first day of every week and then assigned work in the two texts, *Mathematics for Individual Achievement* (1974) and *Mathematics Learning Systems* (1974), accordingly. Shelia put the answers on the bulletin board so children could check answers as they worked. If the lesson was difficult they checked problem by problem. If the lesson was not so difficult, they checked row by row. The bulletin board also had an 'Extra Credit Challenge' page of work for those who chose to do it.

Children's rockets were moving along in the Space Race toward the sun. All children had finished addition and subtraction facts. Ms. Hamilton had ordered certificates to give to those children who reached the sun: she thought it would spur the others on to work a bit harder when certificates were given out.

There were four children on the terminals; all started to play CLAIM GAME (Whole Numbers, D31) as they came in from recess. They had the beginning of their lesson before recess, and so had reached the game slots in their lessons. Each child chose a partner to play the games. Ms. Hamilton said she liked CLAIM GAME because the children helped each other and learned from each other while learning the factors. Harley and Oscar were doing just that as they tried to figure out factors for 25 and 22, but with no success.

Ms. Hamilton gave some extra PLATO time to some children who needed it. Maria was one. The principal said that PLATO had really helped Maria. Maria left a note on PLATO, 'I LIKE PLATO GAME' after playing BATTLESHIP. The principal had been worried about Maria's absenteeism affecting her achievement. Ms. Hamilton agreed to try to give her work time on PLATO more than once a day.

Since the terminals were so much in demand for the children, it was hard for Sheila to find a time to work at the terminal. She had scheduled children from 8 o'clock on in the morning and after school as well. Because of storage problems, the teachers were not supposed to work after school when many of the University courses were running, so even after two-thirty when school was out she could not be assured of access to the Mathematics curriculum lessons and the children's comments.

Ms. Jones came into Ms. Hamilton's room to get some help with PLATO as Sheila and I were talking. She said her name was not being accepted under the COURSE MATH any more. Teachers sometimes had trouble accessing the lessons because they had forgotten the correct procedures or the procedures had been changed. Ms. Jones and Ms. Hamilton joked about it; Ms. Jones said her hand was slapped for trying. PLATO would print a message saying, 'YOU ARE NOT REGISTERED UNDER THIS COURSE', if the course name or procedure had been changed. Teachers usually called CERL to report problems such as these and would be told how to get into the PLATO lessons.

January, 1975

> *Teacher's Log*: *Whole Numbers*. Although we had been working on learning basic facts since the first weeks of school, when we started whole numbers on PLATO *most* of the class was still struggling and not remembering.

> I am very strong on learning facts before getting into complicated computation because when computing the child can grasp the idea much faster with less confusion if he doesn't have to be concerned with counting fingers or drawing pictures. They initially need these methods for understanding, but there comes a time when such are impractical and hindering.

> After a few weeks on the whole number lessons, I could see a definite improvement in these skills — particularly in multiplication. CLAIM GAME was a prime factor in this improvement. I could see it happening on the terminals and the wall chart. Children were helping and prodding each other. At first some did not understand what a factor was. As they began to 'catch on' and play against each other, they began to really concentrate and think about *all* the possibilities. Larry was outstanding. His buddy, Peter, who hadn't been working very hard on facts, was a constant loser. Larry and he played at every opportunity and Peter began improving to the point where he could really rival Larry. His success gave him the self-confidence to take on other opponents. Each time a game took place so did learning.

> The 'off PLATO' version of CLAIM GAME worked for a while, but it soon lost its favor. The 'immediate response' of the terminal, its 'judgement' of what will or will not be accepted, are important factors to learning. *Immediate response* leads to satisfaction, understanding, reduced confusion, elimination of (or at least greatly reduced) bad habits, self-confidence.

> After a month, almost every child had been able to succeed in the fact challenges. Betty was successful in the challenges — remember, she has learning problems, gets special help from the Learning Disabilities teacher, tends to react and learn very slowly. Betty has been coming early — forty-five minutes before class begins — to be on the terminal. Sometimes when she is asked a question she just smiles and looks at the questioner — but no response. Another early comer is Debbie — good student, very outgoing, sometimes rather cruel to those outside her 'group', a popular, alert, energetic girl. She has been a helper to Betty in these before-school sessions. Sometimes she is impatient and blunt with Betty — 'Why don't you know that?' At other times, she is patient and *re*explains how to do something or what something means. They have played the CLAIM GAME many times. There has been a drastic change in Betty's social behavior. She is talking with her peers. She laughs and plays games. She has become

so social that she is talking *most* of the time. For a while, I ignored her *over* socializing because I felt she needed this and *to try to control it too soon might put her back into her shell.* However, after a few weeks, I started reminding her (often by reminding *someone else*) that there were times to talk and times to be quiet. Her response was good — there was no retreat. She was building real friendships. Her parents saw a happy girl at home. We had all been working with Betty before. I must attribute these successes to the early PLATO sessions and the interaction this caused between Debbie and Betty.

SPEEDWAY has been another important factor in developing their skills with number facts. The children have taken pride in their improvement. It is good to see them working against their own achievments.

RUBBER STAMP and ARRAYS are good, but I feel there should be some kind of check-up for understanding at this point. Those who know their number facts and understand what they mean find this repeated process too time consuming and unnecessary. They feel it is too easy for them. PARKING LOT could also be shortened for many. In fact, I would like to see whole numbers set up so that children could progress as rapidly as their understanding permits.

Our terminal problems are fewer. We are having much more regular sessions.

March 23, 1975

Teacher's Log: Fraction Lessons. I am most happy with these lessons and the operation and management of them.

Before we started, I was given a notebook curriculum formulated November 1974; shortly afterward, another updated curriculum, March 1975. These were easy to skim, but detailed enough to be of value. The print-out of *exactly* what will be on the terminal, what the *child* will see is most valuable. Even though I have seen these lessons on the terminal, I can take the guide home to refresh my memory. I use it for planning correlated activities and especially examining areas where some children had problems. I can show a page to a child to refresh his memory and we can discuss his reaction or problem.

I received a booklet of *Excerpts from the Paintings Library* and *Skywriting and Spider Web Library*—samples of student work. This motivated me to go to the lab and make my own copies — something I hadn't realized I could do (though I may have been told).

I have received weekly course data print-outs from the 'overview of performance data'. This and accompanying information about who needs help are very useful. Again, I've almost always seen this data before it comes in the mail, but I don't have to stop and make my own notes each day — or worry that I've missed something if we have a string of after-school meetings or workshops and I can't get into a terminal except a rushed minute during the day.

Parent-Teacher Conferences came soon after we started the Fraction Lessons. I made print-outs of each child's progress in the first two or three chapters and copies of *his* paintings from the paintings library. The 'paintings' were displayed in the hall and later given to each child — they were delighted.

April 9, 1975

On this April afternoon Ms. Hamilton was teaching seven children the sun-moon-earth relationships. She demonstrated the pull of the moon by having two children pull together and then against each other. Five children were working on teacher-made synonym worksheets. Two children were reading books. Nine were reading the Health Science Series and answering questions on mimeographed sheets. Two were fooling around with a calendar and four were at the terminals.

There were many posters around the room. One illustrated tornado action, another illustrated facts of the metric system. GUESS MY RULE problems were displayed on another bulletin board. Scott S. had made a poster showing how long it would take for light to travel from the sun to earth.

186,282 miles light travels each second
93,000,000 miles from sun to earth
499 seconds or 8 min 19 sec for light to travel
from the sun to earth

Outside Ms. Hamilton's room she had displayed the varion prints of children's fractions patterns. Copies of children's work done on PLATO were printed at CERL with a varion printer and given to the teacher (see Fractions). They were 'up' for parents to see on a bulletin board in the hallway by the fourth grade room. Children had chosen other work to display in the hallway. They chose to show their work on the metric system, GUESS MY RULE, Mathematics Crossword Number Game, some papers on graphics that were outgrowths of PLATO Mathematics and CLAIM GAME papers. Ms. Hamilton had made up a CLAIM GAME so children not on terminals could work at similar factoring problems.

Two visitors were intrigued with PLATO mathematics. One wondered if 'slower' children had difficulty understanding the directions and working out the problems. 'Does the program cater to the bright pupils?' he asked. Don and the two visitors were observing as Peter was working on an extra hard GUESS MY RULE, which was one Don had programmed especially for him. It involved quadratics. (See Fig. 2.5.)

Peter did not solve it that day.

One visitor asked Don Cohen what CERL wanted the children to learn in GUESS MY RULE? He mentioned: looking for patterns, variables, open

GUESS MY RULE	Input	Output
	3	18
	4	32
	5	50
	6	72

Figure 2.5:   Peter's GUESS MY RULE problem.

sentences, simple arithmetic and teaching addition, subtraction and multi-plication. He said, 'After problem 25 in GUESS MY RULE exercises children work with negative numbers'.

Ms. Hamilton noted children's progress in mathematics, and also observed children learning from PLATO in other areas, such as language arts and typing.

May 1975

Teacher's Log: Children tend to read school related materials *word* by *word*. Our stress tends to reinforce this type of reading — always looking for main ideas and details. Even though we encourage skim-ming for facts most children are groping word to word — even many of the capable readers. PLATO teaches scanning of the screen — see-ing it as a whole — getting a *whole* image. They learn to pick out key words. If the page is familiar, they are able to glance at the form and pick out enough details to respond rapidly — sometimes immediately. On unfamiliar pages, some of this spotting of valuable information carries over. They want to get to the lessons and games as quickly as possible (so their time isn't wasted). This desire forces them into scan-ning skills. They use the information pages for information — not as an exercise in reading. Many adults have not learned this skill. Very capable students force themselves into scanning. The average student never does this. Most of my class is able to scan read effectively.

They also have learned to appreciate the need for looking at details on (new) material. When a new option comes up — such as SHIFT NEXT for something else — if they don't read these details they may miss important information.

Phase concentration is another important area. Children learn to cope with visual and sound interruptions — learn to *phase* their concentration to their own environment and uniqueness — learn to 'self-pace' concentration. For most, just being able to concentrate (*truly* concentrate) is a new and most valuable experience. Their attention span is lengthened. This is often carried over to other learn-ing areas.

A very subtle idea is that the machine will do as much as they can make it do. It is up to them how far they can go. One can sense in their kid notes that they feel (to different degrees) that they *can* con-tribute worthwhile suggestions — that *their* comments and their notes could make a difference to a particular lesson — perhaps to the entire program.

They have also learned that the *solution* is important — that there are many ways to get to a solution. They are willing to tolerate the sometimes dull repetition of 'arithmetic' to achieve the satisfaction of 'math-number magic'. Their achievement in MAKE A BUNDLE (Whole Numbers, B3) is an especially good example of this.

Hand-eye coordination is developed. At this age, boys in particular develop large muscle control from throwing, batting, running activities. PLATO use teaches not only hand to eye (or eye to hand) coordination but also finger dexterity.

The 'short-cut' student who gets it down *fast* but often incorrectly due to carelessness, learns to be more thorough. The terminal doesn't scold for his mistakes — it simply rejects them and eventually the short-cutter begins to think about what he is doing. Discipline and self-control lead this type of student to success in achieving goals.

I think PLATO is *great*! I hope to remain in the program. If we ever go to 'PLATO rooms', I would like to work with PLATO and children on a full time basis. I wish that *more* children could have use of the terminals.

The Fourth Grade Classroom — Year Two

September 4, 1975

PLATO was not ready for use in September. Note the diagram of the room (as seen in Figure 2.6) for placement of PLATO terminals and table arrangements. Six groups of four children were working together on their folders. The folders contained work assignments for the week.

The assignments for the week were written on the chalkboard. The children were checking their folders to correct mistakes they had made on work in math, spelling, and language arts. Ms. Hamilton marked the papers that were all correct with a star. Others had to be corrected. The children's names were listed on the board. Each child put a circle around his/her name to indicate the folder was ready to be re-checked and taken home. They could also write their name on the board to get help from either the student teacher or Sheila. The children talked quietly and worked steadily on their lessons, exchanging comments about the lessons or getting help from one another.

Ms. Hamilton stopped working with an individual child to tell the whole group how to get help and to circle their names when their folder was ready to be corrected. Two little boys sat on a table and tilted it. She asked, 'Boys, can you see that the table is tilting?' She explained that this created a safety hazard and the table shouldn't be used for sitting, that 'it tipped over several times last year'. The children moved off the table without comment. Then Ms. Hamilton finishd her lesson explanations and told three groups to expect help

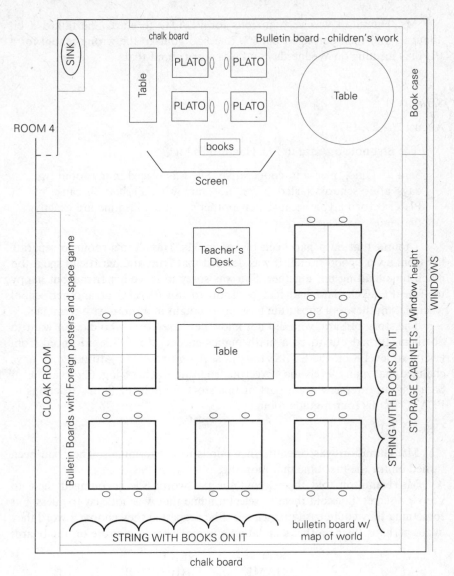

Figure 2.6: Diagram of Ms. Hamilton's fourth grade classroom.

from her and three groups to expect help from Mr. Ebel, the student teacher. Sheila sat down to check folders and the children went back to work.

The room was quite warm. The air conditioners had not been turned on. Air conditioners had been installed in all PLATO classrooms to keep the terminals at an even temperature because the terminals malfunctioned when overheated. Ms. Hamilton turned the air conditioners on when the kids left the room for music.

Ms. Hamilton was very anxious for PLATO to start. She talked a bit about it, and then corrected papers. She had gone to the wrong school for a PLATO meeting on Wednesday and was sorry about that.

Sara

August 26–29, 1975

The first note on Sara in Ms. Hamilton's log:

Sara — Quiet, pleasant, cooperative. She was placed in my room two days after school started. I am not sure why. Perhaps because of PLATO (or maybe because her mother's name and mine are exactly the same). Average worker.

I found that Sara had been placed in Ms. Hamilton's room to separate her from a very good friend. It was decided that Sara and her friend spent too much time 'cutting up' together. She was sorry to leave her friend but happy to have PLATO. Sara had had occasion to use PLATO at another school when her mother — a substitute teacher — taught in a room with terminals.

The story of Sara, who did not know her 'sixes' and who did not want to do them, turned out to be a mathematics success story. She advanced from level 4 to level 8 on the CTBS[9] tests in seven months. Her attitude may have changed that many levels too. Excerpts from the teacher's log, observations of Sara and an interview are a part of this story. Watch for Sara's reactions to PLATO in this fourth grade room.

October 3, 1975

Ms. Hamilton was orienting her pupils to the terminals. They had been turned on for the first time that morning.

Ms. Hamilton told them about the password. She encouraged them to keep it a secret. She told them to select a name that was not easy to guess, but something they could easily remember. She suggested they choose a word they liked, perhaps their mother's or father's name. Then she wrote on the board:

Sara S	NEXT
HAML	SHIFT STOP
PASSWORD	

Sara asked if they should tell Ms. Hamilton their passwords. Ms. Hamilton said, 'You don't need to. Just keep it to yourself'. Another child asked if it could be a number. Ms. Hamilton said it just had to be something they could remember.

She went on to explain the procedure. She said HAML stands for Hamilton. She told the children that this morning they would be asked to write their password two times in order to check the accuracy. (The computer did this automatically whenever a user selected a new password.)

October 6–10, 1975

Teacher's Log: The long awaited day has arrived. *We started PLATO.* It took two days for everyone to get their first session. Since the student teacher is here, I was able to be at the terminals as each child began his first turn.

Many children are not reading directions. They sit for long periods waiting — not noticing the PRESS NEXT. Many are *very* hesitant to respond — asking if their answer is correct *before* typing it. Most read the directions slowly, then don't know what to do or worry that they won't do it right. The directions are clear enough — they just aren't thinking or aren't self-confident enough to try their answer.

When the children look puzzled, I ask them to read the directions again (aloud if necessary) and then they are usually able to tell me what they are supposed to do. Sara, Holly, Wendy, Debbie and Shelly are slow getting started — none of them are very enthusiastic about math. Terry and Erica are okay — rather unsure of themselves.

I like being with them on the first session — to spot strengths and weaknesses, lesson errors, points of confusion, and attitudes. There were almost constant questions. The terminals are arranged so that I can stand in the middle and observe all terminals. Children can see what others are doing, discuss common questions and concerns. Attitudes are all positive.

Second PLATO sessions took two days. The children are slow to read directions and respond — forget to press 'NEXT'. After the second session, there was a notable change. Children read and typed faster — the long waits to remember 'NEXT' were gone. Thursday and Friday everyone had a complete turn. Children were no longer fretting about the responses prior to typing them. We are off to a good start.

Children studied a *number line of historic events in Illinois* — later arranged events in proper sequence. We had taken cameras to Springfield and New Salem last week. Each child had the responsibility of photographing specific buildings. This week they have been working in small groups to develop and print their film. Some were blank, some blurred, a few were very good.

October 15, 1975

On the board Ms. Hamilton had written the schedule.

> Quiet Reading
> Book Reports
> Math: X Challenges, MIA, SRA
> Spelling   Our language mastery
> New Salem Information

The children went to their 'favorite places' to read until 1:10. Then they gave their book reports. Each child who had finished reading a book gave a report. Sara was the first. She read her report very fast and not very loud. The children raised their hands. Sara seemed nervous as she read. Jon was relaxed, but had a bit of trouble reading his own writing. After more reports Ms. Hamilton moved the desks around so they weren't so crowded and started mathematics.

The children were working on pages 68–72 in *Mathematics, Learning Systems Texts*. Ms. Hamilton worked with the whole group. She said, 'Multiplication is a fast way of adding'.

Together the children read the story 'Dirty Digger' which was about a prospector digging for gold. The children looked at patterns and used the blackboard to show how they had to add $10+10+10$ and $8+8+8$. Ms. Hamilton noted that the addition could be done a shorter way, by multiplication, but she reminded the pupils that they could multiply only when the group members are the same. She asked if they could do this problem, 30 + 24 by multiplication. Students said, 'No'.

Then the students and Ms. Hamilton talked about the many ways there are to write ten times six.

$$
\begin{array}{ccccc}
 & 10 & & & 6 \\
10 & 10 & & 6 & 6 \\
\times\ 6 & 10 & 6\ \text{tens} \quad \times 10 & 6 & 6 \quad 10\ \text{sixes} \\
 & 10 & & 6 & \\
 & 10 & & 6 & \\
 & +10 & & 6 & \\
 & & & 6 & \\
 & & & 6 & \\
 & & & 6 & \\
 & & & +6 &
\end{array}
$$

This was the day to start a new kind of multiplication, 'where there are two numbers on the top'.

$$
\begin{array}{r}
18\ \text{ft} \\
\underline{3}\ \text{times}
\end{array}
$$

Few had done this in the past. Ms. Hamilton said, 'Always start with the number on the bottom and work in a pattern. Multiply in the one's column and then in the ten's column'. She showed the children how in:

$$
\begin{array}{r}
23 \\
\times\ 3 \\
\hline
69
\end{array}
$$

It doesn't make much difference which you miltiply first in 23×3 but in 18×3 it does. She said, 'You have to do as you do in addition and carry. We can prove that problem. How can we prove it?'

Children came up with: 18 + 18 + 18. She said, '18 × 3 means the same. If you're not sure, how can you check yourself?' Volunteers said, 'Addition'. Ms. Hamilton said, 'Work a problem on scrap paper or in your heads, 12 × 6'. The answers the youngsters got were: 62, 32, 62, 36 and 22. Ms. Hamilton noted that they agreed on the first column but differed on the 10's column. She said, 'All right, how can we check it out?' Lizzie wrote on the board:

$$
\begin{array}{r}
12 \\
12 \\
12 \\
12 \\
12 \\
\underline{12}
\end{array}
$$

Then the children chanted 'put down 2 and carry 1'. Bob got 72. Ms. Hamilton went over it: '6 × 2 is 12, put down 2, carry 1. 6 × 1 is 6, plus 1 is 7.' Erica said, 'In Mrs. Franklin's class we learned another way.'

Ms. Hamilton responded, 'OK, you may use another way. There are other ways.' She told the children to try 14 × 7. Ted got 141, Tom 98. Other answers were: 84, 152, 81 and 88.

Ms. Hamilton said, 'I hear a lot of answers. They can't all be right for one problem', and told the children to check on scratch paper and then go ahead and work. Ms. Hamilton wrote on the board. 'If you miss the first two problems then see me for special help. If you just go up and change your answer, will that help?' 'No', from her pupils. Ms. Hamilton repeated, 'No, see me!'

After a short break children continued to work by themselves as Ms. Hamilton tested individual children on the multiplication facts with flash cards.

October 20–24, 1975

Teacher's Log: On PLATO, children seem to be generally inaccurate on column addition. I think some of it stems from the finger counting problem — which is still very actively used in addition and subtraction. Jill and Laura are still having the place value problem. They have transferred it from addition to multiplication. Example:

$$
\begin{array}{r}
17 \\
\times\ 2 \\
\hline
61
\end{array}
$$

They carry the '4' because it is the *largest* digit. This problem was apparent when they did EGG FACTORY (Whole Numbers, D28). I think the immediate response will help them become more aware of their errors.

I'm concerned that the children are getting too many new things too fast. I wanted them to be in whole numbers *only* — until they are comfortable, competent and have some degree of success. Game slot gives them options they are not ready to handle. With inadequate directions (PLATO presumes some previous knowledge) the games become frustration rather than reinforcement and pleasure. This wide choice is great for children who participated last year, but too much for newcomers.

October 23, 1975

Ms. Hamilton had four rows of pockets on a bulletin board, which held the names of the children. When children finished on the terminal they turned their card over and went to get the next child on the list for each terminal just as they had done in the previous year.

Ms. Hamilton told the children about leaving a message at the end of a lesson. She said, 'If you don't tell me that something has gone wrong, we won't know. You need to tell me and you need to tell PLATO'. She emphasized that she may be busy and they may have to wait to tell her, but they should be sure to get to her sometime during the day. She told children to also write notes when they enjoyed PLATO and to say whether the lesson was too easy or too hard.

She told children they would use the honor system with regard to passwords and not to watch when others put in their passwords.

This morning she asked the children to work on their folders and to ask the student teacher for help on anything that was wrong. Ms. Hamilton was going to be orienting children to new lessons on the terminals. She told them their typing would be slow this morning but assured them that by next week they'd be faster.

October 28, 1975

Ms. Hamilton worked with children on projects. The children were making quilt pieces. They had been to the Champaign County Historical Society the day before on a field trip where they had made dolls of corn husks. Some children were weaving, others reading or on PLATO. Ms. Hamilton helped children as they worked on PLATO. When a child had trouble with a terminal that refused to respond, Ms. Hamilton told him or her to turn off the machine and wait two minutes; then turn it on again to see if it was OK. The central computer had been down in the morning, now the terminal wouldn't respond to the touch.

After library period the terminals were running, three children asked Ms. Hamilton to stay in and work on PLATO rather than go out for recess. Sheila called the fourth child over to see if he wanted to stay in also and finish his session on PLATO. He wanted to do so. The four children worked intently on the terminals and talked to themselves as they worked. Occasionally they asked each other questions about the lessons. Kathy giggled about EGG DROPPER (Whole Numbers, 2b). Ben asked for help to paint 1/2. He didn't understand all of the directions, and tried to paint it a couple of times.

Ms. Hamilton said, 'Kids have too much trouble with fractions as they haven't had instruction for fractions yet.' She did not want the children to have Fractions as a choice until they had had directions for it. She called the children's attention to the CUT AND PAINT (Fractions, A5) choice and told them not to choose it.

It was time for a reading group lesson. Children signed off PLATO to go to reading. They would finish their PLATO lesson later.

Ms. Hamilton said she helped children for two days to get them started. She explained, 'The children last year did not have trouble with fractions as directions were given when it was in the main slot. When it is a game option the kids don't get the same directions'.

October 28, 1975 (Afternoon)

One of PLATO's problems was with its 'extended core storage'. Everybody called it 'ECS'. Terminals were generally used in the afternoon more than in the morning. When all the computer's core storage was in use new arrivals might not be able to access the lesson they needed. Before PLATO could make a lesson available to a student, the lesson had to be moved from the computer's disc memory (which represented a kind of vast storehouse of computer-programmed lessons), into the extended core storage, a smaller but more accessible portion of computer memory. But if ECS was filled with lessons for students who were already signed on, a newly-arriving student might not be able to get the specific lesson that he or she needed. In such a case the student just had to keep trying until some ECS opened up for them. (This was very much like getting a busy signal on the telephone, and having to re-dial a moment or two later on.)

Sara and three other children were having exactly this problem. Sara tried various keys. She pushed the CLEAR button and tried the touch panel. All to no avail. She asked Ms. Hamilton for help and was told to try different approaches, such as turning the terminal off, waiting a few minutes and then turning it on again. (This was in fact the correct remedy for a different problem; in the present case it could not have helped.) Sara tried every approach a couple of times methodically.

Sara was relaxed and calm to begin with, but became a bit frustrated when PLATO did not respond to her attempts to access a lesson. She hit the keys harder and said, 'PLATO, you're wasting my time'.

After several minutes of waiting, then checking, she went to her desk and brought a Language workbook back to the terminal. She worked in the workbook as she sat waiting for PLATO to become less busy. She was learning the limitations of technology.

October 29, 1975

Since Sara had missed her PLATO turn the day before she was one of the first to be 'on' the next morning. Ms. Hamilton was diligent in her effort to see that PLATO time was shared in an equitable manner.

Sara smiled as she worked. She did a CHECK-UP ON ADDITION (Whole Numbers, B12). She had no trouble following directions or working the problems. Sara typed slowly. She read the directions slowly and carefully as she worked. Her second lesson was RUBBER STAMP (Whole Numbers, Dl). Again she advanced through the lesson with no trouble.

Her third lesson was PARKING LOT (Whole Numbers, D26). Sara finished the 'fives' easily, PLATO informed her that she was ready for the 'sixes'. Sara turned to me and said, 'I don't know the sixes and I don't want to do them.' I knew that most children her age were working on the sixes so I asked her if she didn't want to try them. She said she did not want to.

Not listening, PLATO presented her next problem: 5×6. Sara worked it even though she had said she wasn't going to. Her answer was correct. She clapped her hands and seemed happy with herself.

The authors of the lessons had structured them in such a way that most children continued to be successful, but at the same time, challenged rather than bored. In this instance Sara was afraid to try to multiply by 6. PLATO presented 5×6 and since Sara knew the 5's she worked the problem; was successful, happy and confident at least for the moment. The lessons were structured so that sequencing provided logical direction for the child. At the same time that Sara was saying that she wouldn't do the 6's, PLATO continued to present the lesson and hold her attention. Sara was helped past the threatening situation. PLATO managed to create a positive situation out of a potentially negative one. While this did not always occur with PLATO, from observation it appeared to be a most common case.

Sara then chose SPEEDWAY (Whole Numbers, Bl) from the game slot. She read the directions aloud to herself as she worked at the terminal. Kathy, who sat next to Sara, bragged to Sara about how fast she was working. Sara looked over at Kathy's terminal and asked Kathy which race to do on SPEEDWAY. Kathy said, 'Do GRAND PRIX'. Sara chose GRAND PRIX. Kathy and she discussed the game. Sara entered herself as 'RACER' and named her opponent, 'SLOW POKE'. RACER worked hard to win. She missed 4×1. She got it right on the second try. When PLATO took time-out to say, 'Great, you got it right this time', Sara said, 'OK, OK,' indicating 'Let's get on with the race — I don't need to be told I'm right'.

October 30, 1975

Teacher's Log: Thursday and Friday, Oct. 30 and 31, I was with *Don Cohen of CERL* in Lexington, Kentucky, for the purpose of demonstrating *PLATO at the National Council for Teachers of Math*. Although we were placed with commercial exhibits and had problems with the telephone company getting proper connections, we had a successful trip. To most visitors PLATO was totally new. If they had heard of it, they assumed it was like 'all other teaching machines'. I enjoyed acquainting visitors and exhibitors with PLATO'S mathematics programs and its stimulating and rewarding effect on children and their growth. I 'talked' with Howard in Champaign via PLATO — great excitement there!

In *regular math*, we continue working on multiplication facts. Jeff is the only one to pass. He is working on division. We have discussed and illustrated division arrays (something I started *after* using *PLATO*). The children understand the relationship of multiplication and division (except Karen and Lori). They continue to practice multiplication computation with weekly reviews of column addition and subtraction where renaming is necessary. Half the class is *still* making frequent errors in renaming. Subtraction facts are very poor — most of the pupils finger count and *not* very accurately, at that. They also finger count in addition, but they are quicker and more accurate. These are very difficult habits to break. A few have tried to finger count multiplication facts. I feel that my stress must be on multiplication and division — or we could still be dragging along with subtraction in January. We'll continue weekly reviews and reteaching, but I'll be continually trying to move them forward to new challenges and methods.

November 3–6, 1975

Teacher's Log: We are beginning to receive copies of weekly *PLATO data*. Several children had difficulty with the Addition Algorithm Check Up. I requested detailed data to study these errors at home. Two or more errors place the child in the 'help needed' category.

Billy — two errors because he is multiplying instead of adding.
Wendy — still carrying the wrong number.
Kate — carrying and finger counting errors.
Erica — probably put down the wrong number in the l00's column making it 32 instead of 23 — then didn't add the carry number to the l000's column. I don't know what happened to the other problems.

No school Friday — parent conferences. *I showed each parent a lesson on PLATO*. Their comments were very positive, such as:

'Now I see why my daughter likes it so much.'
'Wendy calls it a fun way to do math.'
'I wish I could come to school and use it.'
'It makes fractions so easy.'
'The kids are always talking about *playing* on PLATO.'
'It's really amazing.'

Bernadine Evans Stake

And many other comments — all indicating that the children are talking about it and like using it. I invited each parent to visit and watch his or her child work a complete session.

Since this was the completion of a grading period, awards were given. Children received honors and certificates for passing mathematics fact challenges. Sara received an award for addition.

November 10, 1975

Pupils gathered around Ms. Hamilton looking at pictures of their Springfield trip. One of the children had brought her pictures in to share. Other children were about the room working on weaving or just talking to each other. School had not officially begun. Four children were working at the terminal.

Ms. Hamilton started mathematics with an old familiar problem on the board. 463×8. All the children were invited to try it, except those at terminals. Kathy went to the board to explain as she worked it. She said $8 \times 3 = 24$, four down here and 2 up here. She continued to work the problem in the same manner: $8 \times 6 + 2 = 50$, 0 down here, 5 up here. $8 \times 4 + 5 = 37$. Kathy finished the problem. Ms. Hamilton reminded the class that you always start with the 8; rather than saying 3×8, you say 8×3. This helps you make sure that you don't multiply with the wrong number. She also pointed out that you go from the 1's to the 10's and then to the 100's column. Then Shelia gave the children another easy problem, 23×10. They did it very quickly. Ms. Hamilton asked them to work another problem in their head. If you have two boxes with ten pencils in each box, how many pencils do you have? with three boxes? with five boxes? She wrote on the board as children answered:

$$\begin{array}{ccc} 2 & 3 & 5 \\ \times 10 & \times 10 & \times 10 \end{array}$$

She asked the children what was true of all three problems. They answered that you add a zero to the number. Then she asked if it always worked out and they tried 50×10. To check it out she made marks on the board as they counted to 500 by 10's. She pointed out there were fifty lines, counted ten for each one, and got 500, so again it worked. Children were repeating with her as they counted: 10, 20, 30 etc. to 500.

In the next problem: 22×10, Ms. Hamilton asked what they would expect the answer to be. As the children prompted her she wrote: 50, 100, 150, 200, 250. Then Ms. Hamilton put a group of problems on the board:

$$\begin{array}{ccccc} 25 & 38 & 43 & 87 & 988 \\ \times 10 & \times 10 & \times 10 & \times 10 & \times 10 \end{array}$$

Pupils volunteered the answers. Ted came up with the 9,880 for the last problem. Next problem:

$$\begin{array}{r} 12,345 \\ \times \quad 10 \end{array}$$

Here they discussed the comma, and she helped them read one hundred twenty three thousand four hundred and fifty. Some of those who were working on PLATO finished. They joined the class discussion. Ms. Hamilton told them not to call anyone else to PLATO until the mathematics discussion was over. Next problem — Ms. Hamilton said, 'Let's switch the problem a bit'. She wrote on the board:

$$\begin{array}{ccc} 2 & 3 & 5 \\ \times 20 & \times 20 & \times 20 \end{array}$$

They counted 20, 40, 60 etc. Ms. Hamilton asked them how they did it and helped them realize they were taking 2 times 2 plus adding 0. Again she used marks on the board. They worked a couple more problems together: 25×20 and 38×20. Ms. Hamilton said she had CERL people remove fraction work from the PLATO lessons for her class. She either wanted the directions for fractions or no fractions. She said she hadn't used extra materials that CERL had provided because they were mostly for fractions. Ms. Hall and a Ms. Martin from England came in to see PLATO.

November 10, 1975

Ms. Hamilton encouraged all parents to come to school to observe their children at the terminals. Sara's mother was visiting to observe Sara at the terminal. Since space was limited around the terminal the lesson wasn't recorded. Sara seemed happy to show her mother what she could do and her mother smiled as she attentively listened to and observed Sara.

November 10–14, 1975

Teacher's Log: Sara and Ann are doing especially well in SPEED-WAY (Whole Numbers, Bl). Bob is faster, but makes more errors. All three are doing multiplication and mixed functions. Sara, along with a few others, is having trouble with EGG FACTORY — WITHOUT THE HEN (Whole Numbers, D9).

Ms. Hamilton and the children had been discussing equations such as $2 \times 3 + 4 \times 1 + 2 \times 5 = ?$ Ms. Hamilton thought the equation should be written: $(2 \times 3) + (4 \times 1) + (2 \times 5) = ?$ She said the children had no difficulty with brackets, and it was much clearer. The previous year her pupils had frequently used equations such as $(4 \times 2) - 3 = 5$ and $4 \times (3 - 2) = 4$ without confusion in HOW THE WEST WAS WON (Whole Numbers, F5). But they found equations confusing when written without brackets.

November 14, 1975

The PLATO data showed Sara needing help with EGG FACTORY — WITHOUT THE HEN and PARKING LOT. Ms. Hamilton sat down at the terminal with the children who were listed in the data as having trouble, and worked on their difficulties with them.

November 19, 1975

Don Cohen came in and talked to Sheila Hamilton for a few minutes about Henry. Don wanted to put Henry on PLATO and said, 'He needs the help'. Sheila said, 'No'. Henry is in a 'control' class for PLATO.

Tom's mother and Kathy's grandfather were observing at the terminals. The student teacher was teaching a lesson on planets. She used slides to show the planets.

An announcement had been made that a balloon ascension was scheduled for the morning. When the time came all kids went out with their teacher to watch. Everyone got very excited as they saw the fire warming up the air to lift the balloon. It was a new experience for all. The class came back to the room and went out for recess. During recess Sheila, Don Cohen and the student teacher were discussing how to figure out the sizes for all planets. They were trying to determine what size to use for Mercury, the smallest planet, so the sun would be in proportion. Sheila tried to get Don to figure it out on PLATO fast. He just kept asking her questions so she'd figure it out herself. She knew how to figure it out but wanted a fast calculation. She decided to use metric measurements. 'It's easier.'

The children came back in. Ms. Hamilton put some children on the terminals. Two little girls were talking about how neat PLATO is. At the terminal Ms. Hamilton helped Martin with the number accumulator. She explained how you move + or − to get to No. 11.

Using the PLATO terminal, Ms. Hamilton had written a note to the folks back at CERL: 'I've had many visitors in to see PLATO today. Parents are interested in writing letters to keep PLATO in operation. Six parents have visited to watch their children have a full session on PLATO. Hurray! All very positive comments! Sheila.'

Sara finished the first chapter on whole numbers this week along with 13 other children. Sara worked at the terminal on SUBTRACTION CHECK-UP (Whole Numbers, C2). She used her fingers to draw imaginary numbers on the screen and answered four out of five problems correctly. REAL LIFE SUBTRACTION STORY PROBLEMS (Whole Numbers, C1) was next. She read the first problem to herself and worked. She turned and said, 'I got 50 points for the open sentence'. Sara was correct on eight out of eight story problems. PLATO AND YOU (Whole Numbers, A1) was her next lesson. As the picture of a terminal and a boy appeared on the screen she said to PLATO, 'I'm not a boy, PLATO.' At an early age Sara recognized sex discrimination in text books. She read to herself and said, 'Hi ya!' She read the question which asked for the location of the terminal and chose, 'Bonnie's answer'. She typed the answer and said, 'Bonnie sends me notes and she knows'.

Bonnie, one of the authors, wrote notes to some of the children in the class. Sara looked forward to those notes. She liked Bonnie. In a PLATO note at the end of the session Sara expressed disappointment that Bonnie hadn't responded to her.

> BONNIE THIS IS MY LAST NOTE TO YOU.
> GET SOMEBODY I CAN DEPEND ON TO WRITE TO ME EVERY DAY.
> GOOD-BYE LOVE DUDE

Sara's next lesson was MAIL BOX (Whole Numbers, G4), a skip counting lesson (counting by 2's, 3's, etc.). The MAIL BOX lesson excited Sara. Other children had been talking about it. She said, 'Oh goody, I get to see the band director!' Kathy, next to her, said, 'You get to see the band'. They were excited about this lesson. Kathy and Sara counted thirteen steps together.

Sara was shown a choice page and asked another friend, 'Which one of these have you tried?' 'How about MAIL BOX?' said the friend. Sara said, 'OK, I know how to do it', referring to counting backwards by 10. As Sara counted she took some candy out of her pocket and ate it. She noticed that Kathy, on the terminal next to her, needed help in changing a sentence in a PLATO note. Sara told Kathy, 'Press LAB, then you can change'. Kathy corrected her mistake by pressing LAB and retyping the line. Sara then chose EGG DROPPER (Graphs, 2b) from the game slot. She asked Kathy how to play it. Kathy said, 'It's more fun to drop the egg on the man'.

The lights went out in the room. The kids at the terminals said, 'ohh' and 'ahh' — 'see how nice it is'. The PLATO screen was much more visible when the room was darkened. The student teacher was showing slides and had pulled the shades.

Kathy didn't want to leave the terminal at the end of her session so Sara typed on another terminal to try to find a lesson for Kathy. She couldn't get into more lessons that day.

At the end of the session Sara wrote a note on PLATO:

> BONNIE I AM GETTING MAD WHY AREN'T YOU SENDING ME ANY
> MORE LETTERS. ARE YOU SICK BUT IF YOU ARE, GET WELL SOON PLEASE ASK SOMEBODY TO WRITE A NOTE TO ME I AM GETTING LONELY I LIKED MY LESSON TO SINCERELY.

(Sara erased the last line when she couldn't add her name and typed 'SINCERELY Sara.') Then she changed the first line to 'I AM GETTING MAD, WHY AREN'T YOU SENDING ME', and changed the second line to 'ANYMORE NOTES. ARE YOU SICK.'

Sara was interested in another little girl who was signing onto PLATO and while she watched the process, PLATO signed Sara out. PLATO was programmed so sign a child out if the child forgot to do so or stopped working for some reason. Sara started over and was allowed to write her note again. Her session was 38 minutes long.

Ms. Hamilton continued to think about the children's progress in PLATO mathematics and how it was working with her regular fourth grade mathematics curriculum. She indicated that she intended to keep PLATO a part of her program rather than a 'do-what-you-want extra'.

November 17–21, 1975

Teacher's Log: Several parents visited again this week: Ann's mother, Sara's father, Ted's father, Bob's mother, Shelly's mother, Billy's mother came after school, both of Sally's parents came after school. All responded very favorably.

One bright ray of sunshine — Ted walked in the room one morning this week and said, 'Good morning, Mrs. Hamilton'. I couldn't believe my ears. What a delightful surprise! Since then he has spoken the same words each morning — always with the same cheerful tone. Ted *communicating* with no pressure applied — just like *anyone* might say it. No matter what happens the rest of the year, I've had my *day*!

We continue to have confusion with EGG FACTORY — WITHOUT THE HEN.

November 24–26, 1975

Teacher's Log: This is a short week due to Thanksgiving vacation. All except Kate and Martin have completed the first chapter of WHOLE NUMBERS.

December 1–5, 1975

Teacher's Log: Ann, Sara and Lizzie have finished the second chapter of whole numbers. I have noticed that especially Ann and Lizzie prefer doing lessons to games. Sara likes games but getting ahead has become more important. Her reading work habits are good, but it takes a lot of prodding to get math paper work completed. We have started a gift project — felt banners with designs of quilted spaghetti and other pastas. There are three pattern choices: three wise men, Christmas tree or a messiah. This week those who are completing assignments in a reasonable length of time (according to ability effort) are starting first. Others will start next week. John, Holly and Sara were the first to start their projects.

December 8–12, 1975

Teacher's Log: Jon is trying division on SPEEDWAY, but doesn't know the facts well enough to have much success. Peter completed the instruction on the subtraction algorithm. He is still making a lot of errors. He doesn't know facts and has trouble remembering how to rename. This is his first real weakness on PLATO math.

Ben, Tom and Sally have completed the second whole number chapter. Of course, Sally's progress is no surprise, but for *Ben and Tom to be among the first eight to complete anything is an accomplishment. I feel it shows how highly motivated they are to use PLATO*. I've tried so many techniques to inspire them — nothing else has been really effective.

January 5–9, 1976

Teacher's Log: No PLATO this week. My how we miss it! The room seems so quiet and dull. In regular math we started long division. I put the whole class together for instruction. We will start with very simple problems such as: 844 divided by 4. I insist that they do all of the steps, even though the problems are so simple that they can be done easily in their heads. We go over and over ... divide, multiply, subtract, bring down until it is automatic. Sara was not having difficulty with long division.

January 8, 1976

In an interview Sara said that she missed PLATO when it was off. She said, 'It's games that I like and also the things PLATO writes on top.... I was playing on PLATO at another school before I started at Johnson. At Johnson we had to do all the Math tests first'. (Referring to the ETS evaluation tests) 'Children at Peterson school had done the tests so', Sara said, 'they got to play on it.' She said, 'My mother was substituting at Peterson so she let the kids play on it'. Sara said she likes doing games, especially HOW THE WEST WAS WON (Whole Numbers, F5). 'In games there is always some fun. It's just fun math. The main slot is just math and it makes you work harder. In math you have to get the right answer in one or two times, otherwise they take you out of the problem. In games if you get a wrong answer or something you can just keep on going. Like in HOW THE WEST WAS WON, if somebody put in the wrong answer for you, you can just go on. When I play with somebody, they sometimes put in the wrong answer before I could put in the right answer. Like if I pick 1 and they put 13, or 14 or something. I've won once or twice in HOW THE WEST WAS WON, but in HOP GAME (Whole Numbers, B14) I always win against PLATO and against a friend. Me and Ted played HOW THE WEST WAS WON and are always playing short games. Ted and I won two games each. First I won, then the second game we tied and the last Ted won. I learn most from the math part on PLATO. I learn more from PLATO than from my teacher cause she teaches off the board and PLATO is like a board. And when you press the things that's a help. Like you just have to press things and you don't have to go up to the board.' Sara thinks she learns some math better with her teacher and some better on PLATO. 'Like long division from Ms. Hamilton and the rest like addition and subtraction I get better on in PLATO.'

'There's one game I really didn't like. I couldn't figure out this one problem. I knew it was right and I couldn't get out. I pressed SHIFT HELP. I knew the answer was right and PLATO said I was wrong. I try not to get that game anymore and if I do, I press SHIFT-HELP and get out of it'.

'I just use the board near the PLATO terminal to make sure it's right (refers to answers to problems). If it's not right I just erase on PLATO and put in the right answer.' Pupils sometimes multiplied, divided, etc., on the chalkboard and then entered their answer on the terminal.

'Ms. Hamilton says you have to do your work before you can do PLATO. Some people were fooling around on the board when they were supposed to be on PLATO — they weren't doing the right thing. They'd do the wrong answer twice to get out and then go on to games. They weren't doing the right thing. Like it's to learn out of, not to play. But the games part is math too 'cept that it's fun.'

I asked Sara to characterize PLATO as an animal. She said: 'It would be a talking animal. It would be an armadillo cause like it has hard skin. Like armadillos you can lift and like PLATO I can lift — an armadillo is talking and it's friendly. PLATO is friendly even though it does sometimes say your answer's wrong, but that's not what I would call mean. PLATO is just fun. I was in Miss Beeman's class and I had to get transferred cause me and my friend couldn't be together. It was worth it to get transferred to have PLATO cause my friend always got me in trouble. We had three friends and we're all in different rooms now. Buffy says she doesn't like Beeman (for a teacher) cause they're in these groups too long. They go to different stations, art, science, ... I like everything in my room. I don't like PLATO being off. My mom said, 'what did you do on PLATO today' and I said, 'well it's off, they're working on it,' and she said, 'oh, that's too bad.' I said, 'yeah.'

January 12 – 16, 1976

> *Teacher's Log*: We had some parent visitors this week. Sara's mother. It seems that after one parent visits the children must go home and say, 'When are you going to visit?' And the next day or so we always have a couple more. All parents are still very positive and appreciative. No school Thursday. Martin Luther King Jr. Day.

January 19 – 30, 1976

> *Teacher's Log*: The children have become very independent in the PLATO sessions. They rarely ask for any type of help and have developed self confidence that they can figure it out. Recent visitors have reminded me of something I had taken more or less for granted — the speed of typing and skim reading the children do. When parents visit, they are always surprised at how quickly the children skim familiar material and understand directions. The parents will comment that they have read only half the page and their child has pressed 'NEXT' and knows exactly what to do. I can see that this is carrying over to

assigned reading. The *Magic Word* group, in particular, had great difficulty understanding directions in the fall. We spent weeks and weeks talking about simple directions and comprehension. Their progress is very good. I feel much of this is due to their PLATO experience.

January 26, 1976

Sara was one of four youngsters (out of twenty-four) recommended to be placed in a review version of Fractions after ETS Check-up B was given. For passing fact challenges during the second grading period, she received a coupon 'good for one extra PLATO session'. Children preferred PLATO to a foreign coin as a reward.

January 29, 1976

Teacher's Log: We started fractions this week. Last year I did classroom fractions two or three weeks before the children used it on PLATO. I decided to let PLATO do the introduction this year. We seem to be off to a very good start.

January 30, 1976

PLATO data says Sara is ready for Meanings worksheets (Meanings 1 thru 10). The worksheets referred to here were prepared by CERL to augment the PLATO lessons.

The data shown in Figure 2.7 is an example of the kinds of information available to the teacher on the PLATO terminal. Sheila referred to the data often to keep track of children's progress and to plan extra help lessons. In whole numbers PLATO data gives the information for each lesson using the following symbols: + fine, √ satisfactory, — unsatisfactory, T terminated, C continuing, L leaving, and F fast state.

February 3

Ms. Hamilton had a lesson on the board for the whole class. She showed them 1/3 of 9. Ms. Hamilton pointed to 3 and said this shows you how many groups you break up into. She asked a child to come to the board to draw a picture of 1/3 of 9.

The child drew:

Ms. Hamilton explained that everyone did well on problems such as 1/3 of 9 so they were ready for something harder. She presented the problem 1/4 of 24, and asked the children, 'What's the first thing we have to do when we show a picture?' Several youngsters suggested making 24 x's. Ms. Hamilton

Subtraction

add concepts	+ and C
sub concepts	+ and C
facts concepts	+ and C
skip counting	+ and C
add – algorithm	✓
sub – algorithm	+
add computation	no entry
sub computation	no entry

Division

concepts	+ C
facts	✓ C
repeated side	no entry
number line	no entry
sharing	no entry
guessing mult	no entry
algorithm	no entry
computation	no entry

Multiplication

concepts	+ C
facts	+ C
repeated add	C
arrays	✓
building up	no entry
doubling	no entry
breaking up	no entry
number line	no entry
algorithm	+
computation	no entry
factors	no entry

General

place value	+
T – F equation	no entry
word problems	+ C
comp. 2/two oper.	– C

Figure 2.7: PLATO data on Sara.

and the children counted as she drew x's on the board: one, two, three, four, ... eight, ... twelve, ... sixteen, ... twenty, ... twenty-four

```
( X  X  X  X  X  X )
  X  X  X  X  X  X
  X  X  X  X  X  X
  X  X  X  X  X  X
```

When Ms. Hamilton asked how many to circle, one child said to circle 4. Ms. Hamilton said if it's fourths, you should have 4 groups that size. Another child said circle 6. Ms. Hamilton said, '1/4 of 24 is 6. How many fours in 24?' Ms. Hamilton explained that ordering things made it easier to find 1/4 of 24 = 6, 2/4 of 24 = 12, 3/4 of 24 = 18 and 4/4 of 24 = 24.

Ms. Hamilton asked how they would find 3/5 of 25. Sara suggested you draw 25 x's and Rhoda said the x's should be in rows to make it easier. They continued in this manner.

Ms. Hamilton told the children who were on terminals to remember to SHIFT NEXT to back out, and get ready for slides of Venezuela.

February 5, 1976

Sara is one of nine children who have reached the PIZZA lessons and are doing well. Sara had a + on MEANINGS OF FRACTIONS (Fractions, A12) and was continuing MIXED NUMBERS AND FRACTIONS. She had +'s on CUT AND PAINT (Fractions, A5), LIGHTS (Fractions, A10),

CHECK-UP FOR MEANING OF FRACTIONS (Fractions, A12) and PIZZA FRACTIONS (Fractions, B4).

February 2–6, 1976

> *Teacher's Log*: A stumbling block in Meaning of Fractions is STICKS 'N' STRING (Fractions, A9) — I think *that* is in the lesson. I even find it difficult to be accurate. Most of the children don't go get the string — they guess. Well it is just too hard to guess. I did it by folding paper. Even that wasn't easy, but it was a lot better than string which is hard to hold and sometimes stretches.

February 13, 1976

Sara was doing CHECK-UP FOR MEANING OF FRACTIONS (Fractions, A1) with a +. She had a check (✓) for MIXED NUMBERS WITH PIZZA (Fractions, B9). She had a + for PIZZA FRACTIONS (Fractions, B4), PIZZA CUTTER STUCK (Fractions, B5), 'c' for PIZZAS FOR 3 KIDS (Fractions, B6), 'c' for MIXED NUMBERS INTRODUCTION (Fractions, B8), + for MAKE-A-MONSTER (Fractions, B14) and for STICKS AND STRINGS (Fractions, B15).

Sara was now ready for the mixed numbers booklet and worksheets produced by the CERL people to accompany PLATO lessons. In whole numbers Sara was continuing in multiplication factors satisfactorily.

February 9–13, 1976

> *Teacher's Log*: This is something that bothers me about this year's program. I want them to *concentrate* on fractions, but when they sign on they immediately have options — some of which are *not* fractions. I can't be there every time someone signs in to make sure they go into fractions — I lose control over what they are doing. The game slot options are fine (if adequate instruction is available) BUT NOT LESSONS.
>
> Sara is doing very well along with Kathy, Rhoda, Ann and Lizzie.
>
> There was an interesting class reaction to PLATO-related worksheets: long faces and groans. But when they got the 'meanings' worksheets and started to do them they really enjoyed them and were ready for more. It was a quick and radical change in attitude. I'm glad the first group was so clever and humorous as it really started them out right.

February 16–20, 1976

> *Teacher's Log*: Sara has gotten so enthusiastic. Remember, she didn't care too much for math at the beginning of the year. This week she brought visiting grandparents to see her session (Mom and Dad,

too). Sara was one who completed mixed numbers. Regular math is all fractions-worksheets of my making and CERL's. This will continue for quite a while.

Ms. Hamilton gave a test on meanings of fractions. Sara missed the following problems:

$$1/4 \neq 2/4$$
$$1/4 = 2/8$$
$$2/4 = 4/8$$
$$8/9 \neq 9/10$$
$$1/10 \neq 9/10$$

February 20, 1976

Sara's PLATO data included the following information:

Whole numbers
    Mult. meaning   ✓
    Mult. and subtraction techniques   +
    Mult. and subtraction techniques   C
Fractions
    Meaning of fractions   +
    Mixed numbers and fractions   +
    Equivalent fractions   C

Sara had a plus on check-up mixed numbers and on check-up number line. She missed some problems on the worksheet — mixed numbers and fractions: $5\frac{5}{12} + 5\frac{11}{12}$ and a problem using minus 1/4.

February 27, 1976

Sara's PLATO data: PLATO said Sara was ready for mixed numbers booklets and worksheets. In whole numbers she was doing fine.

March 5, 1976

Sara's PLATO data

Whole numbers:
    Mult. meanings   ✓
    Mult. and subtraction techniques   +
    Mult. and subtraction techniques   C
Fractions
    Meanings of fractions   +
    Mixed numbers and fractions   C
    Equivalent fractions   C

March 8, 1976

Sara was at the PLATO terminal. She worked at REVIEW AND PRACTICE[10] and did the problems quickly and accurately. She went right through SORT EQUIVALENT FRACTIONS (Fractions, C13). When she got to SORT EQUIVALENT NUMBERS (Fractions, C15), she had some difficulty but managed to get through with PLATO's help. Sara said she'd had TORPEDO (Fractions, C) enough so she shifted out of it. She also shifted out of TOWER PUZZLE (Graphs, 4.p).

Ted was sitting next to Sara and helped her make a whale using the 6, 7, 8 and 9 after SHIFT MICRO. Sara was happy to be able to make a whale on PLATO. Beth wanted to play TORPEDO with Sara, so Sara started but her time was up.

March 8, 1976

Sara helped make scenery for the play since she was one of eight pupils to complete assignments on time. At the beginning of the year she had had to sit by the teacher to work. Sara had completed the equivalent fractions worksheet to complete her assignment. The PLATO data showed nothing new. She was continuing in equivalent fractions and multiplication and subtraction techniques. The children had a couple of days to pass fact challenges: multiplication, division, addition and subtraction facts. Sara was one who completed adding and subtracting fractions and mixed number worksheets without having had the lessons on PLATO. She had teacher help. The children who had PLATO made fewer mistakes than those children who hadn't. Sara's mistakes were in reduction of fractions.

Ms. Hamilton helped children make Munchkin Flowers for the Wizard of Oz performance March 25. Sets for the play were being built by other children. Some children worked on math worksheets and went to Ms. Hamilton to have their progress checked off in her log. Terry was helping Kate on PLATO with fractions. Kate had been in a 'give up' mood.

March 17, 1976

Sara was at the terminal working happily, confidently and with accuracy on CHECK-UP FOR MIXED NUMBERS AND FRACTIONS (Fractions, B23). She said, 'I'm perfect at these, I've never missed one after I learned how to do it'. Then she chose SORT EQUIVALENT NUMBERS (Fractions, C15). Bob said to her, 'I hate those'. Sara responded, 'Well so do I, that's why I'm trying to get out of them'. Sara told me she was going to finish this lesson before she went on to a game. She was on level 2 of 10. After a few minutes, Sara said, 'I'll never finish'. She used the blackboard by the terminals to figure out an equivalence of 32/24. She worked SORTING EQUIVALENT NUMBERS for 20 minutes. Then watched Bob play FRACTIONS BASKETBALL (Fractions, E12) which was new to her. Bob did very well at the game. Sara wanted to play TORPEDO but only if she could play a person rather than PLATO. She found an opponent and played for 7 minutes against >>> . > (symbols pupils used to represent themselves).

Sara noted that Erica was not trying to figure out the answers in TRY THESE: EQUIVALENT FRACTIONS (Fractions, C16). 'Erica is just writing anything to get out of the lesson'. Sara said, 'Erica you shouldn't, I'll help you', and she helped Erica understand how to work the problem.

March 17, 1976

Ms. Hamilton was very pleased with the fractions worksheets. 'They are beautiful worksheets.' Children were working on the worksheets: NUMBER LINE, TRY THESE, MIXED NUMBERS, FRACTION WHOLE NUMBERS, PIZZA AND FUNNY FACES.

The children practised for the Wizard of Oz. The show was going great. The children helped make a corn field, apple orchard etc., and designed many of the costumes. Kate was Aunt Em, Bob was the scarecrow, Sara was one of the Munchkins and Ted the Narrator.

All the children had passed their multiplication, division, subtraction and addition facts except Beth, Ben, Kate, Billy and Peter.

March 25, 1976

Ms. Hamilton was painting kids' faces for the Wizard of Oz performance. Children were milling around the room getting dressed and observing others. Four children were at the terminal. Ms. Hamilton said the children didn't want to lose their turn for the day. Witches and Munchkins sat at the terminals and discussed PLATO lessons and games while waiting for the play to begin. Sara helped Wendy with fractions on PLATO. Ted was concerned with the number of minutes until the play would begin.

The Wizard of Oz was performed on the stage in the auditorium. Children played their parts well. Teachers thought the music and sets were excellent and the audience of children and teachers showed great appreciation.

March 26, 1976

The PLATO data showed Sara passed CHECK-UP FOR EQUIVALENT FRACTIONS (Fractions, C23). PLATO data indicated she was ready for the addition and subtraction of unlike denominator booklets and worksheets. In Whole Numbers she was doing fine in addition, subtraction, division and multiplication concepts.

March 29, 1976

Occasionally Ms. Hamilton had a contest to see who could answer facts on flash cards the fastest and be the winner of the tournament. Sara was a challenge winner in division facts (she could answer 6 divided by 2 and 18 divided by 9, etc. faster than other children in the room when flash cards were presented to her) and had passed all addition, subtraction, multiplication and division facts. She received an extra PLATO session for being a winner.

April 2, 1976

PLATO data indicated Sara was doing satisfactorily in DECIMAL NAMES FOR FRACTIONS (Fractions, G5) and FRACTION NAMES

PLATO Mathematics: The Teacher and Fourth Grade Students Respond

FOR DECIMAL NUMBERS (Fractions, G6) and was continuing in SORT NUMBER NAMES WITH DECIMALS (Fractions, G9). Sara was ready for the MEANING OF DECIMAL FRACTIONS booklet.

April 5–9, 1976

Sara was one of six to work on ADDING AND SUBTRACTING WITH UNLIKE DENOMINATORS. Out of six pages of problems Sara missed only five items. She was doing fine on whole numbers and word problems.

Teacher's Log: This was the second week in study of the linear metric system. The children have done a lot of independent measuring objects in the room or hall, etc.

April 12, 1976

Sara was one of four children who completed the ADDING AND SUBTRACTING WITH DIFFERENT DENOMINATORS booklet. She was doing fine on DECIMAL DARTS (Fractions, G3).

Teacher's Log: Sara has really done an outstanding job. It was so difficult to get her to complete any math at the beginning of the year. In fact it was often necessary to have her work near me to accomplish her daily tasks. She really seems to enjoy math now.

April 13, 1976

The children had a bake sale to study money and banking. They went to other rooms and took orders for cookies, popcorn, etc. and then prepared the food and took it to school. While some children worked with their folders, others were bagging, labeling and marking cookies with the student teacher. The children kept a record of the cookies bagged. They decided to sell three cookies for twenty-five cents. The children had fifty-two orders for popcorn. When the orders were brought, they went to each room to deliver them and made change. The student teacher had the children role-play in order to test their readiness to do business in other rooms. Children who were poorest at making change were paired with those who were good. Ms. Hamilton had discussed the value of coins with the children. They had manipulated the money, figured out different ways to make thirty-seven cents. Children had worked together using paper money and fake coins to make up different amounts of money using the least number of coins. Ms. Hamilton said they had discussed how to present the Bake Sale to kids in other rooms. The children kept track of the cost of ingredients and time spent in order to figure out profits.

From this small business venture, the children went on to study banking and visited Busey Bank. They learned how to write checks and also learned something about stocks.

Ms. Hamilton made up a chart of children's errors in fractions. She checked the specific problems each child had trouble with and helped the child accordingly. Equivalent fractions were difficult for the children.

April 19, 1976

The DECIMAL FRACTION's booklet: Sara was one of eight who completed it. She missed six questions, including such problems as: $30 = 3/100$, $90/30 = 3\frac{3}{10}$ and, $6/0 = 3\frac{3}{10}$.

April 23, 1976

Sara had a 'fine' or 'satisfactory' for Chapters I, II, III and VI. There were no data for IV and V. She had 'unsatisfactory' on STICKS 'N' STRINGS (Fractions, B15) and MAKE-A-MONSTER: COMMON DENOMINATOR (Fractions, C20).

May 3–7, 1976

Teacher's Log: Another set of Sara's grandparents visited.

May 10, 1976

Teacher's Log: Most children had not done adding and subtracting fractions on PLATO at the time standardized tests were given. Sara had done three lessons on decimals.

May 17, 1976

Sara was relaxed and confident as she worked at the terminal. She told me that she had been waiting for decimal fractions so that she could get into like and unlike fractions. Sara repeated, 'That's what I've been waiting for'.

Sara worked quickly and accurately as she reviewed CHECK-UP FOR EQUIVALENT FRACTIONS (Fractions, C23). She went on to SORT NUMBER NAMES WITH DECIMALS (Fractions, G9) and had no trouble. Sara didn't look carefully at the DECIMAL DARTS (Fractions, G3) and was confused by the negative numbers for a minute, but she figured them out. Then she went on to CHECK-UP FOR MEANINGS OF DECIMAL FRACTIONS (Fractions, G11) and did very well. She chose the game, FRACTIONS BASKETBALL (Fractions, D7) and asked me to play. Since it was one of my last visits to the room, I accepted. We had a good time. She won. She had learned a lot of fractions since the time she first tried to sort equivalent fractions.

May 18, 1976

Children worked on folder materials and then went to the design lab. After design lab, they went to the school library to hear stories. After library the children worked on PLATO worksheets. There were no pupils on terminals so Ms. Hamilton said, 'There are four terminals with no one on. I told you whoever's turn it was on PLATO could go on'. She directed four children to the terminals.

Ms. Hamilton conducted a tournament on number facts. She said the same rules as yesterday would apply; accept only the first answer, say it once and if there's a tie go through again. She selected opponents randomly. It seemed to work as well as trying to match according to ability as she had done last year, she said. Ann and Martin were competing on subtraction facts — then others did so.

I had arranged for Sara and I to go to a room next to the gym to discuss PLATO. She talked freely about math and PLATO.

SARA'S VIEW OF PLATO — AN INTERVIEW

May 18, 1976

> *B*: I'd like to find out a little bit about what children think about PLATO and what they think about math.
>
> *S*: Well at the starting, when I was in Kindergarten up to 4th grade, or up to 3rd, I didn't like math.
>
> *B*: Oh, you didn't?
>
> *S*: My sister was on PLATO in second grade. I wanted to be in the room with PLATO and I wasn't last year. And then this year I had to be transferred and I was transferred to a room with PLATO and then I started to really like math. I didn't like it before I started on PLATO. Like Ms. Hamilton didn't rush. She didn't go fast.
>
> *B*: What did she do?
>
> *S*: Like if you were really bad at multiplication then she'd say mmm — she'd just go back and go on with the other kids and we'd have a review and she'd — we could just do it then and you'd figure it out then. And PLATO you can go ahead and you don't have to wait for everybody else. So — that you might lose what you learn.
>
> *B*: Um hum. You don't have to wait.
>
> *S*: Like maybe Bob would be behind in his work and everybody'd have to wait and PLATO — and PLATO you just do your own stuff.
>
> *B*: What other things do you like about PLATO?
>
> *S*: It's fun — Well it helps you type. I used to not be able to type and now since PLATO I type my name real fast. I can do it in five seconds. And I like the games.
>
> *B*: You do?
>
> *S*: And like the games are fun but they also teach you something. Like in HORSE RACE (Whole Numbers, B4).
>
> *B*: Tell me how.
>
> *S*: You put in the right number so you have to be thinking.
>
> *B*: What do you do in HORSE RACE?
>
> *S*: Well, there's some horses and you pick one of the horses you want

and then if you've never done that race before you have a practice. And if you have, you don't have a practice. You go right into it.

B: What kinds of problems are there?

S: Well, multiplications, divisions and all kinds — I think it's real fun 'cause I love horses and I watch every horse race on TV.

B: Oh you do?

S: I try at least.

B: You know who wins them?

S: The one that won the Preakness is Elocutionist and I know a lot of them. One that won Kentucky Derby was Old Forbes.

B: You say you've learned a lot. What did you learn in multiplication?

S: Well, I can do 25×25.

B: OK.

S: (writes)

$$\begin{array}{r} 2 \\ 25 \\ \times\ 25 \\ \hline 125 \\ 50 \\ \hline 625 \end{array}$$

She said, '5×5 is 25, put down 5 carry 2' etc. as she worked, step by step.

B: Can you figure it out another way?

S: You can take 5×25 and add 5 of them. (She did that.)

$$\begin{array}{r} 125 \\ 125 \\ 125 \\ 125 \\ 125 \\ \hline \end{array}$$

B: How do you make sure it's right?

S: You could check it both ways.

B: Is there a hard problem you can do?

S: 165×165.

B: How would you do it?

S: You go on to PLATO and pick a hard problem and work it on PLATO and he'd tell you if you got it right. He'll say 'OK' if you were right and then if not you'd do it over and you'd work it.

B: What if you broke up the problem?

S: You would add 165, 165 times. You could do it by 25 or by 15's.

B: Show me how.

S: Uses algorithm

$$\begin{array}{r} 165 \\ \times\ 165 \\ \hline \end{array}$$

Explains each step. 5×5 is 25 put down 5 carry 2, take 5×6 is $30 + 2$ is 32.

B: OK. Try this. 6×7 is 42 – what would 6×14 be?

S: Double 42. So it would be 84.

B: 17×2 is 34.

Use that number to find 17×7.

S: You can find out 5×17 and then that equals 85 and then you add 34 under here. It's 119.

B: What is an easy way to find 6×14 if 6×15 is 90?

S: Take away 6, it's 84.

B: What did you really learn from PLATO?

S: Well, I don't know. I learned fractions and decimals 'cause Ms. Hamilton didn't teach us any and only me and Ted have done HORSE RACE (Whole Numbers, B4).

B: Did you learn to Multiply?

S: Kind of ... I learned lots from PLATO tests. Kind of ... Well I don't know — well I learned multiplication. I learned by a 1 digit number and by a 2 digit number.

B: Did you learn addition?

S: I learned lots of addition and subtraction. They gave you a check up. I started at Chapter 1. Now I'm on Chapter 8. I finished it and I was so happy. Chapter 8 is adding and subtraction of mixed numbers. I was so happy to get decimals.

B: What do you learn from the games? Or are they just fun?

S: I don't know, but they wouldn't give you anything unless you learn. I played games with Ben, Mrs. Hamilton, or Leslie. I'd get a friend to play rather than PLATO.

B: Did you ever need help?

S: Yes, I'd go to Mrs. Hamilton for help or to somebody else. Usually Mrs. Hamilton. If she's doing something and you shouldn't ask, she'll get mad at you.

B: Is PLATO ever wrong?

S: Sometimes maybe, I tell Mrs. Hamilton. I say I'm right and PLATO's wrong. She says PLATO is wrong.

B: What is PLATO?

S: PLATO's a computer. I don't really know.

B: Does PLATO give you many choices?

S: We have a lot of choice. Why do they have those other things on Thursday and Friday? Like JUMPING BEANS (Fractions, A4) and GIMME (Fractions, E5)? We've already learned all that. I don't like it. If you're at Chapter 8 and you get something from Chapter 1 you think, 'Oh, boy, they think I'm doing real bad'. If you do real good then you get back and on Monday you're always back again.

B: Do you like PLATO as much now as at the beginning of the year?

S: I like math because of PLATO and Ms. Hamilton. I like math a whole lot now.

B: What do your parents think of PLATO?

S: I think they think — 'I'm glad my kids like to go to school'. My Dad and Mom are glad that I like to go to school — 'cause before I always said, 'Oh only 160 days left'. I didn't want to go to school.

B: Do you want to have PLATO next year?

S: I want to go into Mr. Kalisch cause he has PLATO. He's real mean and I hate Mr. Kalisch but I want to have PLATO.

Sara had learned a great deal over the year. She tried things she wasn't sure of (on Oct. 28 she had said, 'I don't know my sixes and I don't want to do them'.) Now she wanted to do everything there was on PLATO. She observed what other children were doing and checked her lessons so she would be able to progress to their levels. Sara had a competitive spirit. When she wasn't excelling in math, she didn't want any part of it. As she worked on PLATO she began to understand math better, and excelled in it. PLATO provided an opportunity for her to be tutored privately without her having to admit to anyone that she made mistakes and she had learned to accept her mistakes more easily as she gained confidence in her ability in math. Sara was unusual within her class on achievement test gains. Her biggest gains were in concepts and applications, whereas other children moved further in computation.

Ms. Hamilton had said Sara was an above average child in everything but math. Math had been something that Sara didn't care about at the beginning of the year. Sara tells her own story of accomplishment and as Ms. Hamilton said, 'She really blossomed this year'.

May 24, 1976

It was the end of another year of PLATO math. On Tuesday after school, those who had earned 800 points during the year for 'assuming responsibility' joined Ms. Hamilton and her husband for a round of miniature golf. Sara was one of the eleven honored.

Ms. Hamilton had her own way of teaching math. She said, 'I don't use text books too much. They don't stress what I want to stress when I want to stress it'. She used the books for some ideas and exercises. Ms. Hamilton also picked up a lot of ideas for teaching from PLATO. She liked the fractions lessons the best as it was consistent with the way she taught math. In whole numbers, Ms. Hamilton did not use many manipulative materials. She said, 'I stress the skills. I don't feel comfortable with manipulatives. It drives me crazy to have toys all around the room.' Sheila said, 'The whole numbers lessons exposed me to a lot of methods of explaining to children who don't have good concepts. Things I had never used before'. Ms. Hamilton didn't get to graphs on PLATO this year. She said, 'From playing BATTLESHIP the children were able to get the coordinates. I did a little correlating'. Sheila had many worksheets that she had used the year before when she learned to teach graphs. She used some of those worksheets this year (1975–76) but said she spent only about 3 percent of her math time on graphs. She said, 'I wish that I had another month of school to teach graphs. I could have helped the children a lot better this year in graphs'.

When asked, 'If you could choose between PLATO and a teacher aide in your room, which would it be?' Sheila answered, 'PLATO'. She didn't hesitate to make the choice and went on to say, 'I think more children profit from PLATO than from a teacher aide. I think they learn things that an aide cannot teach such as concentration, skim reading which is a very difficult thing to get kids to do, they learn to pace themselves, to be intently involved. The trouble with one-to-one with a teacher is the students become so dependent and I think they become independent with PLATO. I have to balance that to say there are times when a teacher has to help at the terminal.'

Student Achievement — Two Years in One?

During the second of these two years Ms. Hamilton came to know the strengths and weaknesses of PLATO for teaching fourth grade arithmetic. It was a personal accomplishment for her. She was treated well by the CERL people and even became a part of the demonstration team at a professional meeting in Kentucky. She was caught up in the CERL enthusiasm. She continued to extoll the virtues of PLATO, 'I think PLATO is *great*! I hope to remain in the program ... I wish that *more* children could have use of the terminals'.

And her students. They never missed a turn. Sara said, 'I want to go into Mr. Kalisch next year cause he has PLATO'. And the rest of the youngsters said the same. Even as spring came to Johnson School, and recess brought the blossom-rich air to their lungs, these children kept banging away at BATTLE-SHIP (Graphs, 1b) and sorting away at SORT EQUIVALENT NUMBERS (Fractions, C15). In terms of time-on-task, the children of this class had more than double the experience pupils ordinarily get on arithmetic problems, without apparently sacrificing time for reading, social studies or aesthetics lessons. According to Ms. Hamilton, 'Beside just math skills, PLATO teaches math concepts, reading skills, spelling and writing. Children try to make their notes more sensible on PLATO. What they get out of PLATO is just tremendous.'

Sheila knew that PLATO often 'CROAKED'. She knew that the software was not available for the rest of elementary school math. She knew that her district could not afford to buy terminals. But it was hard for her to think of these as weaknesses. That's just the way PLATO was.

There are teachers more delimiting in their definition of fourth grade arithmetic than Sheila Hamilton and Don Cohen. Most would accept fractions, decimals, and graphs to go with the basic operations, but some would not include EGG DROP or a student's own creation of SPACE SPIDER. Some would be uncomfortable about counting help given to another child (doing a simpler lesson) as time-on-task. A lot of time was spent in writing notes to the authors. What part of this is mathematics?

Not even Don Cohen would go so far as to say that all the world is mathematics. But clearly within his definition, and that of Bob Davis and the other CERL people, learning mathematics is a matter of incorporating the basic concepts and operations into everyday living. Learning is a matter of experience, much more than of performance. It is a matter of thinking, more than of calculating. The calculating and performance are important, but only if made meaningful. On PLATO the children found fractions in pizzas and found algebra in frontier trains. They found an even better 'tube' than the one they had at home, one that they could talk to and that would talk back to them, and help them learn their lessons.

What socialization here! They wanted to learn. The work ethic ran wild. Sara said, 'I learned lots of addition and subtraction. I started on Chapter 1. Now I'm on Chapter 8. I finished it and I was so happy. Chapter 8 is adding and subtracting mixed numbers. I was so happy to get decimals.' Ted said, 'I'm on level 10 of 12'. He continued in the lesson to level 11 and said, 'Now if I can get here, I can probably pass'. He finished 12 of 12 and said, 'Oh boy, I finished EQUIVALENT FRACTIONS GENERALIZED'.

These were the children Sheila Hamilton was teaching to be responsible. PLATO gave them an instrument, a space of their own, a micro culture (for like King Tut's tomb, it was not the teacher's space) for exercising teacher-like, parent-like control of time, movement, and subject matter, without giving up the opportunity to have fun. It was a field day in responsibility.

It was as if they would race to maturity, two years in one, except that the hard work was all so much fun.

PLATO was not there to give them lessons in adulthood, but in mathematics. Did they learn a year's worth? Ms. Hamilton said, 'Children learned to concentrate. They became very proud of the successes they had. I feel they learned to try not so much in relation to others, but in relation to their own progress. They looked in the chapters to see how they were progressing.' Every child learned on PLATO, even those who didn't like math. The test scores show they gained, on the average, over two years per child. The test scores shown in Figures 2.8 and 2.9 are from the *Comprehensive Test of Basic Skills*. These tests do not conform particularly to the PLATO curriculum and they are more narrow than most people would want an arithmetic program to be, but they do give some indication that certain common problems can be worked well by Ms. Hamilton's pupils.

The tests were administered the second school week in the fall and again with about three weeks to go in the spring. It is known that average children often appear to gain more than a year during this span, but a median gain of 2.2 years is clearly better than the average. Even the two most poorly achieving children, one of whom was Kate, advanced on these test scales well over a year's growth, and stood only slightly below the national norm for fourth grade children.

		Computation		Concepts		Application		Total	
Tom	4th	31	4.9	23	6.8	11	5.3	65	5.4
Martin	4th	17	3.4	10	3.3	7	4.0	34	3.4
Billy	4th	15	3.1	17	4.9	7	4.0	39	3.8
Kathy	4th	37	5.7	21	6.0	17	8.2	75	6.3
Ben	4th	20	3.7	10	4.1	10	5.0	43	4.1
Jon	4th	24	4.1	11	3.5	10	5.0	45	4.2
Bob	4th	40	6.4	21	6.0	17	8.2	78	6.6
Debbie	4th	26	4.3	13	4.1	8	4.4	47	4.3
Leslie	4th	21	3.8	14	4.3	8	4.4	43	4.1
Beth	4th	18	3.5	5	1.9	7	4.0	30	3.0
Erica	4th	23	4.0	20	5.6	10	5.0	53	4.6
Holly	4th	21	3.8	16	4.7	7	4.0	44	4.1
Rhoda	4th	32	5.0	19	5.4	18	8.9	69	5.7
Terry	4th	20	3.7	16	4.7	4	2.7	40	3.9
Wendy	4th	27	4.4	12	3.8	8	4.4	47	4.3
Mona	4th	34	5.3	26	7.8	16	7.5	76	6.4
Beth	4th	31	4.9	27	8.4	16	7.5	74	6.2
Sara	4th	22	3.9	12	3.8	8	4.4	42	4.0
Kitty	4th	29	4.7	26	7.8	11	5.3	66	5.5
Kate	4th	12	2.8	4	1.6	4	2.7	20	2.1
Sally	4th	30	4.8	22	6.4	12	5.6	64	5.3
Shelly	4th	17	3.4	14	4.3	12	5.6	43	4.1
Kenneth	4th	11	2.7	13	4.1	5	3.2	29	3.0
Ted	4th	14	3.0	9	3.1	9	4.7	32	3.2

Each column has raw score and corresponding grade equivalent. Md4.1.
Figure 2.8: CTBS scores for the first year (1975).

But the most important PLATO achievement of all is not in long division, nor in attention to directions, nor in typing, nor in gamesmanship, nor in socialization, but in enthusiasm for learning mathematics. Sara did not want to do her sixes, but at the end of the year she was ready and eager for percentage.

PLATO did teach, and children did learn. The children were happy. The parents and grandparents were happy. PLATO was clearly a success in Ms. Hamilton's fourth grade room.

Complexities of Learning With Plato

Sheila Hamilton accepted and enjoyed the complexities of teaching and learning. PLATO added a new complexity. As Ms. Hamilton taught mathematics using PLATO, she also taught fairness, responsibility, socialization skills and higher order thinking skills. The range and depth of the experiences went from academic to affective as the personalistic exchanges between PLATO, the youngsters and Ms. Hamilton show. Creative responses were evoked. The culture of the classroom and the micro-culture around PLATO was created.

PLATO didn't stand alone, as in some rooms, in Ms. Hamilton's room. She integrated PLATO with her own math curriculum. When children studied graphs on PLATO, they worked graph problems on the chalkboard and on

		Computation		Concepts		Application		Total	
Tom	4th	38	5.9	27	8.4	15	6.9	80	6.9
Martin	4th	33	5.2	18	5.1	12	5.6	68	5.2
Billy	4th	36	5.6	25	7.4	16	7.5	77	6.5
Kathy	4th	45	8.6	28	8.9	17	8.2	90	8.5
Ben	4th	35	5.4	25	7.4	8	4.4	68	5.6
Jon	4th	41	6.6	21	6.0	10	5.0	72	6.0
Bob	4th	43	7.6	24	7.1	18	8.9	85	7.6
Debbie	4th	39	6.1	24	7.1	12	5.6	75	6.3
Leslie	4th	38	5.9	18	5.1	6	3.6	62	5.2
Beth	4th	28	4.5	12	3.8	5	3.2	45	4.2
Erica	4th	38	5.9	20	5.6	15	6.9	73	6.1
Holly	4th	42	7.1	15	4.5	6	3.6	63	5.2
Rhoda	4th	40	6.4	24	7.1	18	8.9	82	7.1
Terry	4th	39	6.1	21	6.0	8	4.4	68	5.6
Wendy	4th	42	7.1	23	6.8	11	5.3	76	6.4
Mona	4th	45	8.6	29	9.5	19	9.8	93	9.2
Beth	4th	45	8.6	28	8.9	20	11.1	93	9.2
Sara	4th	41	6.6	29	9.5	18	8.9	88	8.1
Kitty	4th	0	***	0	***	0	***	0	***
Kate	4th	37	5.7	4	1.6	5	3.2	46	4.2
Sally	4th	0	***	0	***	0	***	0	***
Shelly	4th	30	4.8	23	6.8	15	6.9	68	5.6
Kenneth	4th	36	5.6	15	4.5	10	5.0	61	5.1
Ted	4th	40	6.4	25	7.4	15	6.9	80	6.9

Each column has raw score and corresponding grade equivalent. Md = 6.35.

Figure 2.9: CTBS scores for the first year (1976).

work sheets. When children were learning the facts in multiplication, whole numbers was on PLATO.

The complexity increased as the new materials appeared on the PLATO screen. With the children Ms. Hamilton learned about mathematics and at the same time learned to solve problems related to the PLATO system and to share her knowledge with the children. The PLATO communication system provided a unique experience in learning math. Using PLATO not only increased the child's ability to understand the number system, but it gave the child a special lesson in the complexities of technology. The problems were real and solving them required critical thinking.

Ms. Hamilton individualized instruction not only for the children's progress in academics but also for their progress in socialization. PLATO lessons promoted individual growth and kept children on task. Children were involved not just at the outset but during most of the thirty minute session. It is often not the case for children to be on task more than fifty percent of the time in many classroooms (Tikunoff, Berliner and Rist, 1975; Wiley, 1976).

In the pilot year, 1974–75, Ms. Hamilton reported there were many children in her room at the beginning of the year who would not attend to tasks without supervision, but she also said, 'When the child was on PLATO it was one half hour of the day when I knew each child was being instructed'. In the second year, there were a number of children who were not motivated toward school achievement, for example Sara, but they were consistently attentive to the lessons on the terminal. Ms. Hamilton organized her room to keep children on task. PLATO helped.

With detailed records of each child's strengths and weaknesses in the PLATO program and her curriculum, Ms. Hamilton planned a curriculum to build on strengths and remediate the weaknesses. Programmed to benefit all children in this fourth grade, children worked at their level and continued to progress. To benefit all meant PLATO, as a scarce resource, had to be in use most every half hour of the day in order for each child to have a turn. Ms. Hamilton insisted on fairness. She worked with the developers to see that the hardware was programmed for each child to have a thirty minute session. However, there were many technical problems with hardware and lessons that created frustration for the students when their session was interrupted.

Ms. Hamilton could not respond to each child's problem. She asked children to help each other. At the same time children were learning to multiply they were learning to respond to calls for help from students nearby. In Ms. Hamilton's classroom, school became slightly more a matter of working out problems together. PLATO encouraged children to find a friend to play a game. A teacher who ordinarily required children 'to do their own work' in math encouraged PLATO learners to help each other on the terminal. She also encouraged them to look at the PLATO library section for other children's solutions to problems for ideas on how to solve their own. Two examples of help were: NAMES FOR TODAY'S DATE (Whole Numbers, Fl) and PAINTINGS LIBRARY (Fractions, A8). This setting provided the opportunity for children to be responsible for their own learning when working on the terminals.

PLATO brought many opportunities to increase the repertoire of cognitive and affective experiences of the children. The spirit of competition was strong around Ms. Hamilton's PLATO. Competition can run roughshod over children. We saw the struggles to win. We heard cries of 'Hit'em' and 'I'm the mad bomber'. Are such games subtle practice for more serious hostilities? It is a matter to ponder, but harmful effects were not apparent. The competition appeared benign. Ms. Hamilton was accustomed to a competitive spirit in her classroom, but the cooperative and helpful spirit in the classroom overshadowed effects of competition.

Children played competitive games. They helped each other with lessons. They loved PLATO. At the same time they gained a healthy perspective regarding the use of the technology. Both the benefits and limitations were recognized by Ms. Hamilton and she encouraged the children to recognize them too. She asked children to bring problems to her attention and was quick to point out to the children that PLATO could be wrong. She showed the children how to select lessons, how to shift out of a difficult lesson and how to write notes about their experience. Children did write notes. They wrote notes to say they were angry, to say they had fun, to request more games, to make suggestions to PLATO and to ask for help. The notes helped

Ms. Hamilton evaluate the children's progress and the PLATO system. In turn she kept in touch with the authors to let them know what was good and what was troublesome about the lessons. Ms. Hamilton was key to the success of the innovation.

More than some teachers Ms. Hamilton chose to limit some of the complexity of the children's lessons by working on mastery before venturing on to new materials. She also controlled the selections on PLATO that were available to the children so that they didn't explore the many possibilities of adult lessons on PLATO. She was particularly successful in exercising control over the lessons in the second year when she kept the children practising for mastery of whole numbers and fractions, resulting in very little time to study graphs. At the end of that year, she wished for another month because she could have helped children with graphs more easily in that second year and the time was gone.

PLATO math materials did not celebrate accomplishments of mathematicians and other scholars. Rather they honored the responses of children. Eventually such work would add up to be scholarly and creative accomplishment. Every child believed it. Once given, a student's answers became part of the further lesson. Authors of all lessons — graphs, whole numbers and fractions — attempted to structure lessons so that a child proceeded when he/she was ready to do so without repeating work already mastered. The fractions lessons were especially designed to provide the child with information regarding level and type of mastery. Children were told by PLATO what they had mastered and what they had to do to complete each curriculum chapter. Ms. Hamilton liked fraction lessons because they were the most consistent with the way she taught. Children, on the other hand, were sometimes frustrated by the slow pace and wrote their notes to say so. Never making a mistake became boring. The authors worked to please the children. Striking a balance was a part of the complexity.

In many lessons, making mistakes was the rule rather than the exception. Children who were embarrassed by mistakes when they started to use PLATO later became accustomed to mistakes as part of the process of figuring out problems. The lessons were programmed to expect a range of incorrect and correct student responses. Children were directed in such a way that they felt responsible and were challenged to solve each problem. The study of Sara showed how she used PLATO to make mistakes and eventually succeed.

Personal valuing was a central part of the PLATO curriculum. An underlying assumption of the graphs and whole numbers lessons was that children's ideas were a resource. Children were encouraged to create their own problems. Special lessons, YOUR WAY (Whole Numbers, F14) and EXPERIMENTING WITH LINEAR GRAPHS (Graphs, 1.0) called for a child's own creations. As an example of valuing children's responses, the authors of the graph lessons accepted the answers that the children gave by plotting their answers on the screen. The lesson, SLOPE CHECKUP (Graphs, 1), was an example. The authors tried to anticipate what errors would be made and programmed PLATO to show these errors as correct answers *to a different problem*. The authors said, 'Children often are answering some other problem correctly, one that makes more sense to them. It was the PLATO curriculum developer's job to predict those other problems'.

Easley and Zwoyer (1975) have shown how students cope in school using trusted schemes tempered by experience. Some schemes are inappropriate. Students need the opportunity to try out their schemes. Students using PLATO had opportunities to understand the relationship between their scheme and PLATO's — errors got special attention. If PLATO didn't understand the errors, Ms. Hamilton did.

Case (1975) and others have argued that children gain a better understanding of the principles of mathematics when the learner's errors and justifications as well as correct answers receive attention. PLATO reacted to many responses but could not cope with problems in the way that Ms. Hamilton did.

Bruce Hicks and Gordon Hoke (1974) have written:

Computers challenge society. They can confer benefits or just regiment us. They can serve the many or just the few.

Hoke and Hicks went on to ask:

What are the roles and responsibilities of each educator in helping to insure that computers assist education, but in a humane and humanistic way?

The elementary mathematics lessons on PLATO were more humanistic than most mathematics lessons. They saluted individualistic expression and drew learner attention to the implications of their acts. The space around PLATO was marked by challenge, but also by succor. Competition was usually in the air. The sense of accomplishment endured from session to session.

It was a paradox. At least as used in Ms. Hamilton's room, PLATO individualized the study of mathematics, yet made it possible for children to be more aware of what other children were struggling to learn and how they dealt with their obstacles. It provided a place for children's innate creative and compassionate senses to mix with the cognitive.

Technological systems are a part of our culture. Applications of technology through the use of computers to aid instruction continues. The fiscal costs of equipping children to use technology in a creative and critical way and to live in a technological society may be high, but without such education, the social costs to society may be higher.

Notes

1 PLATO — Programmed Logic for Automatic Teaching Operations.
2 Note: The teacher's name, the school name and all student names are psuedonyms.
3 Students working at their own pace can, of course, mean trouble, especially if some students allow themselves to fall far behind. To guard against such problems, PLATO reported to teachers whenever a student seemed to be making unsatisfactory progress.
4 The description of lessons in the three Mathematics Strands are in the publications *Description of Graphing Strand Lessons* by Donald Cohen and Gerald Glynn, Computer-Based Education Research Laboratory, University of Illinois, Urbana, Illinois, June, 1974; *Description of PLATO Whole Number Arithmetic Lessons* by Bonnie Anderson Seiler and Charles S. Weaver, Computer-Based Education Research Laboratory, University of Illinois, Urbana, Illinois, June, 1976; *The Fractions Curriculum — PLATO Elementary School Mathematics Project* by David Kibby and Sharon Dugdale, Computer-Based Education Research Laboratory, University of Illinois, Urbana, Illinois, March, 1975.
5 SRA — DeVolt, M.V., Frehmeyer, H., Greenberg, H.J., Venuzks, S.J. (1974) *Mathematics Learning System Texts.* Chicago, IL: Science Research Associates, 974 IBM Subsidiary.
6 MIA — Denhalm, R.A., Hankins, D.D., Herrick, M.C., Vojtka, G.R. (1974) *Mathematics for Individual Achievement.* Boston, MA: Houghton Mifflin, ISBM 0-395-14796-4.
7 Ms. Hamilton individualized much of the instruction in the room, which made it easy to fit PLATO into the day's schedule. For whole group activities, she frequently turned the terminals off.
8 Graphing Linear Equation's workbooks were prepared by the authors at CERL to accompany the PLATO lessons.
9 Comprehensive Tests of Basic Skills, published by CTB/McGraw-Hill, Del Monte Research Park, Monterey, California 93940.
10 REVIEW AND PRACTICE was the lesson a child was routed to at the beginning of a session. When the child had finished two or three lessons to a mastery criterion, two or three tasks similar to those in the lessons were presented for review.

References

CASE, R. (1975) 'Gearing the demands of instruction to the developmental capacities of the learner', *Review of Educational Research, 45,* 1, pp. 59–87.
EASLEY, J.A., Jr. and ZWOYER, R.E. (1975) 'Teaching by listening – toward a new day in math classes'. *Contemporary Education, 47,* 1, pp. 19–25.
GUBA, E. and LINCOLN, Y. (1981) *Effective evaluation.* San Francisco: Jossey–Bass.
HICKS, B. and HOKE, G. (1974) 'Instructional Applications of Computers (IAC) in the College of Education.' Working Paper 2, University of Illinois, May 18.
SCRIBNER, S. (1976) 'Situating the experiment in cross cultural research'. In RIEGEL, K. F. and MEACHAM, J.A. (Eds). *The developing individual in a changing world, Vol. I.* The Hauge: Manton, pp. 310–321.
SMITH, L.M. and POHLAND, P.A. (1974) 'Education, technology, and the rural highlands,' in this volume.
STAKE, B.E. (1977) 'PLATO and Fourth Grade Mathematics'. Unpublished manuscript, University of Illinois, CIRCE. A report for the Educational Testing Service. ERIC DOCUMENT ED228–040.

STAKE, R.E. (1975) *Evaluating the arts in education: A responsive approach.* Columbus, OH: Charles E. Merrill. (Out of print but available from University Microfilms, Ann Arbor, MI.)

STAKE, R.E. (1975) *Program evaluation, particularly responsive evaluation.* Occasional Paper No. 5. Kalamazoo: Western Michigan University, Evaluation Center. Also in DOCKRELL, W.B. and HAMILTON, D. (Eds), (1979) *Rethinking educational research.* Kent, England: Hodder-Stoughton

STAKE, R.E., EASLEY, J.A., *et al.* (1977) *Case studies in science education.* Champaign, IL: University of Illinois at Urbana-Champaign, College of Education, CIRCE.

TIKUNOFF, W., BERLINER, D.C. and RIST, R.C. (1975) *An ethnographic study of 40 classrooms of the beginning teachers evaluation study; A known sample.* (Technical Report 75–10–10–5). San Francisco: Far West Regional Laboratory.

TINBERGEN, N. (1971) *The herring gulls world: A study of the social behavior of birds.* Harper Torchbooks, New York, Harper & Row.

WILEY, D.E. (1976) 'Another hour, another day: Quantity of schooling. A potent path for policy'. In SEWEL, W.E., HAUSER R.M. and FEATHERMAN, D.L. (Eds), *Schooling and achievement in American society.* New York, Academic Press, pp. 225–266.

II
Microcomputers in Language Learning

Introduction

In the second section we present two pieces from the mid-1980s that examine the uses of computer technology as a component of second language instruction. In 'Microcomputers in Foreign Language Teaching: A Case Study on Computer-Aided Learning,' Robert Blomeyer offers a multiple-site case study of four secondary foreign language teachers of German, Spanish, and French. The setting for his study is two upper-middle class suburban high schools. In 'Curriculum for Cultural Politics: Literacy Program Development in a Navajo School Setting' by Daniel McLaughlin, we have an account of an innovative secondary school project designed to advance English language and literacy skills and create new communicative functions for both oral and written Navajo through the use of microcomputers as a bilingual writing tool. While the two studies use different theoretical approaches to 'tell the story', they are both accounts of secondary schools where microcomputers were used in innovative programs where CAL became a component of second language teaching and learning.

Blomeyer's study of microcomputer use in foreign language classes was conducted in 1983–84 as fieldwork for his doctoral dissertation entitled *The Use of Computer-Based Instruction in Foreign Language Teaching: An Ethnographically Oriented Study* (Blomeyer, 1985). The unpublished dissertation and the derivative case study offered here concern the use of locally developed foreign language CAI by four teachers in two different suburban school districts. Although Blomeyer's work has methodological and theoretical linkages with the two earlier studies in this book, it does not detail the macro-structure of local culture (Smith and Pohland) or the micro-structure of the classroom (Stake) to the extent of either predecessor. He portrays policy and practice in both settings using *baseline data* (background information about the human, technological, and institutional context of the students, staff and community), *process data* (information derived from observation of CAL activities in both settings) and *value data* (statements taken from observations of and interviews with students, teachers, and program administrators stating what they consider to be important about computer-aided language learning). (See LeCompte and Goetz, 1984.)

McLaughlin's account details a classical participant-observation study wherein an anthropological researcher gathers spoken and written samples of language from the Navajo participants, descriptions of the instructional materials and an analysis of standardized language scores before and after the program. He uses these data within the framework of critical theory to operationalize key concepts of Cummins's (1986) 'Framework for Minority Student Empowerment'.[1] His portrayal of the literacy program shows how the possibilities for empowerment emerged in a Navajo school setting as word processing became a tool for literacy development. This study is important because it demonstrates the potential for replication, adaptation, and the restructuring of formal literacy instruction through a community-school partnership where the creative use of word processing as a curricular tool lead to the empowerment of minority students.

Together, these two very different case studies on computer-aided language learning reveal a possibly important contrast in approaches to the use of microcomputers in curriculum. Blomeyer states that in his case study of foreign language teaching, where drill and practice lessons are the dominant form of interaction, there is little evidence that signals the beginning of a revolutionary change in the dominant conception of schooling. In contrast, McLaughlin's study illustrates the transforming effects of generic microcomputer-based tools as an instrumental medium for literacy acquisition and the social empowerment of Navajo students. The difference between the apparent social outcomes of traditional CAI (the use of microcomputers as a supplement to direct instruction) and the alternative use of microcomputers as emancipatory tools points out a potential asset for new curricula to advance the empowerment of minority students and an important theme for additional research on CAL.

Note

1 The editors would like to thank Dr Antonio Gonzalez in the Curriculum and Instruction Department at the University of Houston for his help in clarifying Cummin's theoretical framework.

References

BLOMEYER, R.L. (1985) *The use of computer-based instruction in foreign language teaching: An ethnographically oriented study* (Doctoral Dissertation, University of Illinois).

CUMMINS, J. (1986) 'Empowering minority students: A framework for intervention', *Harvard Educational Review, 56, 1.*

LeCOMPTE, M.D. and GOETZ, J. (1984) in FETTERMAN D.M. (Ed.) *Ethnography in educational evaluation,* Beverly Hills CA: Sage Publications, pp. 37–59.

Chapter 3

Microcomputers in
Foreign Language Teaching:
A Case Study on Computer Aided Learning

Robert L. Blomeyer, Jr.

Computer-aided learning (CAL) is a powerful educational innovation that has great potential for the improvement of teaching and learning. Books and articles on instructional methods relevant to K-12 computer use are available in abundance. In the last few years, a growing body of professional literature has become available on the subject of school computer use. This includes information from a major national survey on the instructional uses of computers (Becker, 1986), findings from a substantial number of experimental and quasi-experimental studies on computer-assisted instruction (Becker, 1988; Kulik and Kulik, 1986; Sampson, Niemiec, Weinstein and Walberg, 1986; and Kulik, Kulik and Cohen, 1980) and a variety of naturalistic studies on CAL (Blomeyer, 1989).

Existing quantitative research on CAL does little to illustrate links to classroom learning. Research findings provide little clear methodological or policy guidance on how to optimize the instructional effectiveness of computers in the schools. Available survey research provides a general picture of how microcomputers are used in the participating schools, but surveys seldom provide detailed examples illustrating the programs sampled that could make the statistical profile more apprehensible. Experimental and quasi-experimental studies present evidence on the effectiveness of CAI as an instructional intervention in mathematics instruction, but may have limited curricular significance because of limits on generalizability beyond a specific experimental treatment.

Studies on the 'effectiveness' of technological interventions have also been questioned because existing research seldom demonstrates statistically significant findings. Solomon and Gardner have suggested that this may be due to a lack of sensitivity to concomitant changes affecting instructional settings where experimental research was conducted. They call for a more tentative or heuristic approach to inquiry on CAL that can lead to the discovery of instructionally significant questions for future research (Solomon and Gardner, 1986).

Among available naturalistic studies on CAL are case studies and other qualitative research on instructional computing programs in a variety of settings and curricular domains. These studies provide detailed perspectives on the instructional use of computers in schools that have significance for the planning and implementation of new programs and for the integration of microcomputers as a component of instruction throughout the traditional curriculum. Contextually explicit naturalistic research on instructional computing provides heuristic models of policy and practice that allow practitioners to critically examine alternative implementation strategies and curricular applications. Choices can then be made about the acquisition and use of microcomputer applications (Blomeyer, 1989).

The case study described here will examine instructional applications of microcomputers as a curricular innovation in foreign language teaching. Language teachers generally use textbooks, workbooks, audio tapes, films, and other instructional media as instructional tools. At the time this study was conducted (1983–1984) microcomputers were just beginning to be used in support of foreign language teaching. The objective of the study was to provide a detailed portrayal of computer-aided learning in a specific instructional context, with the aim of giving policy-makers and practitioners a practical and relevant basis for making decisions regarding utilization of this new instructional technology.

There is a long history of research on innovation in education and social sciences. Although this study is ethnographically oriented, the intent is to portray characteristics of the innovation rather than the cultural features of the participants. More particularly, the approach to this study is based on studies of the 'diffusion of innovation' that are common to cultural anthropology, rural sociology, and educational research. One of the key concepts from the literature on innovation is that the 'compatibility' of an innovation (i.e., its compatibility with existing socio-cultural values and beliefs, previously introduced ideas, and need for additional innovation) has a great influence on long-range outcomes for continuing adoption or rejection of an innovation (Rogers and Shoemaker, 1971).

Planning decisions about the adoption or rejection of computer-aided learning need to be based on thorough professional understanding of its instructional significance within the established curriculum. When instructional personnel understand the practical significance of new methods and delivery systems, instructional technologies can be integrated as an effective component in any area of subject matter. The present study establishes a measure of the compatibility between computer-aided learning and foreign language teaching. This will allow language teachers and curriculum specialists to examine the potential of CAL as an instructional alternative in foreign language curriculum.

Approach: A Multiple Site Case Study

The model that guided fieldwork and data analysis for this case study was quasi-ethnographic and used two contrasting school sites to establish a basis for a comparative analysis of naturalistic data. LeCompte and Goetz (1984) discuss three categories of data that are generally used to document naturalistic research. These three data types also provide a convenient and logical scheme for the presentation and discussion of naturalistic data. The data categories that are used to describe CAL in foreign language teaching programs in this study are: (a) *baseline data*, or information about the human and technological context of the students, instructional staff and community setting; (b) *process data*, or information derived from observations of CAL activities in these settings and some of their outcomes; and (c) *value data*, or information about the values of the various participants and the values implied by their use of microcomputers in foreign language classes.

The initial study was completed for the author's unpublished doctoral dissertation from the University of Illinois entitled *The use of computer-based instruction in foreign language teaching: An ethnographically-oriented study* (Blomeyer, 1985). The format of the unpublished dissertation allowed for a very comprehensive and detailed treatment of data and conclusions. Separate chapters were included detailing observations and interviews conducted in both locations. Classroom events were reported from both synchronic and diachronic perspectives. Data chapters concerning each of two schools studied included accounts of interviews with students, teachers, and administrative personnel.

This case study provides an abbreviated version of the data and conclusions from the earlier work. Although particular data segments used to document this case study comprise only a small portion of that used in the unpublished dissertation, the substance and tone of the original work is maintained. References are provided to more detailed sections of the original work when appropriate. It is the intent of this study to illustrate the significance of CAL as an instructional innovation used in support of foreign language teaching. In addition, the conclusions suggest broader questions regarding the role of CAL in other areas of curriculum. The concluding section will examine some of the broader implications of this study for an increased understanding of computer-aided learning's potential impact on teaching and learning.

Fieldwork Strategies

This case study is based on a fundamental concern that educational research should improve professional understanding of relationships between educational policy and practice and translate this knowledge into information used for improving educational practice. One of the first published multiple-

site case studies of CAL by Smith and Pohland (1974) was a significant influence on the conceptual direction and methodology of this case study. They
believed that anthropological methods grounded in cultural theory would
produce research findings useful for educational improvement.They expressed
their concern in the following way:

> It seems to us that it is incumbent upon the profession to narrow
> the gap between educational theory and practice in terms that are
> both appropriate and understandable to the practitioner. (Smith and
> Pohland, 1976, p. 265)

The methods employed during the fieldwork conducted for this case
study were specifically chosen to maximize applicability of findings for
the improvement of instructional practice and to minimize potentially dis-
ruptive effect of classroom-based naturalistic research. Naturalistic inquiry
techniques minimize intervention into the routine functioning of the classroom and school settings and are preferred by many researchers for school-
based educational research (Guba, 1978).

The case study offered here used a standard approach to site access and
field methods. Site access was negotiated between the researcher and the
school district with the support of a foreign language specialist employed by
the state board of education and faculty members from a major university.
Fieldwork strategies included participant and non-participant observation
and interviews. Interviews were conducted with teachers and other school
staff members. Additional interviews were conducted with students to
broaden the database, triangulate preliminary data with additional emic
perspectives, and to generally increase the representation of the students'
viewpoint on using CAL in foreign language classes.

Initial observations were unstructured and utilized time-sequenced observer field notes and (when possible) audio recordings to document the classes
observed. Most field observations remained unstructured, but 'progressive
focusing' on clusters of events and potentially significant issues refined the
study's 'foreshadowed problems', evolved new data categories based on the
observed phenomena, and led to an 'expected evolution and redefinition' of
the questions suggested by prior case studies of instructional computing
(Blomeyer, 1985).

Data was gathered in both research sites. Audio tape recording was used
to document a sampling of the classes observed and to record all of the staff
and student interviews. Observations provided questions and concerns that
were later formalized as interview questions that were used with the cooperating teachers and selected students. These were conducted after the
classroom observation was completed in order to: (a) check the accuracy of
the preliminary data, and (b) control for contamination that might result
from imprudent conversations with teachers or students.

Classes observed included both traditional foreign language classes and

Table 1: Classes observed and class microcomputer use

Classes Observed	Class Time Observed	Classes Observed Using Micros	Time Using Micros (Class periods and hours)
Woodville West High School (each period = 50 min.)	35	26 hours	10 per./7.5 hours
Hilldale Community High School (each period = 45 min.)			
Teacher S1	18	13.5 hours	3 ½ per./1.3 hours
Teacher S2	13	9.7 hours	3 per./2.25 hours
Teacher G	16	12.0 hours	6 ½ per./2.25 hours
SUB TOTAL	47	39.0 hours	7.5 per./6.25 hours

(Source: Blomeyer, 1985, p. 118)

classes meeting in microcomputer laboratories where the students made use of CAL. In School One (hereafter referred to as Woodville West High School) nearly all the regular classes conducted away from the microcomputer site were tape recorded. In both schools it was found that the sound level was too high in the microcomputer sites for effective audio recording. Because teachers in School Two (Hilldale Community High School) specifically expressed concern that the use of a tape recorder would intrude on their normal classroom settings, audio taping was more selective and generally confined to the classes that were observed toward the end of the fieldwork in their classrooms.

The approximate time required for this study was one school year. Original plans called for completion of the classroom observation and staff interviews. Table 1 shows the number of classes and time spent observing each of the four participating teachers and what portion of the classes observed actually included CAL. Use of CAL by the cooperating teachers only school included preliminary visits, two to three weeks of inclusive observation, and three day follow-up visits for the purpose of conducting student interviews. Table 1 shows the number of classes and time spent observing each of the four participating teachers and what portion of the classes observed actually included CAL. Use of CAL by the cooperating teachers only accounted for a small percentage of overall class time devoted to foreign language instruction. Table 1 contains a summary detailing classroom observations and the portion of that time that was devoted to CAL by each of the cooperating teachers.

The French teacher at Woodville West had the largest percentage of time observed that was devoted to CAL with 28 percent, and one of the Spanish teachers at Hilldale High School had the smallest percentage of observed time using CAL with 9 percent. Time devoted to observation tends to favor the impression that CAL was used to a greater extent than was actually the case. Teachers arranged for the researcher to visit their schools at times when they planned to use CAL. It was their understanding that the study was about computer-based language learning and they discussed the idea that days when the researcher was present probably did not accurately reflect the total percentage of use during the school year.

In some respects the two suburban sites for the field study were alike in size and in terms of their overall educational programs. However, they were very different in the way that they approached instructional computing at the school level and in the hardware resources that were available. It is necessary to have an idea of the similarities and differences between the two schools selected for the study in order to appreciate the events observed in each location. The following section provides background information on the two participating schools and their respective instructional computing programs.

Baseline Data

One of the earliest findings of the study was that as of May, 1983, foreign language teachers were actually using microcomputers as an organized part of their instructional delivery in only a very small number of high schools in the state where the study was conducted. Although instructional computing had been a reality in some state school districts for three to five years, it appeared that use of CAL as a component of foreign language curriculum might be confined to less than a half-dozen suburban schools around the metropolitan area where the two schools were located.

The language teachers who cooperated with this study were leaders regarding their use of microcomputers in foreign language curriculum. This was the case even though the overall instructional computing programs in their schools were already well established. Stated in terms of Rogers' (1983) innovation adoption categories, the cooperating teachers were 'innovators' within the state-wide population of foreign language teachers using computer-aided learning in secondary school curriculum. By outlining the histories of the instructional computing programs in both schools, it becomes more apparent why the cooperating teachers were among the first foreign language teachers in their state to begin using CAL as a component of comprehensive foreign language instruction.

Woodville West High School

Woodville West was located about ten miles from a nearby metropolitan area in a middle income suburb (median income about $32,000.00), having a population of about 33,000 persons. It was a four year comprehensive high school with Basic, Regular, Accelerated, and Honors (Advanced Placement) course offerings within its curriculum. Weighted grades were given to the accelerated and honors courses. Advanced Placement (A.P.) courses included English, calculus, European history, US history, biology, chemistry, physics, German, French and Spanish. The size of the total 9–12 enrollment was about 2200 students. According to school district statistics, about 77 percent of the graduating class usually went on to college. Records showed that 10 percent of the graduating class took the A.P. calculus and English exams. Out of 291 A.P. scores in a given year, 192 were 3 or better (A.P. scores range from a low of 0 to a high of 5).

At the time of the study, the school had a professional staff of about 165 persons with a pupil/teacher ratio of about 13 to 1. The foreign language department had a staff of twelve full and part-time teachers and an instructional supervisor who was also a part-time language teacher. The foreign language department offered classes in Latin, Spanish, French, German, and Russian. In 1983–1984, eighty-four students were enrolled in Latin, 584 students in Spanish, 288 students in French, eighty-seven students in German, and nineteen students in Russian. Foreign language classes were offered at four levels with an optional advanced placement course. Among foreign language students taking the A.P. test in a given year 85 percent reported 3 or better in French and 100 percent reported 3 or better in German. In that same year, of students taking the A.P. Spanish language and literature test, 35–45 percent reported receiving a 3 or better.

The educational computing program at Woodville West included use of both a mainframe computer and microcomputers. Initially, Cobol and Fortran were taught on the school's mainframe computer in applications programming courses oriented toward an advanced business curriculum. About two years before the study, an effort from the district superintendent's office led to the purchase of about thirty Apple microcomputers and the setting up of a single microcomputer site that was referred to as the 'Apple Lab'. The site was located in the wing of the school which housed the mathematics department. The microcomputers were to be used for 'instructional computing' as opposed to learning programming languages, and the use of the site was opened to all classroom teachers on a 'sign-up' basis. A computer 'site manager' was permanently assigned to the Apple Lab to manage the scheduling, assist classroom teachers using the facility, maintain the lesson disks for the various classes, and maintain the site hardware.

At about the same time that the Apple Lab was opened, the district hired a chairman for their mathematics department who had a background in business computer applications. This individual was retained at a salary level competitive with private industry and given the responsibility for overseeing the district-wide 'Computers in Education' program. In addition to his other duties, the math chairman/computer coordinator offered basic 'computer literacy' and programming courses to interested staff members in all the school's departments. These in-service courses included beginning to advanced level programming using a 'business applications' approach. Training involved providing the interested participants with enough information to develop their own applications and to integrate resources for educational computing into their own classes when and if they considered it appropriate. Money was made available in the department budgets that could be used for software purchases but final decisions on authorization of software purchases were left to the instructional supervisor or head in each department.

The French teacher at Woodville West who collaborated in the study had learned Basic programming techniques by attending the in-service courses offered by the math department chairman. She began attending these courses when they were first offered to the teaching staff and created her first computer-based language lessons as projects during those sessions. She piloted these lessons with her students during the year prior to this study by fitting her use of the microcomputer lab around the existing schedule for math, science, and business classes by checking with the individual instructors. She submitted her lessons to a foreign language publisher for review and subsequently had them accepted for publication. The school district granted her sole ownership of the materials for commercial publication although they had been developed as a direct outcome of district sponsored in-service training activities. These lessons continued to be used by the teacher during the period of the study.

Additional developments during the study included the purchase of a 'Corvus' hard-disk system and replacement of older model Apple II microcomputers with newer models having sufficient memory for programming in the PASCAL language and for administrative applications used by the principal's office. The French teacher who participated in the study continued to attend in-service training courses and studied the PASCAL language while the study was in progress.

Hilldale Community High School

Hilldale High served an area that included nine suburban communities about fifteen miles southwest of a large urban metropolitan area. The combined population of these areas was about 80,000. The communities in the immediate vicinity of the school itself were comprised of professional and managerial class families. However, the mean income for the school district was just around the $30,700.00 level; at or slightly below the median income for middle class families. The average income of the area had dropped considerably because the district redrew boundaries to include two low income areas in the catchment area for the school district. At the time of the study, 182 students attending the school were eligible for free lunches under the Chapter I guidelines.

Like Woodville West High School, Hilldale High was also a four year comprehensive high school, with a grading system which gave weighted class rankings to Fundamental, General, Regular, Superior and Honors A.P. course levels. Advanced placement courses included three English and literature courses, calculus, algebra, computer science, European history, US history, biology, chemistry, physics, music theory 1 and 2, German, French, Spanish, Latin, and Russian. Students were assigned to course levels on the basis of test scores, achievement and teacher recommendations.

The school was housed on two campuses located about ten blocks apart. The total enrollment for grades 9–12 was about 3600 students. According to available school district statistics, about 72 percent of the graduating class usually went on to college. Records showed that in 1982, 202 students took 308 advanced placement examinations. Of these students, 81.8 percent reported scores of 3 or better.

Hilldale High had a professional staff of about 232 persons with a pupil/teacher ratio of about 11.5 to 1. The foreign language department had a staff of twenty-two teachers and an instructional supervisor who was also a part-time language teacher. The foreign language department generally offered classes in Latin, Spanish, Italian, French, German, and Russian. In 1983–1984, 105 students were enrolled in Latin, 1085 students were enrolled in Spanish, 105 students were enrolled in Italian, 408 students were enrolled in French, 212 students were enrolled in German, and seventy-one students were enrolled in 'Word Clues' (an etymology course). This means that a total of 1955 students, or 56 percent of the student body, chose to enroll in foreign language courses. Foreign language classes were offered at four levels with an additional advanced placement course as an option. The exception to this pattern was Italian, which was taught at three levels. In 1982, twenty-four students took the A.P. French exam, twenty-one took the A.P. Spanish exam and eight took the A.P. German exam.

The educational computing program in Hilldale also included the use of both a mainframe computer and microcomputers. The school had over 250 TRS-80 Model III microcomputers located in six general usage sites which were spread out over the two campuses. In addition to the mainframe computer terminals and TRS-80 Model III's, IBM Personal Computers were available for use in an Advanced Placement PASCAL programming course.

Hilldale High had a course in 'computer literacy' that was required for all incoming freshmen. Some students were allowed to substitute other more advanced computer courses if they had computer literacy courses in elementary or junior high school. The only formal policy effecting instructional computing in Hilldale High School was the requirement for student 'computer literacy'. Computer literacy was defined by the school's administrators in terms of the following objectives:

1　Students will become familiar with computers, their history, and essential vocabulary pertaining to them.
2　Students will see how computers are used, what they can do, and what they cannot do.
3　Students will learn about the microcomputers' impact on society, vocational implications, and controversial issues (e.g,. privacy, electronic crime).
4　Students will interact with computers by practising keyboard skills, observing sample programs, observing how different statements alter a program, and writing simple programs themselves.

5   Students will apply computers in subject-related areas and in specific courses in their daily schedule.

One of the broad assumptions guiding the implementation of the instructional computing program in Hilldale High was stated as follows:

An infused computer literacy program taught across all departments by all staff reaches more students and diminishes negative impact upon curriculum. (Blomeyer, 1985)

The instructional computing program had four initial components:

1   definition of computer literacy;
2   teacher training;
3   instructional courseware development;
4   implementation of computer literacy units for the students.

The operational definition of computer literacy detailed above was applied first to developing a model for staff in-service training. Then, the teachers who received the training used the model to implement the student computer literacy units.

During the first year of Hilldale High's instructional computing program (1980–81), goals and objectives were formulated, an initial number of TRS-80 Model III microcomputers were purchased and the first teacher training seminars were initiated. The first computers purchased were not used by the students, but rather for teacher training. Initially one outside consultant trained eight teachers. These eight teachers then trained thirty-five more teachers, who eventually trained the remaining staff of 240 teachers. All three of the foreign language teachers who collaborated with this study had been participants in the training program between 1980–1982.

In all, twenty hours of training occurred over a period of fifteen months. After completion of the initial training experiences, free access to the microcomputers and peer assistance continued to be available to those teachers who wished to further develop their skills. Toward the end of the formal training experience, teachers were 'encouraged' to identify curriculum content that was suitable for delivery in the computer-based medium.

The administration also encouraged the staff to submit formal proposals for courseware development. These were reviewed and proposals which were accepted were implemented in 'summer computer curriculum development' workshops held during the summers of 1981 and 1982. During these workshops, teams were selected which included subject matter experts (teachers whose proposals had been accepted), designers (teachers knowledgeable in both implementation and curriculum), and professional programming consultants (college students with programming background). All participating teachers were paid at a rate equal to their regular salary rate and the outside programmers were paid approximately $10.00 per hour.

The outcomes of the summer materials development workshops at Hilldale High were limited amounts of instructional software produced by teachers from twelve departments. The level of training that was attained by the 65 participating teachers was one of the most significant results of the program. Additionally, courseware of variable quality became available for use in a variety of subject matter areas. After the software was screened and evaluated, much of what was produced during the first workshops was either revised or never actually used for student instruction. Those materials that were considered suitable for classroom use were utilized by classroom teachers as an optional mode of instructional delivery as soon as the micro-computer sites were installed during the 1981–1982 school year.

The two Spanish teachers who collaborated in the present study had participated in a materials development workshop as 'subject matter experts' during the summer of 1982. During that workshop they had produced the prototypes for the computerized language lesson materials that they used with their students during my period of observation in their classes. Some of the lessons were written by using authoring systems and 'driver programs'. These included basic vocabulary recognition and grammar review exercises. Additionally there were some 'tutorial' lessons (oriented toward teaching recognition and production of basic grammatical distinctions in Spanish) that were written from the ground up using Basic. Only a limited amount of materials were developed and use of the computerized lessons during class time was generally sporadic. Both Spanish teachers were still occasionally revising features of these lessons and updating the subject contents of the 'driver programs'.

A collaborating German teacher in Hilldale High School had not been a participant in the materials development workshops, but instead worked with other teachers who were more experienced in the use of authoring systems and 'drill drivers' for the presentation of various types of subject matter. The German teacher consulted with other staff members to determine what kinds of lesson formats were available (translation drills, grammar drills, quizzes, etc.), wrote out the lexical contents of the display and the correct response for each question, and finally had these contents inserted into the 'driver' programs by a school staff-member.

In the case of the German teacher, the lessons were actually implemented with the help of the other two more experienced materials developers and a 'computer aide', a non-academic employee who assisted with the instructional computing program. These lessons tended to be less oriented toward a 'tutorial' approach and more oriented toward 'drill and practice' or computerized quizzing formats than those written from scratch in Basic by the other two cooperating language teachers. However, the flexibility of these lessons for adapting them to different lexical and grammatical materials meant that it was possible to develop review exercises for virtually every unit in the German teacher's instructional plan. These materials were used by the German teacher's students on a regular basis during the school year.

Recent hardware and software developments influenced the Hilldale instructional computing program. These included the evaluation of various microcomputer systems as possible replacements for the 250 TRS-80's and the ongoing evaluation of new instructional applications. During the period of the study, all six of the microcomputer sites were 'networked' so that software programs could be loaded into all of the student workstations from either a workstation under teacher control or from a 'file server' under student control. At the time of the study a significant factor influencing decisions on hardware being considered as possible replacements for the TRS-80 workstations was the school administration's requirement that networking be an available option with all hardware systems under consideration.

Another factor affecting microcomputer use was that the curriculum in each department was under review for determining what portion of the required subject matter could be delivered effectively in the computer-based medium. This meant what in addition to their regular instructional and extracurricular duties, the foreign language teachers who collaborated with this study were consulted on the evaluation of other hardware systems and involved in the location and evaluation of commercial software.

Two Contrasting Policy Models for Computer Aided Learning

As can be seen in the accounts above, while the two schools and their respect-ive communities have striking similarities, the treatment of CAL as a component of the curriculum in the two schools was very different. In sum-mary, the two schools present contrasting examples illustrating the impact of distinct policy scenarios on instructional computing programs. At Woodville West High School we can describe the situation as *the default definition of instructional computing as math, science or computer technology.* In this case policy was a consequence of actions taken by the first teachers who became users of the microcomputer laboratory. Use patterns were established on a 'first come, first served' basis and teachers from curricular areas that were not early adopters apparently had difficulties obtaining access to the micro-computers.

At Hilldale High School the policy situation can be described as *in-stitutionalization of instructional computing in comprehensive curriculum.* In contrast to Woodville West, a district planning initiative resulted in the for-mulation of a curriculum policy that mandated use of microcomputers by all students enrolled in the school. Administrative practices affecting personnel and resource allocation also supported an instructional climate where the use of microcomputers as an ancillary component of instruction was common in all areas of curriculum.

The policy frameworks in both schools had distinct implications for instructional practice as it was observed in the classes of the four cooperating teachers. The general business of foreign language teaching and the traditional methods of foreign language specialists were common to both schools, but interactions involving the students, teachers, and CAL materials were different. By sampling process data from observations of conventional foreign language classes and classes where CAL was used as part of the instructional delivery system, the next section will illustrate some of the unique instructional events that occur when CAL becomes a component of foreign language teaching.

Process Data

The foreign language teachers who cooperated with the field study used computer-based foreign language instruction as a supplementary instructional strategy in beginning and advanced classes in French, German, and Spanish. In all cases the interactive computer-assisted lessons used were designed and implemented or modified by the cooperating teachers or other instructional personnel in the respective schools. Although both schools had large foreign language departments, only the four teachers whose classes were observed during the study made use of available CAL materials.

The cooperating teachers were generally knowledgeable about instructional use of microcomputers and three of the four were designing and programming their own materials. As discussed in the previous section, both schools offered training opportunities where their teachers could contribute to the design and implementation of CAL. Because of the special problems of designing computer-based instruction as distinct from other computer applications (management, record-keeping, answer judging, etc.) and the additional technical requirement of foreign language characters (accents, tildes, etc.), much of what the teachers learned in their initial training experiences had to be adapted or discarded as new techniques were devised by trial and error.

One of the observations made in a Spanish class at Hilldale High School provides an illustration of the approach used by the teachers to field test and revise their locally developed computer-based lessons. During this particular observation, the teacher used her lunch period loading the required BASIC program into each of about eighteen student workstations from a disk before class. The class was in session for a twenty minute period prior to the break for lunch. As the last student returned from lunch, the teacher announced the protocols for using the prototype interactive lesson materials.

1. Don't push the <BREAK> key; 2. Don't push the <CLEAR> key; 3. Don't push the orange <RESET> button; and don't turn the computer off!

She continued:

You will see 'PRESS RETURN TO CONTINUE' written onscreen. After doing so you will have to type 'RUN' and go through the program. Please understand that this is a lesson I am developing and it is not finished yet. I would appreciate your comments and questions. Please hold up your hand if you have any question about the lesson and I will try and come around and help you. I will be circulating through the class and I will try and check with each of you sometime during the period.

A female student was observed using the lesson. The screens began by presenting clear directions about using the lesson. The first part is an on-line review of preterite verb forms. The first few pages give examples for regular verbs using -ar, -er, and -ir endings. Then the students began using an interactive drill where they were to key in the preterite form of a given infinitive verb.

The students finished the first part of the new program quickly and the teacher came around to question a female student about the prototype lesson. She asked:

Were the directions clear? Was anything about the instructions or the design of the program confusing? Were the screen displays too crowded? Or were they designed in a way that made the answer obvious?

After the student responded to all of the questions about the lesson, the teacher noticed that there was only about ten minutes left in the period. She asked the students to turn off their computers and began a discussion with the class. She reviewed the materials covered in the drill and asked the class:

What was the program trying to teach about preterite and imperfect? What were the words that enabled you to distinguish between the two types of past in the last group of sentences requiring identification of verb tense? I don't intend to always give you translations of the phrases. I want you to figure out the answers in context from the language given in the exercise.

(Adapted from Blomeyer, 1985, pp. 238–241)

In the example given above, it is evident that field testing a prototype lesson was a very labor intensive undertaking for the teacher. Once revised and completed, the grammar drill would probably be a significant resource for the Spanish classes in the school. However, the time required of the teacher for design, prototype development, field testing and revision was significant.[1]

An element that was common to the instructional style of the teachers observed was use of a wide variety of learning activities and instructional strategies in their classroom teaching. Typical activities included both oral and written practice on vocabulary and grammar as well as presentation of cultural aspects of the lessons. The teachers used microcomputer-based lessons as one strategy within eclectic but traditional foreign language syllabus design that included both oral and written learning experiences.

In the classes observed, integration of computer-based instruction into the foreign language syllabus design was accomplished by incorporating subject matter from traditional classroom materials that were already in use as the content items for the computer-based lessons. The courseware used by students during this study was all designed or modified by the classroom teachers. As a result, the contents of the computerized lessons were closely tailored to the particular content of the individual classes.

The individual lessons generally used the format common to drill and practice exercises covering the same vocabulary and grammar as the regular lesson materials in a different instructional medium. In addition, computer-assisted testing was used in an Advanced Placement French class as preparation for the grammar test that the students would be encountering on the A.P. examination. The following example illustrates the way that these A.P. prep lessons were used by the French teacher at Woodville West:

A boy and two girls are seated at microcomputer stations near the back of the room. Conversations between students in this situation tend to be in English. The three students are seated as follows:

Jon   Patricia   Louise

All three students were working on their grammar review. Louise had a small technical difficulty and had to request help from the 'site director' in locating a computer that will work properly. She moved over to the right one station and borrowed a lesson disk from Jon to reload the BASIC program into her Apple computer.

At 12:13 Jon and Patricia were going through the pre-test but did not appear to be taking notes on their own performance. They did not appear to be getting many correct. The questions are 'fill-in's' and their scores were not good. They went through eight questions without getting any correct responses. Jon remarked:

'Whatever I think is right ... is wrong!'

Jon and Patricia finally finish the exercise and the program gives them their cumulative scores and a percentage. Jon got ten out of twenty questions right for 50 percent and Patricia got eight out of twenty correct for 40 percent. Both appeared discouraged. In order to restart with another exercise, they needed to have a lesson disk that contains the program to reload. Jon retrieved the lesson disk from Louise and both reloaded their microcomputers to continue with the computer-based A.P. diagnostic lessons.

About 12:17 the teacher switched the fifth year group to 'un petit exercise en classe' so that she was free to zero-in on individual students who were having problems with the on-line exercises. She repeated her instruction that they should be writing down the diagnostic information on the items they miss and using this information to study the review materials in the printed lesson documentation. She tried to encourage those students (like the two under observation) who were becoming discouraged by their initial failure on the pre-tests. She talked with a few individuals and at about 12:20 moved to the back of the room to work on English grammar with two French speakers.

At about 12:20, after the teacher's words of encouragement, Jon, Louise and Patricia went on to another exercise that had a multiple choice format giving a French target sentence with a preposition deleted. The students were given one chance to choose the correct preposition and indicate the answer by pressing the correct number on the keyboard. The program judged the answer as in the previous exercise, and offered information on the location of remedial grammar information in the documentation. A typical multiple choice item from the interactive lesson is illustrated here:

Regardez _____ la fenênre. Il pleut.
1) par (correct)
2) de
3) à
4) hors de.

All three students tended to get more of these multiple-choice items correct. At 12:29 Patricia finished twenty multiple choice questions and scores twelve out of twenty for 60 percent. That was a better score than her previous 40 percent. The students noticed that the lab period was over and began to switch off their microcomputers.

While the students were finishing up the bell rang. The French teacher began to pick up the microcomputer disks from the students as they left the microcomputer lab.

(Adapted from Blomeyer, 1985, pp. 152–156)

In the schools observed, support was available for software purchase as a discretionary item in the departmental budget. Allocation of funds within foreign language departments in the cooperating schools was determined by the department heads in consultation with the teaching staff. In Woodville West High School other budget items presently had a higher priority than the purchase of instructional software. At Hilldale High efforts were underway to locate and preview materials. Staff in both schools indicated that when commercial software materials became available that met their standards for usability, appropriate materials would be purchased as regular items within the department's annual budget.

After approximately sixty-five hours of classroom observation in both schools, preliminary analysis of field notes indicated that the use of CAL in foreign language classrooms appeared to be resulting in some structural and procedural changes in teaching practice. Gradual accumulation of documentary and observational information pointed to a number of potentially relevant issues that required further study. During the final days of classroom observation, an interview schedule was designed to address these emergent issues and interviews were scheduled with the cooperating teachers and administrative personnel.

The perspectives of the teachers and instructional supervisors were needed to provide their interpretations of events and their attitudes toward computer-aided learning and its role in foreign language instruction. In turn, their interviews further refined the issues and questions to a point where the students' interpretations and attitudes became necessary information. In particular, the students' descriptions of the teacher-developed software and their attitudes toward CAL as a component of foreign language instruction were a particularly revealing perspective on the observational data.

In the next section, the value data presents viewpoints of the students, teachers and supervisory personnel on seven key issues that emerged from the classroom observation as critical for understanding the role of computer aided learning in foreign language teaching. The text will be illustrated by some quotes from student interviews and paraphrased material taken from staff interviews. Direct quotes will not be used from interviews with teachers and administrators to avoid compromising the identity of the individual respondents.

Value Data

The seven issues used here to categorize the value data from the interviews conducted in both schools provides a summary of concerns and questions relevant to understanding the particular role of CAL in foreign language teaching and considering the more general role of CAL in support of discipline-based subject matter in secondary school curriculum. The seven issues are addressed in terms of the following questions:

1 What are the similarities and differences in implementation strategies?
2 What are the human costs of integrating CAL as a component in foreign language curriculum?
3 What is a possibly optimal level of operational computer literacy for foreign language teachers?
4 What policies might optimize the effective use of CAL as a component of foreign language instruction?
5 If policies are appropriate, how should they be formalized to maximize positive impact on language teaching?
6 What is the potential impact of CAL on the 'dominant core' of teaching practice as apparent in language teaching?
7 What are the implications of CAL for broad policy initiatives concerning the efficiency, equity and quality of foreign language education?

1 Similarities and differences in implementation strategies

Some of the similarities and differences between the strategies used in the two schools to adapt microcomputers as a part of language teaching have been discussed in preceding sections. As discussed in the section on baseline data, differences in implementation strategies were attributable to each school's policies effecting CAL. This is particularly evident regarding policies defining student and staff computer literacy and policies influencing use of microcomputer-based instruction in the foreign language classes.

A. Student access to microcomputer workstations

One major area of difference relates to either de facto or explicit policies governing access to microcomputer sites. For instance, the French teacher at Woodville West appeared to have a difficult time scheduling the use of the microcomputer lab because it was fully booked with computer math and programming classes. When asked whether their usage of microcomputers was generally regular or irregular in occurrence, students from French classes responded in the following way:

> She (the French teacher) had to work her classes in around the computer classes. Sometimes we would go to the lab and there would be a math class there. Then we would have to re-schedule and do something else that day.

In contrast the teachers at Hilldale High apparently had little trouble obtaining the use of microcomputer labs because there was a larger number of workstations available for use by all departments and because administrative practices favored integration of microcomputers throughout the curriculum. When students from one of the Spanish classes in Hilldale High were asked an identical question about regularity or irregularity of usage, they responded this way:

> Use has been pretty regular. Sometimes once a week, sometimes twice a week. It evened out over time. The variation is probably because of other classes using the lab. We went in when she could schedule the room.

B. Site implementation and hardware differences

Other differences in instructional practice involving microcomputers were consequences of decisions on the purchase and disposition of hardware resources. Different brands and configurations of microcomputers (Apple, Tandy, IBM, etc.) vary according to hardware features, capacity, and whether they are used as free-standing microcomputers or workstations in a local area network (LAN). Configuration and disposition of hardware appear to have a pronounced effect on both integration and management of computer aided learning.

At Woodville West Apple II microcomputers were configured with $5\frac{1}{4}$ inch floppy disk drives and programs were loaded from disk. This required the teacher to spend time duplicating, distributing, and recovering the students' lesson disks. When insufficient disks were available for the number of students present, it was necessary for the students to 'boot and run' the programs, remove the disks, and pass them to another waiting student. All of the students interviewed at Woodville West reported that there were never enough copies of the disks for all the students. They said that they had to 'pass them around' to load the programs into the microcomputers. Students also indicated that they generally had to share workstations with other French students in the computer lab.

In contrast, Hilldale High School configured their TRS Model 80 microcomputers without disk drives and linked them to a master workstation through a local area network. The teacher loaded the available program into the RAM of the master workstation and the students then loaded the program into their own workstations through the network. Disk duplication and distribution was unnecessary and lab management appeared to be generally easier in the networked environment. All of the students interviewed at Hilldale High indicated that there were nearly always terminals and programs sufficient for each student to work independently. One student said:

> Yeah, there were enough terminals. Nobody had to share. There were a couple out of adjustment, and someone had to come in and adjust them ... but there were enough.

C. Lesson design similarities

Some of the similarities in practice were due to the design of the computer-based materials themselves and their dependence on similar presentational paradigms. In response to an interview question asking them to describe the foreign language lessons they had done on microcomputers, a Woodville West French student from an intermediate class responded this way:

> She would present the lesson ... then we would read it. Then we would press the return key and read more. And then she would give us example problems that we could fill in. If we would put down the wrong answer ... it would say 'No, try again' and then it would show us the page in the lesson that it applied to. Then we would read it over again and then we would have another chance to do it.

Another Woodville student from Advanced Placement fifth year French gave a different account of the grammar exercises the teacher devised to help them prepare for the A.P. French exam:

> It was grammar. She had a big packet of all the most difficult stuff in the French language. (Written materials detailing the grammar rules with examples or grammar squibs.)

> First we studied real hard ... all the stuff in the pack ... then we'd
> have a test on the problems. (A computer-based test simulating the
> format and content of the A.P. test.)

After the on-line test was completed, scores were generated automatically and
the indicated areas of deficiency led the students back to study the materials
appropriate for a particular aspect of French grammar.

The descriptions of CAL materials given in response to the identical
question by language students at Hilldale High School were generally similar
regarding content, but tended to be more elaborate regarding details
describing the interactive lessons. A German student described the computer-
interactive lessons as follows:

> The lessons were mostly vocabulary or verb drills ... Conjugations
> where you type in the right verb, but mostly vocabulary drills. These
> were simple translation exercises where you translated a word from
> English to German or vice versa.

Overall, students from both schools reported seeing both grammar and vocabulary exercises in computer-based form. These were always drill and practice in classical CAI interactive format. One exception to the standard drill
and practice format was the computer-based tests administered as practice for
the A.P. French test at Woodville West.

D. Sources of lesson materials

Another point of obvious similarity between the implementation strategies in
Woodville West and Hilldale High School was that the teachers produced the
computer-based lessons themselves using subject matter taken from materials
already in use. Student interviews in both schools confirmed this apparent
correlation between the curriculum materials used during conventional
language classes and the CAL materials.

In Woodville West all the students interviewed said that the CAL
materials were consistent with the other materials used in the class. Five
out of six students indicated that they were aware the teacher had developed
the materials specifically for their classes. Eighty-two percent of the students
interviewed at Hilldale High indicated that the computer-based lessons
they used were consistent with other instructional materials and assignments
necessary in their language classes. One student put it this way:

> The computerized materials were basically a supplement to what we
> were doing in class. They fit into the overall class plan pretty well. It
> is just another way of presenting the same materials in a different
> form.

E. Similarities attributable to foreign language teachers

Other similarities were possibly due to complex factors like the instructional
practices common to conventional foreign language teaching and the training

of the individual teachers involved. The cooperating teachers were all asked how they came to be involved with using computer-based language instruction. Teachers at Woodville West and at Hilldale High said that they became involved because the microcomputers were available and they thought that it offered potential as an instructional resource.

Teachers at Hilldale High School indicated that their initial introduction to CAL had been in response to participation in required 'in-service' workshops. They also stated that they continued to voluntarily participate in developing and using computer-based lessons because they felt a strong personal and professional responsibility to take any opportunity available which might provide additional instructional options that could benefit their students.

It is important to note that at the time of the field study the American Council of Foreign Language Teachers (ACTFL) was actively involved in implementation of programs intended to increase the emphasis on oral proficiency in foreign language curriculum. Teachers in both schools were members of a state ACTFL affiliate organization and they discussed their commitment to improving the oral proficiency of their classes. They expressed their belief that the use of computer-based drill and practice over grammar and vocabulary allowed students to progress over materials faster than conventional classroom methods. This was important to them because they felt it allowed them to re-allocate class time for additional practice on oral proficiency.

F. Similarities attributable to teacher computer literacy

Another important similarity of all of the cooperating teachers was that they all had sufficient functional competency using microcomputers that they could confidently use the technology for instructional purposes. Individual levels of expertise varied from the French teacher at Woodville West who had experience programming commercially published drill and practice materials to the German teacher at Hilldale High who professed to have no interest in programming computers.

It seemed that generally the teachers were more able to make creative use of the technological resources to generate new applications as their level of literacy increased. In this respect the computer literacy of the teachers seems to be a critical component of instructional computer use by foreign language classes in both schools. This was true for four of the five teachers. However, the German teacher at Hilldale said she was interested in knowing only enough about operating the microcomputers to preview the lesson materials prepared for her by others. She indicated that this was necessary to check the materials for spelling and grammar accuracy.[2]

2 Optimal levels of functional computer literacy for foreign language teachers

The integration strategies that the teachers in both schools were using to make instructional computing a functional part of their foreign language teaching programs required the ability to make determinations of the 'fit' between computer-based resources and the existing instructional materials. Making these judgments required that the teachers be familiar with the available alternatives and criteria for software evaluation and also have adequate knowledge about the pedagogy of computer-based language teaching. The teachers had become materials developers themselves and actively participated in the design and implementation of the computer-based language lessons used by their classes.

The teacher in Woodville High designed her French lessons 'from the ground up' using the BASIC language. Her technical proficiency as a programmer was increasing through continued study and experience gained by writing and 'field testing' her lessons on the students in her classes. In interviews the teacher expressed her belief that she could profit from additional advanced course work in the design and implementation of computer-based materials.

Two of the language teachers at Hilldale could write programs in BASIC, but many of the materials used in their classes were produced from flexible utilities or lesson templates developed by other teachers in the school. Their technical literacy included the ability to use flexible resources like authoring programs and open-ended drill templates to develop applications that were appropriate for the specific grammar and vocabulary of their current lesson materials.

> All teachers participating in the study said that they believed that the 'in-service' training they had received was adequate to enable their own use of CAL. They indicated that 'more of the same' was needed for other foreign language teachers in their departments when they become more interested in similar instructional applications of computer-based lessons. Teachers in both schools also expressed similar opinions that the majority of foreign language teachers in their schools were not ready to begin using CAL because of the limited availability of appropriate instructional software.

3 The human costs of integrating instructional computing into the foreign language curriculum

Data presented in previous sections indicates that integration of instructional computing into the foreign languages curriculum was accomplished by using locally developed computer-based materials. In both cooperating schools the teachers themselves were the source of the subject matter content for these materials. In some instances they actually coded the interactive lessons themselves using authoring tools or program templates. The lesson materials used in the two schools had a high degree of compatibility and even overlap with the materials used in the regular classroom settings. However, the cost of this close fit between instructional computing and classroom teaching was high. The teachers who contributed to developing the materials paid a high price in terms of their time and energy.

In interviews, the teacher at Woodville High School revealed that she had voluntarily taken a reduction to half-time status in order to have sufficient time to study programming techniques, to revise her existing lessons and to develop new interactive lesson materials. In her case the development costs for the computer-based language lessons were absorbed by the teacher. The teacher seemed willing to accept the reduced salary in part because the ownership of the materials remained with the author and was not claimed by the school district. Her lessons had been published by a company specializing in foreign language instructional materials, and she was already receiving royalty payments during the period of this study.

At Hilldale High School the school district had made a sizable investment in an ambitious in-service training program. Initially, in-service training was provided to all teachers in the school. These first experiences were followed by voluntary summer workshops in which the participating teachers worked with student programmers to develop and implement materials to be used in the following school year. The participating teachers were paid a stipend to subsidize their attendance. After the initial workshops they used summers, weekends, and evenings to write and revise instructional programs.

The teachers who continued to work on materials development and teach a full schedule of classes simultaneously said during interviews that the time necessary to maintain existing lessons and work on new projects cut deeply into their personal time. They reported giving this time willingly because of their professional pride, but it was evident that this commitment was taking its toll. The description of the Spanish class period already given in the section on Process Data is a good example of the extra work involved in teacher-based software development. All the cooperating teachers remarked in interviews and conversations that they did not consider it to be reasonable for administrators to assume that teacher-produced materials would be a primary source of instructional software.

Perhaps significantly, the teachers at Hilldale High who actually worked on the development of computer-based language lessons were not regular users of the microcomputer labs. The one teacher who was a regular user (once every two weeks) of the computer labs had provided the language materials for the lessons, but had not participated directly in the mechanics of developing the lessons nor in writing the programs for student use. According to the students of the 'regular' microcomputer lab user:

> We used the lab about once every two weeks. Now (about three months after completion of the fieldwork) it's getting to be every

three weeks. It depends on when the teacher can get the materials prepared.

At Hilldale some of this demand for time and specialized skills was filled by providing 'computer aides' and programming consultants to assist with the development of new materials in high priority areas. However, the maintenance and revision of existing materials was still the job of the individual teachers. The 'aide' and 'programmer' positions seemed to be filled by persons without professional education background. Their salaries were not competitive with industry and the positions appeared to have a high turnover rate. Additionally, these staff members lacked skills in instructional design which could make possible the production of more sophisticated and useful courseware.

Although successful integration of computer-based materials into a syllabus was probably the result of developing and using teacher produced interactive lesson materials, their design and implementation of CAL materials is technically demanding and time-consuming. Based on this, it seems logical to assume that using commercially produced computer-based language teaching materials would be easier than undertaking local software development. However, for the teachers who were observed during this study, this did not appear to be true. As new foreign language courseware continued to be released by publishers, the foreign language teachers found the task of locating, pre-screening and selecting suitable computer-based instructional materials to be both time-consuming and difficult.

When computerized materials were made available for preview, thorough review of content and technical implementation required a large amount of time and good understanding of the pedagogy involved in the design of computer-based language lessons. At Hilldale High School the cooperating teachers were in demand to review software that was being considered for purchase by the foreign language department. The teachers found errors in the grammar and spelling of the courseware they previewed and found much of it to be of questionable relevance.

In some of the programs that had already been purchased, the teachers felt they had to edit the commercial programs to remove the errors. This was also time-consuming and required a high degree of technical skill. In addition, copyrighted commercial lessons were usually protected from modification by law and by elaborate disk protection schemes. All these factors made editing or modification of commercially produced lessons problematic.

In summary, integration of CAL in foreign language teaching appeared to be a labor intensive activity whether the interactive materials were locally developed or purchased from vendors. In either case, the classroom teachers spent a substantial amount of time on tasks required to prepare computer-based materials. Because there was no accompanying reduction in instructional load, activities related to computer-aided learning increased the foreign language teachers' workloads. Time that the cooperating teachers

were investing in activities related to instructional computing was a voluntary addition to their normal teaching load. It was questionable whether
they could continue to carry full instructional loads and maintain their
microcomputer-related activities indefinitely.

4   State, district and individual school practices affecting the classroom use of
computer-based foreign language instruction
There was little evidence found during this study that any educational policy
originating with the state office of education was having an influence on
the instructional computing programs in the cooperating schools. In fact,
the absence of any guiding state or district policy provided both schools
studied with an opportunity to develop their own unique responses to community mandates for increased microcomputer use in the schools. As discussed, school district initiatives at Woodville West High School placed
microcomputers in the math department of the school with the intention that
they be used for general instructional purposes. However, observations in the
school showed that the microcomputer site was used primarily for teaching
programming and that teachers outside the math department actually had limited access to the microcomputers.

At Hilldale High School, district and school policy were more in agreement. District policy established 'student computer literacy' as a requirement
for all students and local principals and curriculum directors encouraged all
departments in the school to make use of the available microcomputer
resources. According to administrators and teachers who were interviewed at
Hilldale High School, the formal policy and local implementation was a
comprehensive response to local community pressure on the school district to
make instructional computing a component of curriculum (Blomeyer, 1985).

5   Instructional and administrative practices with long-range effects on
continued commitment to use of instructional computing
Hilldale High School had a required course for all incoming freshmen which
provided basic information on the use of microcomputers for instructional
purposes. The course was intended to give them some basic concepts of programming and advice on the vocational choices and special training necessary
to pursue careers in computer technology. Woodville West had no requirement for computer literacy and exposure to computer-use skills was a function
of elective choices or experiences outside of school for the students in that
school.

Interviews with students in both schools showed differences between their
respective abilities to discuss and describe their experiences with computer-
aided language learning. Quotes given below come from responses to identical
interview questions asking the students to describe fill-in format items from
the lessons they had used and tell whether the computer-based lessons used in
the language classes were in learning the assigned materials.

Generally, the students in Woodville West, who had little previous experience using microcomputers before French class, tended to give relatively few detailed remarks about the strengths and weaknesses of microcomputers as a tool for language study. Although they were not uncritical, most tended to be positive in their attitudes toward computer use and felt that instructional computing would somehow help them in their foreign language studies.

What you had to do was fill in a blank or choose a, b, c, or d ... whatever was the right answer for a multiple choice grammar quiz. The other was a fill-in-the-blank where you had to fill in the right word or words.

Well, the computer is a little more fun to play with ... It's something different from just sitting in the classroom. You're doing things yourself. You're punching things into the computer. Computers themselves are exciting ... At least I think so, 'cause I'm in computer class now.

In contrast, the students at Hilldale articulated a more detailed view of the strengths and limitations of computer-based foreign language instruction. Overall, the students at Hilldale appeared to have a stronger sense that computerized lessons had limits to their instructional effectiveness. They were also generally more skeptical in their attitudes toward the benefits of microcomputer use:

The lessons were mostly vocabulary or verb drills. Conjugations where you type in the right verb, but mostly vocabulary drills. These were simple translation exercises where you translated a word from English to German or vice versa.

It was some help, but it wasn't unique. It could have been done a lot of other ways in class. I don't think that there was any specific benefit just because we were using a computer. I think some people like using computers because they are new ... It is new and innovative, but I'm not really convinced how useful it really is right now.

Observations suggested that at Woodville West the students using computers in the foreign language classes were often less efficient and less comfortable using microcomputers as a medium for foreign language instruction. The foreign language students required a great deal of in-class instruction on the basics of using the microcomputers as an instructional medium. Conversations of the students at Woodville with the teacher sometimes demonstrated either unrealistic expectations of the microcomputer's contribution to learning or (occasionally) an outright aversion to using the computer.

In contrast, at Hilldale High where students all had a basic computer literacy course it was seldom necessary to use class time for instructing the students on the use of the microcomputer. The students were all able to use the computer-based language learning programs with relative ease. When present in the computer labs with their classes, teachers supervised the use of the materials and answered questions about lesson content. The teachers spent more time monitoring the work of all the students and evaluating student progress than the teacher at Woodville West.

In summary, student computer literacy is apparently a major factor effecting use of microcomputers in foreign language curriculum. Simply stated, students whose repertoire of learning strategies included an introduction to the use of interactive CAL and other instructional applications were apparently able to use computer-based drill and practice lessons as a supplement to other instructional strategies. Students lacking this introduction to computer literacy appear less able to use CAL efficiently.[3]

6   The impact of instructional computing on the 'Dominant Core' of teaching practices.

Although computer-based instruction was being used as part of the foreign language curriculum by the teachers observed in both schools, the overall impact of this microcomputer use on teaching practices appeared to be minimal. Some activities that might have been conducted by the teacher during regular class time were vocabulary reviews, verb conjugation, and adjective or pronoun agreement, which seemed to be the subject matter that was most suitable for the computerized drills used by the students. These drills were most often used as a means of studying for tests. Only one teacher out of the four made the use of the computer-based lesson a regular part of her lesson plans and in that case the ratio of time was about one period in the computer lab to nine days of regular classroom study (Blomeyer, 1985). The instructional computer use and the regular foreign language class activities that were observed in the two schools seem to support the notion that the use of microcomputers in the classroom may not have any strong effects on dominant classroom practices. It seems more likely that the 'core practices' will dominate the conception of computer-based instruction more than they themselves will be changed.

The teachers in both of the participating high schools had integrated the use of computer-based lessons as a limited portion of the curriculum design in their respective classes. The majority of their class time was still spent on more traditional classroom language learning activities. The traditional classes that were observed in both schools followed closely the teaching practices that have persisted in American education since the later nineteenth century. These practices are characterized by whole group delivery, teacher dominated conversation, reliance on textbook materials, desks arranged in straight rows, and classroom interactions structured in a 'question and answer' framework (Cuban, 1983).

These same teachers had begun to evolve routines and procedures for conducting classes in the microcomputer laboratories. Their instructional and management strategies that were observed in the microcomputer labs were probably influenced by individual observation of colleagues using the microcomputer laboratories or adapted from past experiences using 'language laboratories' during the post-Sputnick era. However, it was unclear whether any of the teachers had specific preparation for using the microcomputer labs with student groups. At Woodville High School the teacher had taken in-service classes in programming with the mathematics department chairman. At Hilldale High the teachers had all participated in training experiences organized by the school district. It seems reasonable to assume that their own training in the use of microcomputers had an influence on instructional use of computers in their classes.

There has been vocal speculation among advocates of computer use in the schools about the 'transforming' and 'restructuring' potential of micro-computer use on public education. In the most optimistic scenario, micro-computers have been viewed as having the potential to 'revolutionize' the existing educational system. Far reaching speculation has suggested that increasing availability of microcomputers and powerful computer-based 'tools' for problem solving will provide instructional experiences far superior to those available now, and will shift the dominant conception of formal learning toward individualized learning based outside the school setting (Papert, 1980).[4]

Some shift in the 'dominant core' constellation of practices toward greater individualization was noted during the observations, thus to some extent bearing out the predictions just mentioned. This apparently shifted the teacher's role from direct instruction to a resource provider who monitors self-pacing, individualized instruction. Once the programs were loaded and the majority of the class was working on the lessons, the teachers were free to cir-culate through the class and assist individual students. However, within the framework of the language classes observed in these schools (which used com-puter-based materials oriented toward either identification or recall of specific factual material), there seems to be little evidence that signals the beginning of a 'revolutionary' change in the dominant conception of schooling (Blomeyer, 1985).

During these work periods on the computers, there was some margin for student conversations and for collaboration by students on the specifics of particular answers. However, this shift away from the constraints of a tra-ditional 'teacher centered' classroom environment was limited. If these student interactions exceeded a level that was acceptable to the teacher, management procedures were initiated and the dominance of the teacher was reaffirmed.

Much of the teachers' time in the microcomputer labs was spent in the logistics of getting the programs loaded into the student workstations. This was particularly true at Woodville West, where the programs were loaded into the microcomputers from diskettes. It was also the case that the French teacher in Woodville High had to spend more in-class time tutoring the students on the use of microcomputers in the classroom.

Direct instructional operations were necessary to some extent in the computer classes in both school districts. They required the teachers to give instructions to the whole class in group mode and to provide answers to individual questions as needed. Although these 'classroom management' operations took place in the computer laboratories, they were nonetheless very traditional in form.

Another significant characteristic of traditional classroom practice is the overall reliance of teachers on textbooks as a source for instructional materials. For some years, foreign language textbooks have been accompanied by Spirit duplicator masters, workbooks, audio tapes, slides, films, and a variety of other integrated instructional media. In an effort to integrate the use of computer-based instruction into their foreign language classes, the teachers in both schools had used vocabulary and grammar materials common to the other more traditional instructional materials already in use.

In this sense the teacher-produced interactive lessons were still dominated by the traditional textbook materials. The strong assertion, made by both teachers and curriculum directors interviewed during the study, that the majority of foreign language teachers will not use computer-based lessons until integrated materials are produced by the textbook publishers, reinforces this point about the centrality of the textbook for most foreign language teachers (Blomeyer, 1985).

Another aspect of traditional classroom organization is the recurrent pattern of desks arranged in straight rows. In the computer laboratories in both schools, the student workstations were fixed in rows probably because of hardware connections, space limitations, and hardware security. These arrangements were even less flexible than movable classroom seating. Although more flexible options allowing movement of workstations in and between classrooms and lab settings may exist, they were not observed in the two participating schools.

The last characteristic attributed by Cuban to traditional classrooms is the predominance of 'question and answer' frameworks in classroom interactions. As previously noted, the teachers observed spent a portion of their time in the computer labs giving direct instructions on loading lessons or explaining the particulars of using a specific interactive lesson. They also questioned individual students on their progress and answered student questions on the subject materials or instructions for using the programs. However, most of the students' time was spent using the interactive lessons.

If we consider the teachers' and students' accounts of the interactive lesson's contents and analyze the structure of the programs observed in use, it is obvious that the pattern of 'question and answer' interactions is dominant in the lesson materials. The obvious difference is that the questions and answers are in a written form on the microcomputer display instead of being part of the oral interactions that predominate in traditional classroom settings (Blomeyer, 1985).

7 Effects of policy on instructional computing with regard to equity, efficiency and instructional quality

Data gathered through both direct observation and interviews in the two cooperating schools provides limited information from which to draw conclusions about the effects of instructional computer use on the equity, efficiency, and relative quality of foreign language teaching. Broader conclusions about the effects on equity of the two schools' approaches to instructional computing within the total curriculum have been discussed above.

Observation and interview data suggest that a stated policy requiring universal 'student computer literacy' may have a positive influence on the equity of instructional computer use in terms of encouraging female students to learn to use computers. It also appears that the use of microcomputers as a curriculum-wide instructional resource provides greater equity within a school than restriction of computer use to one area in the curriculum.[5]

Much of the current inefficiency involved in using microcomputers in foreign language teaching is due to the apparent lack of professionally acceptable commercially produced materials. The high 'human costs' and low level of sophistication displayed by the locally developed foreign language courseware raises questions about the value and efficiency of using these materials and about the effectiveness of local software development in school districts. Using these teacher-produced materials has probably speeded the rate of adoption for instructional computer use in the foreign language teaching program and contributed to increased equity in the use of computers within the student population. Unfortunately, the trade-off may be a sacrifice of efficiency and quality.

Because the focus of this study was on relationships between policy and practice, little or no clear information is available about the influence of computer-based language teaching on instructional quality. To reach conclusions of this sort will require different research strategies and different fundamental research questions (Blomeyer, 1985).

Conclusion

Previous research on instructional technologies has often taken an optimistic view of computer-based instruction. This is typical of most studies of educational innovation. In general, researchers who are already advocates of a particular innovation conduct studies that confirm their 'pro-innovation' position. This classical 'technological perspective' on instructional innovation has been based on the primary assumption that innovation has an inherent positive value. Modernity has often been conceptually linked with educational improvement and, according to House (1979) 'To be modern was to be innovative' (House, p. 2). Until the instructional use of computers can be examined dispassionately and rationally by a greater number of researchers using a variety of approaches, little concrete information can be expected about the effects of microcomputer applications on student achievement and the quality of education.

Research funded by the National Institute of Education (NIE) has focused on broad aspects of computer use in elementary schools, i.e., access to microcomputers, changes in teacher roles, integration of CAI into curriculum, the quality and quantity of available software, teacher preparation for micro-computer use, and the effects and outcomes of microcomputer use. The research was conducted on schools in three pioneering districts, but the authors, Sheingold, Kane and Endreweit (1983), concluded that their findings lacked specific information on how microcomputers will affect educational practice. Instead, they stated:

> The results suggest that the effects of microcomputers on education, will depend to a large extent, on the social and educational contexts within which they are imbedded. (p. 431)

Experimental and quasi-experimental studies comparing CAL to other instructional methods often show 'no significant difference' between the per-formance of experimental and control groups (Solomon and Gardner, 1986). Meta-analysis of the available experimental studies indicates only a small 'effects size' from CAL interventions (Becker, 1988). These weak findings may result from use of inflexible or unreliable quantitative measures or because no agreement exists on whether the chosen measures reflect professional consen-sus on the goals and objectives of the program (House, 1980). Interpreting these quantitative findings may also be problematic for teachers and curricu-lum specialists because they offer little contextual information within which to judge the 'fit' of particular treatments for possible transfer to new curricular settings.

The findings from this case study suggest that the effects of micro-computers on foreign language instruction are indeed context dependent. Within that context, there may be particular domains of influence that war-rant special consideration for understanding the complex process by which microcomputers and other instructional technologies are integrated or re-jected as a component of discipline-based curriculum. A historical perspective on the relationship between curriculum and instructional computing is essen-tial to interpret the significance of CAL for classroom learning. In these terms, it may be particularly important to document the life histories of the instructional specialists involved in the development and use of instructional computing applications (Goodson, 1988). Other specific domains of influence warranting careful examination may include the following:

1 hardware and site implementation (including logistic and technical concerns);
2 availability or access to microcomputer workstations;
3 design characteristics of the software (with particular attention to the interactive characteristics of CAL);
4 curricular and disciplinary sources of lesson materials;
5 pedagogical characteristics attributable to the content domain or the particular training of teachers as content specialists; and

6   the effects of specialized technology training or 'computer literacy' on the functional ability and attitudes of students and teachers.

In this study of computer-aided language learning, the unavailability of sufficient acceptable foreign language software seemed to be the greatest hindrance to using computer-based foreign language instruction as a systematic component of foreign language teaching. Both the local production of computer-based foreign language materials and the review of commercial materials for their eventual acquisition were tried as alternatives and proved to be time-consuming, expensive and inefficient.

In both schools studied, the teachers and foreign language department chairpersons had very definite ideas about what acceptable foreign language CAL should be. Their concerns were grounded in professional expectations about necessary vocabulary, pedagogy and the technical accuracy of acceptable foreign language materials. Their analysis was that the commercially available materials were not suitable. Their position was that until suitable materials might become available, use of CAL in foreign language classes would be limited to use of the few existing acceptable options.

Teacher-based materials development efforts provided a limited number of computer-based lessons that fit well with the ecology of the existing foreign language teaching program. Interviews with both students and teachers revealed that these interactive drills were a useful and efficient supplement to traditional instruction. Even so, the teachers were outspoken about their belief that existing commercially produced materials were inadequate and that foreign language textbook publishers should take the initiative to produce computer-based materials as comprehensive supplements to series books.

Foreign language teachers in both schools expressed their belief that publishers should actively solicit the opinions and ideas of experienced classroom teachers having discipline-based experience using and developing CAL. Teachers at Hilldale High suggested that until nationally prominent publishing houses were willing to invest in the development of comprehensive computer-based materials for use with their books, the majority of public school foreign language teachers would not be able to make effective use of CAL.

Since the study was completed in 1984, a large variety of new computer-assisted language learning materials have become commercially available. One particular publishing house (D.C. Heath and Company) has published foreign language series books for French and Spanish that have computer-based vocabulary acquisition lessons as optional supplementary materials.[6] Foreign language curriculum specialists have also responded to the need for pedagogically appropriate CAL materials by screening the available commercially produced lessons and developing additional interactive computer-based lessons based on standard foreign language pedagogy and technically accurate linguistic materials.[7] Additionally, a number of easy-to-use authoring programs and specialized programming utilities are now available to aid foreign language and English-as-a-second-language teachers who want to create their own interactive lessons without unnecessarily complicated 'ground up' programming.[8]

No data exists presently that could give an indication of the impact that the more recent series supplements and authoring utilities are having on current foreign language teaching. Information from the case study reported here suggests some significant concerns about the feasibility of attempts to utilize CAL as a more systematic component of foreign language teaching. It is clear that unless professionally acceptable materials become available to foreign language teachers, regular use of microcomputer-based language lessons seems unlikely.

It is also questionable whether the majority of foreign language teachers will be able to make use of the more recently available CAL materials. Scarcity of hardware resources, monopolization of available hardware by curricular areas more traditionally viewed as being 'computer users' and insufficient experience or training on the technical and pedagogical fundamentals of foreign language CAL are all areas of concern.

Given the perspective on CAL offered here, it seems unlikely that major reforms or changes in the central characteristics of the American educational system will be brought about solely by the introduction of instructional computing. On the other hand, if the CAL can be introduced in a way that promotes a review of course content in the various areas of curriculum, perhaps it can provide educational practice with new resources and a renewal of professional interest and enthusiasm. If the foreign language teachers themselves become active participants in the development and implementation of computer-based lessons in ways that encourage review and revitalization of curriculum content, then the effect is likely to be a positive one for foreign language instruction.

Finally, the most serious concern suggested by this case study may be that the foreign language teachers who were the innovators working to integrate microcomputers as a curricular resource increased their workload without a decrease in their instructional responsibility. Pioneering classroom applications of new instructional technologies is difficult and time-consuming work. Unless the teachers who take significant roles in the integration of technology to discipline-based curriculum can be supported by availability of adequate planning and preparation time, it seems unlikely that instructional staff will become involved voluntarily. In last analysis, it is the teachers in the classrooms who will determine whether or not microcomputers and other instructional technologies make any significant contribution to educational improvement.

Naturalistic case studies can broaden our understanding of CAL to include the socio-cultural context of computer use in curriculum and provide a view of its effects on teaching and learning from the perspectives of the classroom teacher and the students. Additional naturalistic research on instructional computing could help foster more appropriate applications of microcomputers as an instructional medium throughout the curriculum and help monitor the effects of instructional technology on teaching practice and the organization of schooling. These concerns should be important questions for studying curricular integration of microcomputers in other areas of discipline-based curriculum besides language learning. This can be accomplished by adopting the following agenda for future research activities:

1 The ethnographic documentation and substantive evaluation of instructional computing in discipline-based applications;
2 The application of new knowledge about the role of CAI in educational settings to the development and implementation of prototype systems for instructional delivery; and
3 Measurement of the outcomes of the instructional use of computers in terms of the students' achievement, attitudes toward school computer use in general, and specific attitudes toward computer use in the full range of the curriculum.

The approach to research on computer-assisted instruction proposed here is potentially relevant to all of the subject areas in the comprehensive curriculum. In the next few years research findings on new curricular applications will hopefully become available to broaden our knowledge base on the effects of using CAL applications in a variety of disciplines. Interest in the areas of curriculum where instructional computer use is more frequent (i.e., math, computer science, natural sciences, and business applications) should not exclude computer use in the humanities. It is critical to work toward establishing a viable model for educational computing that includes the delivery of instruction in all subject areas.

The results from this and other naturalistic studies of instructional computer use raise questions about the overall efficiency and effectiveness of computer-based instruction as a classroom tool. More research on the integration of instructional computing into the curriculum is necessary before any broad policy recommendations can be made. One direction for this research is the continued study of how teachers and students use and apply instructional technology in educational environments. Another necessary direction is research on the impacts of instructional computer use on educational quality, equity and efficiency.

It is our hope that this case study and others like it will contribute to the future development of exemplary instructional computer applications in foreign language education and other related areas of the curriculum. Without continuing systematic efforts to study educational policy and instructional practices affecting the integration of computer-aided learning, most of the resources expended on purchasing microcomputers for the schools, and on lesson design and implementation of CAL materials, may ultimately be limited to demonstrations of technological capacity and will lack true instructional value.

Notes

1   During the observations conducted at Hilldale High School, this class was the only occasion when the particular Spanish teacher was observed to use the microcomputer laboratory. When questioned about her infrequent use of the microcomputer labs, the teacher explained that the amount of time necessary to assure technical accuracy and a pedagogically sound lesson design made regular use of the microcomputer labs very difficult. The teacher said that she was not able to find commercially published materials that were suitable, and insufficient time was available to produce a substantial amount of locally developed courseware.

2   It is interesting to note that the German teacher had the highest ratio of classes observed using microcomputers to total classes observed (see Table 1). This could suggest that the one teacher studied who was not spending time developing CAL materials was able to actually use computer-based materials with greater regularity. An implication of this anecdote could be that developing CAL materials makes use of computer-based materials with ongoing classes more difficult.

3   A related observation may be that students having a 'computer literacy' class were able to discuss the use of computers with better fluency and more appropriate use of technical terminology. Students who had computer literacy classes also seemed to be more critical in their perceptions of CAL as an instructional tool. This suggests a possible correlation between the ability to use microcomputers effectively and conversational fluency regarding their use and significance.

4   It is interesting to note that the protocols and procedures used in the computer laboratories by the language teachers in this study may show more similarity to the traditional core of teaching practice than to any radical change. Some computer-instruction advocates might maintain that the software these teachers were using was unsophisticated and did not fully exploit the creative potential of the interactive medium. However, in interviews the teachers said that the locally developed computer-aided language learning materials fit within the existing foreign language curriculum. Though use of CAL was limited, it was consistent with the goals and objectives of local curriculum.

5   This approach to increasing the equity of instructional computer use appears possible only for school districts having the financial resources to invest large amounts of capital resources in microcomputers and instructional software. The use of instructional computing throughout the curriculum is dependent on having sufficient financial resources to afford a substantial investment in microcomputer hardware. Additionally, a school taking this approach must either purchase commercial software or support local software development. In cases of smaller school districts with more limited resources, transferral of this approach would probably require external funding specifically earmarked for the purchase of microcomputer and software. Without some form of state-mandated assistance, it is doubtful that equity can be achieved in less wealthy school districts.

6   D.C. Heath and Company publishes Spanish for Mastery Software and French for Mastery Software for their related series books.

7   Lingo Fun Inc. of Westerville, Ohio and Gessler Publishing Company of New York are good sources of computer-based foreign language materials.

8   Athelstan Publications of La Jolla, CA has just published a new book on ESL/FL courseware authoring by Sandra Hampson (1988).

References

BECKER, H.J. (1988) 'The impact of computer use on children's learning: What the research has shown and what it has not', Center for Research on Elementary and Middle Schools, Johns Hopkins University.

BECKER, H.J. (1986) 'Instructional uses of school computers: Reports from the 1985 national survey', Center for the Social Organization of Schools, Johns Hopkins University, Issues 1–3.

BLOMEYER, R.L. (1985) *The use of computer-based instruction in foreign language teaching: An ethnographically-oriented study* (Doctoral Dissertation, University of Illinois).

BLOMEYER, R.L. (1989) 'A naturalistic perspective on computer aided learning: guidance for policy and practice in higher education', *Journal of Educational Policy*, 4, 3, pp. 259–74.

CUBAN, L. (1983) 'How did teachers teach, 1890–1980' *Theory Into Practice, 12*, 3, pp. 159–65.

GOODSON, I.F. (1988) 'Teachers' life histories and studies of curriculum and schooling', in GOODSON, I.F. *The making of curriculum: Collected essays*, Philadelphia PA: Falmer Press, pp. 71–92.

GUBA, E.G. (1978) *Toward a methodology of naturalistic inquiry in educational evaluation*, (CSE Monograph Series in Evaluation No. 8), Center for the Study of Evaluation at UCLA.

HOUSE, E. (1979) 'Technology versus craft: A ten year perspective on innovation', *Journal of Curriculum Studies, 11*, 1, pp. 1–15.

HOUSE, E. (1980) *Evaluating with validity*, Beverly Hills CA: Sage Publications.

KULIK J.A. and KULIK, C.C. (1986) 'Effectiveness of computer-based education in colleges', *Association of Educational Data Systems Journal, 19*, 2–3, pp. 81–108.

KULIK, J.A., KULIK, C.C. and COHEN, P.A. (1980) 'Effectiveness of computer-based college teaching: A meta-analysis of the findings.' *Review of Educational Research, 50*, pp. 525–44.

LECOMPTE, M.D. and GOETZ, J. (1984) in FETTERMAN, D.M. (Ed.), *Ethnography in educational evaluation*, Beverley Hills CA: Sage Publications, pp. 37–59.

PAPERT, S. (1980) *Mindstorms: children, computers, and powerful ideas,* New York: Basic Books.

ROGERS, E.M. (1983) *The diffusion of innovation* (3rd ed.), New York: The Free Press.

ROGERS, E.M. and SHOEMAKER, F. (1971) *Communication of innovations* (2nd ed.), New York: The Free Press.

SAMPSON, G.E., NIEMIEC, R., WEINSTEIN, T. and WALBERG, H.J. (1986) 'Effects of computer-based instruction on secondary school achievement: A quantitative synthesis', *Association for Educational Data Systems Journal, 19*, 4, pp. 312–26.

SHEINGOLD, K., KANE, J. and ENDREWEIT, M. (1983) 'Microcomputer use in the schools: Developing a research agenda', *Harvard Educational Review, 54*, 4, November pp. 412–32.

SMITH, L. and POHLAND, P. (1974) 'Educational technology and the rural highlands', in STAKE R. (Ed.) *Four evaluation example: Anthropological, economic, narrative, and portrayal* (AERA Monograph Series on Curriculum Evaluation No. 7, pp. 5–54), and in this volume.

SMITH L. and POHLAND, P. (1976) 'Grounded theory in educational ethnography: A methodological analysis and critique,' in ROBERTS J.I. and AKINSANYA, S.K. (Eds) *Educational patterns and cultural configurations*, New York: David McKay Co., Inc, pp. 264–79.

SOLOMON and GARDNER (1986) 'The computer as educator: Lessons from television research', *Educational Researcher*, 15, 1, pp. 13–19.

Chapter 4

Curriculum for Cultural Politics: Literacy Program Development in a Navajo School Setting

Daniel McLaughlin

Purpose and Overview of the Chapter

This chapter is about a model educational program for language minority students. It describes a project designed by secondary school educators to advance English language and literacy skills, create new functions for oral and written Navajo, and promote the empowerment of Navajo students. In promoting standard and vernacular forms of communication and in developing students' language, literacy, thinking, and word-processing abilities, the project works from critical theory to operationalize key aspects of Cummins's 'Framework for Minority Student Empowerment' (1986). Possibilities of empowerment in one Navajo school setting have emerged, as a way for students to develop confident cultural identities and to question and transform, rather than merely serve, the wider social order.

Cummins' theoretical framework basically encompasses a continuum between two divergent poles. The educational system can empower the child and hence the student is able to realize success in school, or the child is disabled and does not succeed. Empowerment is facilitated by including the child's cultural and linguistic characteristics in the school's curriculum and instruction, or the educational system becomes an impediment to the child by not including those characteristics.

Cummins identifies the educator's role as additive or subtractive relative to students' cultural/linguistic incorporation. The educational institution includes community members by either collaborating or excluding them from the education of their children. Teachers themselves can either teach in a reciprocal-interactive mode whereby students are active participants in their education, or they can be passive as the teacher merely lectures. Finally, the assessment of the child is oriented to either legitimizing the perception that the child is incapable of performing and being successful, or the educational system becomes an advocate of the child by using assessment as a source of diagnosis and direction to more completely meet the needs of the child.

Six sections of the chapter follow. In the first section, I tell the story of one man's disablement, both literal and figurative, on the Navajo Reservation. In so doing, I identify processes of illiteracy, joblessness, and social dysfunctions, against which any educational program in reservation schools must operate. In the second section, I bracket this same individual's experience in terms of critical theory and Cummins's framework, and analyze what we can understand from the experience to conceptualize issues affecting learning, teaching, curriculum, and literacy program development. In the third and fourth sections, I explain how a model language and literacy project in a Navajo secondary school puts into practice key aspects of critical theory and Cummins's ideas. In the fifth section, I examine how the project measures against its stated aims. In the last section, I relate the significance of the project to educators concerned with the empowerment of Indian and other minority students.

On the Need for Empowerment

Empowerment looms as a crucial issue in reservation communities. Its reverse takes the form of identity cliffs over which people are regularly and pervasively thrown. Evidence of the carnage is ubiquitous. The dropout rate for Indian students is three to ten times the national average. Students who do graduate tend to leave high school with academic skills on a seventh-grade level, barely half the national norm and well below the tenth grade benchmark deemed necessary for competing successfully in the job market. Beyond school, staggering rates of joblessness set minimal ceilings of opportunity. Alcoholism and other social problems follow, figuring prominently in the biographies of many young people on Indian reservations.

Jimmie Chee's situation is illustrative. He was raised in a reservation community close to the Navajo Nation's capital, where English is quickly becoming the unmarked language of oral communication. Although he was a standout basketball player, Jimmie was otherwise an unremarkable student. He graduated with sixth grade skills, similar to most of his peers across the reservation. After high school, Jimmie pursued an A.A. degree in physical education at a nearby community college. There, he met his wife. After one semester, he dropped out, as did his wife, and moved to his in-law's community, living without work in the home of his wife's parents, subsisting on welfare and waiting for seasonal, temporary employment as a forest fire fighter.

One summer day, a call went out for crews of forest fire fighters. Jimmy was one of the first to arrive at the staging point, the community trading post, and off he went to Flagstaff, Phoenix, and eventually Montana, where a huge blaze was in progress. Two weeks into fighting the fire, Jimmie slipped, fell on his axe, and nearly severed his thumb. He was airlifted to Great Falls, stitched back together, and flown back home. The fire raged on. Jimmie's crew did not return to the community until the blaze was under control two weeks later.

Three weeks after he got home, Jimmie received a letter from a claims examiner at the Office of Workers' Compensation in San Francisco. 'Your notice of Injury/Illness was received without sufficient medical evidence to adjudicate the claim,' the letter began. 'It is your responsibility to arrange for submission of medical evidence to substantiate your claim.' Jimmie had filed no claim papers and had little idea of what the letter said. 'Refer to items checked,' the letter continued, urging Jimmie to submit 'a medical report by each physician who has treated you for the condition ... a medical report on form CA-16, (and)... a completed CA3 form.' None of these forms was included. Moreover, the letter was written at a reading level well beyond Jimmie's comprehension abilities.

Ten days passed, and a second letter arrived. Addressing Jimmie, the same claims examiner wrote, 'It has been determined that the facts of the injury and employment support Jimmie Chee's contention that he was a federal employee who sustained a traumatic injury in the performance of duty. You should, therefore, continue his pay for the period of disability not to exceed forty-five days.' Taken literally, then, Jimmie — nonsensically — was to continue his own pay. Because of the confusion, as well as the difficult level at which the letters were written, Jimmie looked for people who could read and write well for help. He came to me.

At the time, I was doing fieldwork for an ethnography of English and Navajo literacy (McLaughlin, forthcoming). I had known Jimmie's wife, had taught several of his in-laws in high school for four years, and as part of my fieldwork had fought the same forest fire in Montana. I looked at the letters, called the fire dispatcher in Flagstaff, and found out that seasonal, temporary employees, such that forest fire fighters are, apparently had no claim to worker's compensation benefits. I was told to get hold of the claims examiner who had written Jimmie the letters.

From one of two pay phones in the community, Jimmie and I tried to get hold of this person for twelve days. We called person-to-person. The examiner was out. She was busy. She was on another line. She would call us back. We left messages. We waited by the phone. No calls came in. We called back, having rehearsed the conversation many times, and waited, and waited. Finally, the examiner called, one hour after an appointment we had set and reset with the examiner's two secretaries a half-dozen times. I fixed a telephone microphone to the ear piece, having arranged to help in exchange for any literacy-related data we would be able to collect, and handed Jimmie the receiver:

Jimmie: Hello.
Examiner: Good morning, may I speak with, ah, Jimmie Chee, please.

Jimmie: Yeah, this is he.

Examiner: OK, this is the office of Federal Employees Compensation. I'm returning a phone call you made to the office.

Jimmie: Yeah.

Examiner: OK, may I help you?

Jimmie: Ah, who is this, is this Helen [the examiner's first name]?

Examiner: Yes.

Jimmie: OK. Well, you sent me a letter on the, August the ninth and the August the nineteenth, and I don't really understand what you're saying.

Examiner: What, um, what do the letters say?

Jimmie: [clears throat] Which one?

Examiner: OK, see, I, um, you had called up a few days ago, and I requested a case-to-case. It shows on the computer here that it is in there, but it isn't. So, I made a search, and I don't have the case. And, um, because of that –

Jimmie: [to me] Dan! [Come here, take the phone.]

Examiner: -ah, I can't, I can't look at the case file and tell you, so, but I have a note down that you were waiting for my phone call today at this time, so that's why I'm responding to your call, but, ah, I don't have your case in front of me. *You'll have to read the letter to me to give me some idea, you know, what I said.* I have too many cases to re-member what I wrote you.

Jimmie: OK.

Examiner: Are they both regarding the same issue?

Jimmie: OK, OK. [Jimmie hands the phone to me.]

We had planned for the call. We had practised telephone etiquette and had role-played Jimmie's questions and the examiner's answers. We had envisioned different things the examiner might say, different questions she might ask. We had written some questions and answers on paper. Jimmie would use these as props as required. But we had not figured on the identity cliff that materialized. We had not figured that the examiner would ask Jimmie to read the letters. He couldn't. His fall was quick. He gave me the phone, knowing he was lost.

Conceptualizing Language, Literacy, and Learning Issues

What does Jimmie's situation tell us about issues that affect the education of minority children? What does it tell us about language, literacy, and learning? What does it say about teaching and curriculum? How does it fit within com-peting sets of theory that explain individuals' apparent inadequacies, such as Jimmie's, as well as educational failure on a massive scale, such as that which characterizes Navajo schooling and Indian and minority student performance in general?

If we ask, 'What's going on here?', and the unit of analysis is the individual, we locate the source of Jimmie's difficulties in Jimmie himself. He could not read the letters or communicate effectively over the telephone because he did not have oral and written skills adequate for the tasks. Perhaps the problem stems from Jimmie's home language background. Perhaps the issue involves a lack of adequate training in school. Perhaps the difficulty is an 'innate processing deficit', a question of Jimmie's raw intelligence.

Whatever the root of the problem, again, if the unit of analysis is Jimmie himself, the pedagogical solution is to stress skills, which need to be taught one after another, sequenced according to cognitive complexity, and mastered singly before moving ahead. Quality input is key, consisting of standard varieties of language. Vernacular forms of Indian English as well as oral and written forms of Navajo have no validity, much less any utility, in the classroom. A definition of learning follows. It happens inside the individual. It develops as a function of internal processes that allow learners to sort, compare, contrast and synthesize external experiences. Given these notions, curriculum becomes the development of more and more skills, organized according to cognitive complexity, to be mastered singly before moving ahead, and to be taught as lessons in and of themselves, with few (if any) references to the learner's direct experience. The focus is on Jimmie, not on his world.

If, however, we ask the same question, 'What's going on?', and our unit of analysis is the scene — the cultural context — in which Jimmie's actions and beliefs take place (as well as those of others with whom Jimmie interacts), then an understanding of the problem is quite different, as are understandings of language, literacy, learning, and curriculum. We look at Jimmie's total situation. He comes from a community with an unemployment rate of 85 percent. As a temporary forest service worker, he has no benefits, few rights, and access to few and distant resources for redress. He is a product of an educational system that produces failure on a massive scale. He lives on a reservation that is utterly dependent on the mainstream world, where institutions and ideologies speak to the unique legacy, language, culture, and needs of the Navajo people, but where, to get things done and to get ahead, one must speak, read, and write English.

If we assume that Jimmie's pathology is as much the world's as it is his, then the approach to remediating the difficulty must go beyond blaming individual victims for their apparent inadequacies. It must include more than skills. It will include more than a set of objectives and standard forms taught in isolation from the kind of politically charged context in which Jimmie's interaction with the claims examiner takes place. The need, then, is to understand language and literacy as sets of concepts and practices that operate within a cultural context. Rather than view culture apolitically, as a functional expression of society or as a set of mentalist imperatives, however, the need is to see culture — indeed, Jimmie's situation — in terms of the individual's interactions with dominant truths and power relations in society. Consequently, the meanings of language and literacy depend upon social institutions and ideologies that structure forms, functions, and topics of communication. It also follows that curricula constitute, and are constrained by, key aspects of social structure, such as domination, stratification, and empowerment.[1]

Cummins's 'Framework for Minority Student Empowerment' (1986) specifies the connection between language and literacy as a cultural phenomenon and pedagogical practice. What Cummins emphasizes is that students like Jimmie will succeed educationally to the extent that political processes in schools reverse those that legitimize the domination and disablement of members of the minority group. Aspects of these processes are four-fold: first, the minority student's language must be incorporated into the process and content of schooling; second, community members must be involved collaboratively in making curricular and administrative decisions at school; third, pedagogical practices should encourage student-student dialogue in collaborative learning contexts that foster intrinsic, rather than extrinsic, motivation; and last, assessment should consist of procedures which locate the problem of minority student failure not within the mind of the individual, thereby legitimating transmission models of learning, but within a larger context of unequal power relations marking dominated and dominating groups in society.

With Cummins's framework, notions about teaching, learning and curriculum become fundamentally different from those which derive from a skills or transmission approach. Teaching becomes more than the impartation of pre-sequenced, disembedded knowledge. It is designed to reinforce the cultural identities of the students and to integrate standard and vernacular varieties of cognitively complex language into all aspects of classroom life. Learning becomes more than a collection of concepts inside the learner's head. It is designed to happen between people. As a function of dialogue, it consists of reciprocal-interactive strategies planned to build the learner up, not probe the student until requisite deficiencies are found. Curriculum changes, too. It becomes more than a sequence of decontextualized, apolitical skills. Rather, it is designed to help the learner connect academic concepts to a problemized world.[2]

As the classroom focus shifts from curriculum that is arbitrary to curriculum that scrutinizes problems immediate to the lives of the students, the teacher's role changes. The teacher becomes coach, an expert who can help the student solve problems. In the process, pedagogy becomes problem-solving, and curriculum becomes cultural politics, structured according to themes immediate to the lives of classroom participants. When explored as a medium that decodes what is powerful and problematic, language and literacy assume new meaning. With the power of understanding, students can use what they know not only to make gains in school but also to understand and act upon the world.[3]

A Model Language and Literacy Project

A secondary-level language and literacy project in a K-12 Navajo bilingual school was conceived in 1983 to do what Cummins advocates.[4] Created for a student population of 160 Navajos, funded with federal monies from Title V of the Indian Education Act, and staffed by a team of four teachers and one evaluator, the project specifies a range of products which develop students' thinking, reading, writing, and speaking abilities in Navajo and English. On a quarterly basis, the products constitute elements of a community bilingual newspaper as well as programming material for a low-power community television station. All of the products measure against a model of thinking that ensures cognitively complex activity. Students work within an immediately comprehensible world at the same time that project staff members challenge the students to think critically.

The curriculum is organized along three dimensions. The first dimension consists of four content areas: Navajo Research, English Research, Computers, and Performance. The second dimension, underpinning the first, consists of cognitive goals specified for different grade levels. Knowledge consumption is for grade seven, comprehension and application for grade eight, analysis for grade nine, synthesis and evaluation for grade ten, and meta-cognition — awareness of the processes of learning — for grades eleven and twelve. At the intersection of the content area and the goals for cognitive development, constituting the third dimension, are headings for nine-week learning activities.

In eighth grade, for example, students divide equally into the project's four content areas. In Navajo Research, the teacher helps students develop an historical text from an interview with someone locally. Class participants learn to use interview equipment, transcribe text, summarize main points, and use reported speech where appropriate in producing a written document. Next, students develop, practice, and perform lessons for teaching the document to elementary students. At the end of the nine-week quarter, the document becomes part of the elementary library's collection of student-produced materials. The same thing happens in English Research. In computers, students learn to type at a rate of 45 words per minute and to use a Navajo-smart word processing program. In Performance, students develop video paragraphs, complete with main points and supporting ideas.

In twelfth grade, students again divide equally into the project's four classes. In Navajo Research, they develop an editorial-style article in Navajo, first articulating research questions, next interviewing at least two experts (with contrasting points of view) on their research topic, then evaluating and synthesizing opinions, and finally writing editorial articles for publication in the bilingual community newspaper. Seniors in English Research follow the same set of procedures, only in English, to develop editorial-style articles for the same newspaper. In Computers, with the Navajo-smart word processors, students learn to use different word-processing and D-base programs, which they will encounter at work or in higher education. And in Performance, they analyze a topic of critical importance to the individual, the school, the community, or the Navajo Tribe, by preparing videotape products to be aired over the community's low-power television station, which propound change.

All of the students in grades seven through twelve take the classes. The program is for everyone. It is neither a remedial, pull-out program, nor one only for 'gifted' children. At any given point in the academic year, the individual student is involved in one of the four activities for his or her grade level. At the conclusion of the nine-week quarters, the students rotate from one activity to the next. In this way, each grade's four groups take the four class activities, albeit in different order, by the end of the school year.

How the Program Works

One student's newspaper article about Billy Mills, the Pine Ridge Sioux who won a gold medal in the 1964 Olympics and on whose experiences the movie *Running Brave* is based, illustrates how the classes actually work. The writer of the article about Billy Mills was in the tenth grade, had a keen interest in sports, and in her senior year would become the reservation's 'Female Athlete of the Year'. For the first three weeks of English Research, this student and her seven classmates worked to develop article ideas.

A five-day instructional sequence dictated activity for the course's first three weeks. On Mondays, the class began with twenty questions derived from articles and headlines in recent newspapers and magazines. 'What does "termination" mean, and how did it become headline news last week?' was one question. 'Where is Beirut, and what happened of consequence there over the weekend'? was another. 'Who is Billy Mills, what is he famous for, and where is the movie about him showing on the reservation this week?' was a third.

Scanning the periodicals, the students raced to answer all of the questions. The aim was to answer as many as possible *as a group*. On Tuesdays, the teacher reviewed the group's answers, and at the end of the class period, the students picked a lecture topic for further expansion. On Wednesdays, class began with a twenty-minute lecture. 'Navajos and the Federal Government: A 30-year cycle of termination and self-determination' was the title of one lecture, stemming directly from the twenty-question exercise that happened the previous Monday. Immediately before the lecture, the students received an outline form which guided the process of note-taking. With this form, the students took notes, then compared strategies for listening, note-taking, and outlining. On Thursdays, using their notes, the students wrote essays on the lecture topic. The proficient use of thesis statements and topic sentences was the main point of the writing assignment. On Fridays, the students had to correct the essays. Read-arounds took place, when all mistakes were to be corrected by peer readers.

At the end of the three-week sequence, the students had to write thesis statements for feature articles. Having recently seen the movie *Running Brave*, the student-athlete initially piqued by Monday's question about Billy Mills chose quickly to write about the former Olympian champion. 'I want to interview Billy Mills to find out who he is, what he was, and what he did to become a superior athlete', this tenth grader wrote.

In week four of the course, the writer of the Billy Mills article and her classmates prepared for their interviews. One would interview a Tribal Council Delegate about the Navajo-Hopi land dispute. Another would interview a professor at a regional community college about the origins of Arab-Israeli strife (as it was being played out at that time dramatically in the streets of Beirut) and the events of the Jewish Holocaust. A third would interview a U.S. Senator about a comment he made in the Navajo tribal newspaper, that 'all Indian schools are deplorable'. A fourth would interview an official with the Bureau of Indian Affairs to chronicle the history of relations between the federal government and Indian tribes.

The writer of the Billy Mills piece, meanwhile, focused on how the Olympian prepared for his gold medal quest. 'Did you ever think in your earlier days that you would be famous?' was one interview question. 'What did you do to prepare yourself to be a good runner.... How do you feel about the movie about you?' were others.

She called the former Olympian, asked for permission to tape record an interview with him, and recorded his answers for more than forty minutes. In response to the student's first question about fame, Billy Mills said:

I don't think I'm anybody famous. But, ah, from the time I was a sophomore in high school, I wanted to make the Olympic team. I didn't think in terms of being famous. I thought in terms of making the Olympic team. Here's what I have to do. Here's what, here's the commitment I have to make. Here's the type of training I have to do, go through. And maybe, if I do that, I have a chance. You don't think in terms of I want to be famous. If you do, nothing will ever happen. But if you think in terms of something you want to accomplish, a specific goal, and you try to do it and you understand the type of work, preparation, training, and knowledge that it's going to take to do it, then you start having a real understanding of the possibilities.

This student taped the answers to her questions. Then, working with a partner, she transcribed the entire interview on butcher paper. Afterwards, she and her teacher edited the transcript and made note of frequent switches in voice, from first to second person, as well as incomplete, sometimes incoherent grammatical constructions in the text. The student then summarized Billy Mills's main points, and quoted him whenever it seemed best to do so. Finally, during weeks seven through nine of the course, she typed the article on a word-processor and helped with its layout in a bilingual community newspaper. Here is part of the final piece which was worked from the interview passage quoted above:

> I asked if [Billy Mills] ever thought in his earlier days that he was going to be famous. He said that from the time he was a sophomore in high school, he wanted to make the Olympic team. He thought then about making a commitment and following through on it. If he had thought about being famous, nothing would've probably happened. Said Mr. Mills, 'If you think in terms of something you want to accomplish, a specific goal, and you try to do it, you understand the type of training, preparation, and knowledge that it's going to take, then you start having a real understanding of the possibilities.'

In conducting the interview with Billy Mills, transcribing it, then editing and finally producing a finished product, the student spent considerable time scrutinizing oral speech and shaping it into written form. The same happened with an article another student wrote about alcoholism, based on an interview with an individual from the local community. This time, however, the transcript was characterized not only by false starts and tense and voice inconsistencies, but also by many of the phonological and grammatical features of Indian English[5]:

> My own experience, drinking on the Navajo Reservation, things I think was more moderate. You don't see many of these Navajos, even young people, drinking at the time I was young. You wouldn't see too many bootlegger, too many of 'em, and then bootlegging was very strict, too. Also, you didn't see too many young people drinking at all these ceremonial like it is today. But nowadays, you see too many, lot of drinking at all these social gathering going on all over the reservation. Anytime you see social gathering going on, for sure you'll see lot of drinking.

In this case, the writer had to make hard decisions. Which parts of the interview were important to summarize? Which parts were good for quoting verbatim? To what extent did the quoted passages need to be rendered in standard form? In correcting any 'mistakes', how much violence to the original meaning would take place? Were the non-standard forms really 'mistakes' in the first place?

In answering these questions, this student and others like him were having to interrogate standard and vernacular varieties of English and Navajo. They were having to examine the appropriateness and utility of each. In posing these kinds of questions, not only about the content of the interviews but also about the language itself, project staff were making the pedagogical more political, problemizing skills, and celebrating the cultural and linguistic resources of the community. They were involving parents and community people, positioning the students as critical agents, and ultimately, making skills and knowledge more meaningful.

Measuring the Success of the Project

Do the classes work? Do the students become better readers and writers? Test scores, insofar as they provide accurate indices, indicate yes. For each class in the project, there are criterion-referenced tests (CRTs), which chronicle the individual students' step-by-step completion of products specified in the curriculum. In the program's first year, the students' success rate on CRTs was 91 percent. In the following two years, the rate was 95 percent. Students' standardized test scores (on the California Test of Basic Skills) also indicate significant growth. Over the life of the project so far, students have averaged eight months' growth between pre- and post-tests of reading comprehension in English, more than twice the average growth of students in nearby BIA schools.[6]

More telling than the statistics, though, are students' responses of an anecdotal nature, and gains in speaking and writing abilities — charted for the first time in the 1987/88 academic year with pre-and post-test measures designed by project staff — that demonstrate the students' orientation to classroom activities as actors, rather than people acted upon. One student, writing about the project in the community newspaper, expressed her feelings about the project this way:

> It is good the way students write articles on what they think is important to them. This way, they feel that they are not writing for nothing, and it is easy for them to express their thoughts. Our newspaper is the only one made this way, and the only one to have articles in Navajo. If we keep up with newspaper production, our language will remain strong.

Other students, at graduation giving farewell speeches, echo their classmate's sentiments: 'Ours is a great school ... and has an excellent bilingual program....' 'The [model literacy] program is outstanding ... and has taught me to communicate effectively in English and Navajo....' 'This school is where I have learned to read and write my own language and to be proud of myself....' 'I have been prepared to go out into the adult world....' All of which, of course, would stand Jimmie Chee in good stead.

Daniel McLaughlin

Significance of the Project

The significance of this project for educators of Indian and other minority children concerns replicability. The project is not replicable in its entirety. To the degree that language and literacy situations differ from one community to the next, the content of effective language arts programs must change. The process of developing a model language and literacy project such as the one described here, however, is replicable. The project's central concern for the politics of oral and written communication, the structuring of cognitively complex varieties of standard and vernacular language across the curriculum, and the empowerment of project participants, need to be considered in the design of any successful literacy program, especially ones for students of dominated minority background, such as Jimmie Chee.

In this case, interactive microcomputer technology became a viable tool which supported literacy instruction by allowing the students to manipulate both the native and second language in a highly interactive manner. The students experienced accelerated reciprocal interaction with language in written form. Navajo and English were written, reviewed, and revised without distorting critical relationships between message content and the cultural frame of reference.

The point here is one stressed by Cummins. If school programs for economically depressed and politically disenfranchised communities are to succeed, they must do more than superficially reorder the content of curriculum or the language of instruction. As long as curriculum and pedagogy do no more than reshuffle practices that fundamentally disable, without positioning students to scrutinize and transform what goes on around them, schools will continue to reproduce the structural inequities that characterize society in general and that render social dysfunctions and the widespread pattern of minority student failure inevitable.

Notes

1 To view culture in this way and to see how the world arranges for Jimmie Chee to appear inadequate is to use critical theory, as developed by Freire (1973), Bowles and Gintes (1976), Bourdieu and Passeron (1977), Apple and Weiss (1983), and Giroux (1983). To view oral and written communication as a highly charged political tool, with positive and negative possibilities, is the central thesis of Street (1985), Cook-Gumpertz (1986), Bakhtin (1986), Freire and Macedo (1987), Aronowitz and Giroux (1988), and McLaren (1988).
2 Reciprocal-interactive teaching strategies stem from the notion that concept formation happens twice: first, as a dialogical process between individuals; then, as an intrapsychological process inside the mind of the learner (Vygotsky, 1962 and 1978).
3 Positioning the teacher as coach, and thus orienting the teacher and the students collectively to solve problems, is a process advocated and described by Freire (1973), Heath (1983), Kozol (1985), and Wigginton (1985).

4   For anonymity's sake, I have not said which school has designed and implemented this project, nor have I specified the actual name of the program.
5   Grammatical and phonological features of Indian English were first described by Leecham and Hall (1955), later by Dillard (1972), who compared Indian English to Black English, and then Leap (1977). More recently, it has been described by Bartelt (1986), who argues that a variety of Apachean English has developed as an interlanguage pidgin, used to establish an intermediate Indian identity among Navajo and Western Apache speakers.
6   CTBS test gains cannot be attributed solely to the project. Previous to the project, the school's test scores on standardized measures compared as favorably with those of nearby, comparable schools as do the ones reported here. More accurate indices of project participants' gains in speaking and writing will be available as the project's pre-and post-test data in the two areas becomes available.

References

APPLE, M. and WEISS, L. (1983) *Ideology and practice in schooling*, Philadelphia, PA: Temple University Press
ARONOWITZ, S. and GIROUX, H. (1988) 'Schooling, culture, and literacy in the age of broken dreams: A review of Bloom and Hirsch', In *Harvard Educational Review*, *58*(2).
BAKHTIN, M. (1986) *Speech genres and other late essays*, Austin, TX: University of Texas Press.
BARTELT, H.G. (1986) 'Language contact in Arizona: The case of Apachean English,' *Anthropos*, 81,4/6.
BOURDIEU, P. and PASSERON, J.C. (1977) *Reproduction in education, society, and culture*, Beverly Hills, CA: Sage.
BOWLES, S. and GINTES, H. (1976) *Schooling in capitalist America*, New York, NY: Basic Books.
COOK-GUMPERTZ, J. (1986) *The social construction of literacy*, London: Cambridge University Press.
CUMMINS, J. (1986) '*Empowering minority students: A framework for intervention,*' Harvard Educational Review, 56 (1).
DILLARD, J. (1972) *Black English: Its History and Usage in the United States,* New York, NY: Random House.
FREIRE, P. (1973) *Pedagogy of the oppressed*, New York, NY: Seabury.
FREIRE, P. and MACEDO, D. (1987) Literacy: *Reading the word and the world*, South Hadley, MA: Bergin and Garvey.
GIROUX, H. (1983) *Theory and Resistance in Education: A pedagogy for the oppressed.* South Hadley, MA: Bergin and Garvey.
HEATH, S. (1983) *Ways with words: Language, life, and work in communities and classrooms*, New York, NY: Cambridge University Press.
KOZOL, J. (1985) *Illiterate America*, Garden City, NY: Doubleday.
LEAP, W. (1977) *Studies in Southwestern Indian English*, San Antonio, TX: Trinity University Press.
LEECHAM, D. and HALL, R. (1955). American Indian pidgin English: Attestations and grammatical pecularities. *American Speech*, 30.
MCLAREN, P. (1988) 'Culture or canon? critical pedagogy and the politics of literacy,' *Harvard Educational Review*, 58 (2).
MCLAUGHLIN, D. (forthcoming) *When literacy empowers: An ethnography of uses for Engl ' and Navajo print*, Alburquerque: University of New Mexico Press.

STREET, B. (1985) *Literacy in theory and practice,* New York, NY: Cambridge University Press.

VYGOTSKY, L. (1962) *Thought and language,* Cambridge, MA: MIT Press.

VYGOTSKY, L. (1978) *Mind in society.* COLE, M., JOHN-STENINER, V., SCRIBNER, S. and SOUBERMA, E. (Eds), Cambridge, MA: Harvard University Press.

WIGGINTON, E. (1985) *Sometimes a shining moment: The Foxfire experience,* Garden City, NY: Anchor Books.

III
Macro Views of Computers in Education

Introduction

It has become apparent that the large financial expenditure required by school districts to implement the new technologies is not a one-shot commitment, but an ongoing and potentially increasing commitment as the technologies continue to change. Expenditures on instructional computing programs have become the proverbial black hole in some school budgets, and many school boards are starting to demand accountability for such programs. These factors have put tremendous pressure on decision makers to plan and to make programmatic choices about policy and practice regarding microcomputers in the schools. This, in turn, has created a demand for more research and additional data to justify support for microcomputers and other emerging instructional technologies.

In this section we present two studies that examine the process of implementing computer technology at the school district level. The first study, 'Stakeholder Perspectives on the Implementation of Micros in a School District', was conducted in 1986 by Dianne Martin. It is a multiple-site case study illustrating the mobilization and implementation stages of introducing microcomputers into a 'majority adopter' school district (Rogers, 1983). In this particular case, the process is examined from the viewpoint of the program's 'stakeholders' at three levels: (1) district central office personnel, (2) teachers in the individual schools, and (3) students in the affected classes. Factors contributing to institutional change, the unique characteristics of microcomputers as an instructional innovation and the particular concerns of individuals at all three of the levels mentioned are taken into account in the analysis. Data from the field study included structured and unstructured interviews, direct observations in the classrooms and microcomputer labs, administrative and historical documents, computer usage statistics and a survey of teacher concerns.

Martin's use of a microcomputer to handle the large volume of ethnographic data during the fieldwork is an interesting methodological sidelight of this particular case study. The use of the microcomputer enabled the researcher to perform the data collection, analysis, and presentation more efficiently, allowing more time to be spent on preparing the case study. The conclusions suggest that the classroom teachers are the primary stakeholders in the implementation process. Teachers who used the microcomputers as a tool to help them improve their on-the-job performance and teachers who participated in the development of computer-curriculum units were the most enthusiastic users of microcomputers with their students. This finding suggests a real need for the training of teachers beyond basic 'computer literacy' courses and an increased emphasis on training in the use of open-ended tools like word processing, database management and statistical modeling.

The second study in this section, 'Successful Change Agent Strategies for Overcoming Impediments to Microcomputer Implementation in the Classroom', was conducted in 1986 by Neil Strudler for his doctoral research focusing on the importance of computer coordinators as key agents for curriculum and technological change. His research examines the roles of three elementary computer coordinators in an Oregon school district. Data gathered for the study consisted of questionnaires and interviews with the three coordinators, their instructional supervisors, teachers in their respective schools, and parents from the community. Observations of representative coordinators' activities and examination of relevant documents provided independent verification of the coordinator responses to survey and interview questions.

Strudler's study emphasizes the importance of human relations skills, as well as technical skill with microcomputers and knowledge of curriculum resources, for coordinators to be effective agents for the implementation of district computer programs. He also discusses some of the typical obstacles encountered by coordinators and administrative personnel when computers are introduced across a school district. His conclusions include suggested guidelines for implementing the coordinator's role, an injunction for undertaking long-range planning at the district level, suggestions for the selection and training of coordinators, and implications for educational policymakers. In particular, he suggests that predictable impediments to significant educational change make the curricular integration of microcomputers unlikely without the direct support of well-trained computer coordinators.

Both of these studies are important because they look at the problems encountered when implementing microcomputer technology in school districts. Since the approximately 16,000 school districts in the United States face this issue in one way or another, the lists of critical factors outlined at the end of both reports provide valuable resources for decision-makers who may be planning for the initial integration of microcomputers with an educational program or reexamining existing implementation plans to assess their effectiveness and recommend modifications. In either event, increased attention to teacher training and support provided by coordinators or other specialized personnel are liable to be high priorities.

Introduction.

Reference

Rogers, E.M. (1983) *The diffusion of innovation* (3rd ed.), New York: The Free Press.

Chapter 5

Stakeholder Perspectives on the Implementation of Micros in a School District

C. Dianne Martin

Introduction

During the early 1980s there was widespread demand for the integration of microcomputers into the instructional delivery system at all grade levels. Microcomputers represented an innovation with a potential to have a major impact upon education, but there were no clear guidelines about how school districts should implement them. In order to understand the process by which an innovation is introduced into an educational setting, previous researchers identified the need to examine the process at the school district level from the perspective of all of the stakeholders.

In this study the mobilization and implementation stages of introducing microcomputers into a majority adopter school district were examined. The research was conducted as a multiple-site case study using structured and informal interviews, naturalistic observations, content analysis of historical documents, computer usage statistics, and stages-of-concerns data. Interaction within the institutional context, characteristics of the innovation, and concerns of individuals were examined within the loosely coupled operational units of a school district: the central office, schools, and classrooms.

The use of ethnographic data collection techniques produced a rich reservoir of information in which several conflicting themes were found. The data revealed resistance to innovation, strong grassroots support for microcomputers, fear of microcomputers, high motivation to use microcomputers, the influence of early adopter school districts, and the importance of the individual in the implementation process. Characteristics of the implementation process were identified that contributed to and detracted from eventual institutionalization of microcomputers by the school district.

Background

The clarion call of the early 1980s was for the widespread integration of microcomputers into the instructional delivery system of education at all grade levels. During this time, microcomputers became affordable for instruction and had the characteristics of an innovation defined to be 'a practice or plan new to a particular school or local educational agency ... [and] because it is new, requires some degree of modification or change in behavior of the principal actors' (Berman and McLaughlin, 1974, p. 1). Microcomputers represented a new and different technology with the potential to have a major impact upon education, but there were no clear guidelines or precedence about how to implement them for district-wide instruction. While PTAs held bake sales to purchase microcomputers, prestigious national organizations such as the National Council of Teachers of Mathematics (NCTM) called for integration of microcomputers into all aspects of the curriculum and stated that widespread use of computers would significantly change the emphasis of education from product to process (NCTM, 1980). There was a concurrent public perception that schools were in trouble and that microcomputers could be used to modernize and improve the instructional delivery system (OTA, 1982).

All of these factors created a tremendous pressure on school districts from the grass roots level and from the national and state levels to introduce computers for instruction. It quickly became apparent that school district-wide introduction of this new technology required dealing with significant technological and financial issues. It required a massive commitment of time, staff development, curriculum changes, expenditure of large amounts of money, and redistribution of resources. Ironically, however, the largest obstacle encountered during the introduction of microcomputers for instruction turned out to be the acceptance of the innovation by all of the stakeholders involved in the process — district administrators, principals, curriculum specialists, the classroom teachers and, ultimately, the students.

Educational settings are particularly resistant to change. There is a regressive tendency to revert back to pre-existing patterns of behavior unless all of those affected by the process participate in its development (McLaughlin and Berman, 1978). Unlike other settings in which the primary problem is to succeed in having an innovation adopted, in education the decision to adopt is only the beginning of a highly unstable and variable implementation process that can best be described as evolutionary (Miles, 1964). Because of its complex and evolutionary nature, implementation is difficult to study but it is important to study because it illuminates the consequences of policy (Pressman and Wildavsky, 1984). In examining the process by which an innovation is introduced into an educational setting, Berman and McLaughlin (1978) identified three phases: mobilization, implementation, and institutionalization. Past research revealed that implementation of an innovation leading to institutional change does not take place unless the institutions and individuals involved in the process had both the willingness and the capability to change. Applying the designation by Rogers (1983) of innovation adopters, the innovators (first 2.5 percent) began using microcomputers for instruction in education during 1978–80, followed by the early adopters (next 13.5 percent) during 1980–83. The majority adopters (next 68 percent) began implementing microcomputers for instruction in 1983–84.

This study described the process of implementing microcomputers for instruction in the elementary and middle schools of a majority adopter school district. The philosophy of the selected majority adopter school district toward innovation was best expressed by the county motto: '*I byde my time*'. During the 1982–83 school year, school district officials made the decision, with the approval of the local School Board, to introduce microcomputers for instruction in three of its twenty-three elementary schools and in all four middle schools of the school district starting with the 1984–85 school year. There had been prior use of microcomputers for instruction in the high schools, but none in grades K-8. The district was able to implement this decision using district-wide planning that drew from the set of computer implementation models available from neighboring districts. Several were innovators and early adopters, using microcomputers for instruction in their elementary and middle schools during the past five years.

Research Design

Implementation of a technological innovation like microcomputers for instruction involved many activities: acquisition of the necessary computer hardware and software, staff development to support the innovation, curriculum development to incorporate the innovation, and participant willingness to use the innovation. These activities do not proceed in a linear sequence but are both simultaneous and iterative. Because implementation is a dynamic process that involves the interaction of institutions and individuals with an innovation, the decision was made to adopt the qualitative paradigm as the framework to study the district-wide implementation of microcomputers for instruction. Within this paradigm a field-based methodology was chosen as the most appropriate approach for studying this process within the schools in a school district.

In recent years the field-based approach has become more prominent in educational research. 'The orientation of field-based research is to attempt to understand schools in terms of the complex patterns of social interactions. It focuses upon the "culture" of school life ... data are collected in a "natural setting" while schooling and the social interactions ... are taking place' (Popkewitz, 1981, p. 1). The field-based methodology allowed the researcher to analyze the implementation of microcomputers for instruction as it was understood by the administrators, teachers, and students of the school district (Rist, 1982).

In their review of the evaluation literature pertaining to educational innovations up through 1978, Berman and McLaughlin cited evidence that it was inappropriate to attempt to measure the effects of implementing an innovation using quantitative data. Past attempts to tie student outcome data to a particular innovation produced tenuous causal links at best (Berman and McLaughlin, 1978, p. 1). Similarly, collection of survey or anecdotal data from school district personnel as a means of measuring the results of an innovation have proven equally unsuccessful in providing a realistic picture of the actual implementation of the innovation. 'Much of the literature on change in education consists of single-case studies that evidence little methodological sophistication — research characterized as ... "show and tell" local education authority project reports ... containing descriptions of "exemplary projects" or "innovative" programs' (Berman and McLaughlin, 1974, p. 3). Therefore, the most appropriate research strategy to use to capture the essence of a dynamic process like implementation was a phenomenological approach (Rist, 1977) using purely descriptive data (Berger and Luckmann, 1967) gathered from naturalistic observations (Becker and Geer, 1957; Spradley, 1980), structured interviews (Spradley, 1979), and content analysis of historical documents (Webb et al., 1981) by someone outside of the school district (Merton, 1972).

This research was conducted as a multiple-site case study using naturalistic observations, structured and informal interviews, content analysis of historical documents, computer usage statistics, and teacher concerns data. All research activities were done with the permission of and in coordination with the public school officials. The observations were conducted in the natural classroom and computer labs of three pilot schools, two elementary and one middle school. The research was conducted over the six month period from January to June, 1986.

Demographics of the school district

The school district coincided with a county local government unit encompassing 527 square miles of land area with a total population of approximately 70,000 people and a median family income of $43,393 as of April, 1986. Until recently, the county had been mostly rural, but with a rapidly expanding population migrating from the neighboring county, it was quickly becoming suburban with the attendant new demands on its school system. Demographic data obtained from the county planning office revealed that the county had a population that was predominantly white, with less than 10 percent black and less than 5 percent other minority members combined. It was located one county removed from a major metropolitan area, and its eastern side was rapidly becoming a suburban extension of the metropolitan area. It was representative of school districts in the second ring of suburbanization around a major metropolitan area. The twenty-two square miles in the eastern part of the county accounted for 33,000 members of the total population. In the center of the county was a small city of 10,000 people making up the county seat. The remainder of the county population was spread over approximately 500 square miles of rural land. The school district with an enrollment of 13,000 students from both a rural and suburban constituency was in the upper 3 percent of school districts by size in the country and fell within the third of six class sizes used by the National Center for Educational Statistics to classify school districts by size.

The research population for this study was made up of district staff, school staff, and students involved with the implementation of microcomputers for instruction in the elementary and middle schools. The district staff were selected from recommendations by other staff members, based upon their knowledge of and participation in the process of implementing microcomputers in instruction.

Gaining access to the population
Permission to conduct this study was granted by the Assistant Superintendent of Instruction in agreement with the school principals and the classroom teachers. A blanket permission was granted, allowing the researcher unrestricted access to the schools during regular working hours. Upon arrival to a school the researcher would check in at the office and would then go to any classroom where the computers were in use. The teachers were informed that the researcher would be coming and going during the months of the study, but the teachers would not know ahead of time when the researcher would be in their classroom. Whenever the researcher entered a classroom, she introduced herself to the teacher and obtained permission to remain in the classroom. The researcher never encountered any difficulty gaining access to any school or classroom during the study and received full cooperation from those being interviewed or observed.

Initially, the reciprocal benefit to the school district for allowing the researcher unrestricted access to the schools was to be a copy of the findings at the end of the study. The district officials felt that they would benefit from the findings of an outside observer. While the research was being conducted, however, another reciprocal benefit for the school district was free access to the researcher's expertise on the use of microcomputers for instruction. Since the researcher was the only person who was actually observing the use of microcomputers in the schools, district officials would occasionally ask the researcher how the implementation of the microcomputers was going in the schools. They would also ask for advice about future staff development or curriculum plans.

Another reciprocal benefit was the willingness of the researcher to answer any technical questions that arose about microcomputers when she was on site. This fostered positive feelings on the part of teachers and administrators toward the researcher and insured continuing access to the schools. It was understood that the research data belonged to the researcher who guaranteed the security of the data. The names used in the study are pseudonyms to protect the privacy of those interviewed and observed.

Data Collection

A major concern of qualitative research is data reliability. Qualitative data carries with it an inherent internal validity since it tends to be deep data gathered in such a way as to determine the perspective of the subjects rather than the researcher. To increase the internal reliability of this study, at least three types of ethnographic data were collected to allow for triangulation of data sources (Denizen, 1978). The three main data sources were naturalistic observations in the classrooms and computer labs, structured and informal interviews, and historical documents from the school district. These data were collected at the three operational levels of the district, the school and the classroom. In addition, other sources of data were computer usage figures and stages-of-concern data from the county-contracted, graduate level computer education course conducted on site at two middle schools.

Structured interviews
There were data from ten structured interviews, seven with school district staff personnel and three with the principals of the participating schools, to obtain their perspectives on the innovation, the decision-making process to adopt the innovation and the implementation process.

For each structured interview the researcher scheduled an hour-long appointment with the staff person in advance, stating that the purpose of the interview was to discuss their view of and participation in the implementation of microcomputers for instructional use in the elementary and middle schools in the school district and/or in their school. The researcher arrived with a set of broad questions that varied according to the staff position of the respondent. The questions were general enough to allow the respondent to address themes and events regarded to be important by the respondent. The questions were asked in a conversational manner by the researcher, and the answers were recorded by the researcher with pen and paper in a narrative fashion. The researcher recorded the answers in the respondent's own words. The interviews were then typed by the researcher into field notes within forty-eight hours after recording them.

Informal interviews
Fifty-two informal interviews were documented by the researcher. Informal interviews were different from the structured interviews in that the respondents did not know ahead of time that they were going to be interviewed. The purpose of the informal interviews conducted with three principals, three school librarians, and twenty-seven teachers was to answer specific questions about how the microcomputers were being used for instruction in a school or in a particular classroom.

Informal interviews lasted from five to fifty minutes each, depending upon the nature of the question(s) and the amount of time that the respondent had available for the interview. An informal interview was conducted with every teacher observed, before or after the observation period, to determine the teacher's purpose in using microcomputers with the students. Several informal interviews were conducted with the librarians of each school since they were responsible for scheduling the use of the computers and the software. Informal phone interviews were also conducted with a planner from the county planning office to obtain demographic data about the county, and with an official of the US Department of Education to obtain national school enrollment data as the basis for categorizing the school district by size. The responses to informal interviews were recorded by the researcher in a narrative fashion at the time of the interview using pen and paper. The interviews were then typed by the researcher into field notes within forty-eight hours after recording them.

Naturalistic observations
Fifty-three naturalistic observations were conducted by the researcher in regular classrooms or the computer labs of the schools in the study. The purpose of the naturalistic observations was to determine how the teachers and students were using the microcomputers in the classrooms of the school district by documenting the kinds of interaction observed between teachers, students and computers.

The researcher went to the school district two days a week and stopped in at one or two of the three schools each day. The researcher based the observation schedule upon the microcomputer activities that were going on at each school. In two of the three schools, the teachers had to sign up for the computers ahead of time so the researcher planned in advance to see certain activities. Overall, the researcher spent twelve to sixteen hours of observation in each school and observed each kind of instructional use of the microcomputer at least once. Each observation lasted from thirty minutes to two hours for a total of forty-five and a half hours of naturalistic observation. The length of an observation depended upon the activities going on in the classroom being observed and the researcher's own schedule. As long as one or more microcomputers were being used by one or more students, the researcher remained to record the activity.

When the observation took place in a regular classroom, the researcher documented the other activity, if any, that was occurring in the room while the computer was being used. During an observation the researcher sat beside a microcomputer and documented the activity that occurred as the child or children used the microcomputer. In the cases where there was more than one microcomputer in a classroom, the researcher sat by each of the computers for a complete session with a child or children. (In most cases the children would be at a computer for some amount of time specified by the teacher.)

In the lab observations, the researcher first sat in the middle of the room to record the general activity and then walked around the room to record individual activity at the computer. The researcher documented the overall atmosphere of the lab and the teacher's role in managing the lab situation. For both the lab and classroom setting the research notes were taken in longhand with a pen on a shorthand pad in a narrative style.

In both the lab and classroom setting the researcher noted the type of software being used on the computer, the teacher's role, if any, in assisting the children to use the software, the children's reaction to the software and the computer, the result of the interaction with the computer, and the interaction between the children in the room while using the computer. In addition, the researcher noted any reaction on the part of the children or the teacher to the presence of the researcher and the teacher's attitude toward having the students use the computer.

For all observation sessions, the researcher attempted to remain as unobtrusive as possible. However, the teachers occasionally asked the researcher questions since the teachers considered the researcher to be a computer expert. When doing observations in the computer lab setting, the teachers occasionally asked the researcher for assistance with students since several students would be asking for help at the same time. In such instances, the researcher assisted the teacher and then returned to recording the field notes. All such instances of researcher intervention were documented in the field notes. The researcher typed up the field notes into a narrative format within forty-eight hours from the time the observation took place.

Use of key informants

A teacher was identified by the researcher in each of the three schools to be a key informant. In each case the teacher chosen was highly motivated and positively disposed toward the use of microcomputers for instruction in the classroom. In each case the teacher chosen was eager to speak to the researcher about the computers. In the middle school the home economics teacher was chosen since she was experimenting with computer uses beyond the prescribed home economics curriculum. She had taken a computer course the previous semester. At the large elementary school a fourth grade teacher was chosen since she was using the computer in the greatest variety of ways of the teachers in her school. She was enrolled in a computer course at the time of the data collection and had taken the inservice training at her school. At the small elementary school the Chapter I teacher was chosen since she was using the computers with her students more than any other teacher in the school. She had taken a district-sponsored BASIC programming course and the inservice training provided at her school. Numerous informal interviews and observations were conducted with the key informants at each school to determine if there was any common pattern to be observed among these computer enthusiasts.

Other data collected

The historical documents included school board minutes, district planning reports, reports produced by school staff, demographic data and curriculum and course materials. They were examined for policy statements, goals, plans, budget allocations and concerns related to microcomputers. The computer usage statistics were compiled by the researcher from the librarians' sign-out logs for the software and hardware. They were used to establish patterns and levels of use of the microcomputers. The stages-of-concern data were gathered from the participants of county-contracted, graduate level computer education courses directed and taught by the researcher. The Stages-of-Concern Questionnaire (SoCQ$^{\copyright}$) was used to measure the stages of concern felt by an individual toward an innovation using the stages-of-concern taxonomy: awareness, informational, personal, management, consequence, collaboration, and refocusing (Hall, George, and Rutherford 1979). In this study the SocQ$^{\copyright}$ was used to measure the levels of concern felt by administrators and teachers toward microcomputers.

Data management
There were over two hundred pages of field notes from the ethnographic interviews and the participant observations. There were data from 138 stages-of-concern questionnaires (SoCQ) and four sets of computer usage figures. There were a dozen historical documents. To evaluate this large volume of data, the ethnographic field notes were typed into computerized data files for easy retrieval of information during data analysis. They were also coded into the computerized data base program FileMaker on a 512-K memory Macintosh computer to allow the researcher to determine the distribution of the ethnographic data and to find occurrences of common themes (Gillespie, 1982). A record was established in the data base for each informal interview or naturalistic observation in the following format:

field	*description*
fn	identification number of source field notes
site	site of the interview or observation
date	date of the interview or observation
name	name of person(s) interviewed or observed
title	title of person(s) interviewed or observed
concerns	concerns of person(s) interviewed or observed
use	use of the microcomputer classified by CAI (computer-assisted instruction), database use, word-processing, simulations, LOGO programming, computer literacy instruction or other
intervene	intervention by researcher and what kind
data type	informal interview or observation
time	duration of the interview or observation
attitudes	toward the microcomputer of interviewed or observed person(s)

Since the identifying number of each set of field notes was cross-referenced in the computerized data base, the data base was used by the re-

Data type

1 Structured Interviews	4 Historical Documents
2 Informal Interviews	5 Computer Usage Statistics
3 Naturalistic Observations	6 Stages-of-Concern (SoCQ) Data

Factor/Operational unit	School district	School	Classroom
Institutional structure	1, 4	1, 2, 4	2, 3, 5
Innovation characteristics	1, 4	1, 2, 4, 5	2, 3, 5
Individual concerns	1, 4	1, 2, 3, 6	2, 3, 6

Figure 5.1:   Data analysis matrix with related data.

searcher to locate appropriate descriptions needed to describe specific phenomena.

Data Analysis

Obtaining a precise description of implementing an innovation in an educational setting requires examining the institutional context (Berman & McLaughlin, 1978) and the impact on the setting in terms of organizational change (Miles, 1964; Havelock, 1969; Elmore, 1978; Firestone and Herriott, 1982), the characteristics of the innovation itself (Rogers *et al.*, 1985), and the concerns and participation of the individuals involved (Hall, George and Rutherford, 1979; McLaughlin and Berman, 1978). Since the operational units within a school district are the school district, the individual schools, and classrooms (Berman and McLaughlin, 1974), all of which enjoy a high degree of autonomy (Weick, 1976), any meaningful analysis of implementation must look at each operational unit. Thus, the study examined three major factors at three different levels using a 3×3 data analysis matrix. The six types of data collected were used to inform the components of the data analysis matrix shown in Figure 5.1.

Distribution of the ethnographic data
Once the data base was created, a profile of the ethnographic data was developed by doing searching and sorting based upon the various fields. The distribution of data by type and site was determined. These data were collected in the central office and three schools, identified by the pseudonyms:

a)   District — the central office staff
b)   Longfellow Middle School — the middle school
c)   Crestwood Elementary School — the smaller elementary school
d)   Fairview Elementary School — the larger elementary school

The distribution of data collected by source, site and kind of contact was calculated using the computerized data base to produce the table shown in Figure 5.2.

Location	Structured	Informal	Observation	Total
District	7	1	0	8
Longfellow	1	21	16	38
Crestwood	1	16	15	32
Fairview	1	23	22	46
	10	61	53	124

Kind of contact

district adminstrators: 8   principals: 6   librarians: 6
teachers: 51   students: 53

Figure 5.2: Distribution of ethnographic data.

Within each site, data were collected from the staff shown in Figure 5.3. The distributions by computer usage and attitudes of participants were also determined. The computer usage figures were tabulated into four tables and used as an indication of the level of usage of the innovation. The data from the individual SoCQ's were aggregated into composite profiles by semester to show the overall levels of concerns about microcomputers by participants in a district-sponsored computer course for teachers and administrators.

Institutional Characteristics and Implementation

Examination of the institutional characteristics of the school district revealed the presence of broad, district-wide educational goals for the innovation. All of the data supported a high degree of autonomy between the operational units of the school district both in general and as it related to the implementation of microcomputers. Based upon the data, the operational units of the school district were characterized as loosely coupled (Weick, 1976). The picture that emerged regarding the organizational structure was one of shared responsibility and authority. There was a clear-cut hierarchy of decision-making that extended across all operational levels of the school district and was characterized as both centralized for policy decisions and decentralized for implementation decisions.

The aspects of the mobilization stage that were examined were the base of support for the innovation, the allocation of resources needed to implement the innovation, the resistance, if any, to the innovation that occurred during mobilization, and the influence of early adopters on a majority adopter school district. The support for microcomputers in instruction that emerged from the data was broad-based and included parents, the School Board, administrators, teachers and students. The resources allocated for the innovation included money for planning, equipment and software, staff development, technical support, and curriculum development as well as space to house the microcomputers. There was resistance on the part of central office staff to rush into the implementation of microcomputers for instruction without careful planning, and there was indication that innovator and early-

District:	Number of interactions:
assistant superintendent of instruction	1
supervisor of instructional services**	2
supervisor of special education**	1
director of vocational education	1
supervisor of home economics**	1

School 1: Longfellow Middle School

principal: Mr. Jones**	1
librarian**	2
teachers:	
Mrs. Burton (Home Economics)*, **	6
Mrs. Riseling (Math)	1
Mrs. Lee (LD)	2
Mrs. White (English)**	1
Mrs. Todd (Remedial Reading)**	1
Mr. Delaney (in-school restriction teacher)	2
Miss Lincoln (Language Arts)**	3
Mrs. Gray (Music)**	2
8th grade math teacher**	1

School 2: Crestwood Elementary School

principal: Mr. Smith	3
librarian	2
teachers:	
Mrs. Johnson (Chapt.I)*, **	5
Mrs. Jackson (1st)**	2
Mrs. Black (3rd)	1
Mr. O'Connell (4th)	1
Mrs. Gordon (5th)	2
Mr. Brown (physical education teacher)	1

School 3: Fairview Elementary School

principal: Mrs. Engle	2
librarian**	2
teachers:	
Mrs. Merlin (K)**	2
Miss Lang (1st)	1
Mr. Wilson (1st)	1
Mrs. Harrison (2nd)	1
Mrs. James (2nd)	1
Mrs. Hogan (2nd)**	1
Mrs. Green (3rd)**	1
Mrs. Washington (4th)*, **	5
Mrs. John (4th)	1
Mrs. Emory (5th)**	3
Mr. Watson (5th)	2
Mr. Lane (speech therapist)**	1

* *key informant*
** *participated in a computer course*

Figure 5.3: Staff involved in the data collection (with pseudonyms used).

adopter school districts were consulted when developing the implementation plan.

The central office staff realized from the beginning that the implementation process was multifaceted, involving curriculum changes, staff training, selection and preparation of secure facilities, equipment purchases, software distribution, and finally equipment maintenance. They proceeded slowly, implementing the plan in stages from the high schools to the middle schools to the elementary schools. The implementation process began in fall, 1985 and was planned to be carried out through the spring, 1988.

During 1985–86, the first full year of implementation of the microcomputers in the middle schools and the three pilot elementary schools, the researcher determined that the following activities were going on simultaneously: graduate courses for teachers, inservice training in the schools, curriculum development, distribution of more software to the schools, computer maintenance, use of the computers in lab and classroom settings by students, and use of the computers by teachers to do lesson preparation and administrative tasks. All of this activity was driven by the educational goal to eventually provide every child in the school district with experience using computers.

The teacher training, curriculum development, distribution of software, and computer maintenance were directed and coordinated by the Media Specialist from the central office. However, the actual use of the computers was in the schools. Each school in the study was managed by a principal who was in favor of the microcomputers and who had a set of goals related to the use of computers in that school. Within the classrooms the teachers were ultimately responsible for the use of computers with the students, and the informal interviews showed that most of them accepted that responsibility with enthusiasm. Although there were some delays and changes to the original plan, implementation proceeded on all fronts during the 1985–86 school year. Because the implementation of microcomputers for instruction involved the efforts and cooperation of so many people at all operational levels of the school district, the data supported the premise that implementation was enhanced by the presence of diverse goals, autonomy between operational units, and distributed decision-making.

As a majority adopter, the school district waited until broad-based support was generated, a long-range plan based upon the experiences of early adopter districts was developed, and the necessary resources were marshalled to proceed cautiously with the implementation of microcomputers for instruction. Such an approach could be characterized as mature mobilization leading to implementation. This was contrasted to Schimizzi's finding based upon information from 400 schools in early adopter school districts that the major stumbling block to implementing microcomputers for instruction was the lack of systematic and long-term planning (1983).

A unique characteristic that contributed positively to the implementation process of the school district in the study was its size. A technical innovation such as microcomputers required a critical mass of technical expertise and financial support. With 13,000 students the district was large enough to allocate the $250,000 to pay for computer hardware, as well as the additional resources needed to pay for the multifaceted commitment required to implement microcomputers for instruction district-wide. On the other hand, it was small enough to allow for the decentralized decision-making necessary for a successful implementation. There were few layers of bureaucracy to impede implementation, and the high degree of autonomy given to the principal and teachers fostered a sense of professionalism at all levels.

Innovation Characteristics and Implementation

Berman and McLaughlin (1979) stated that the innovation itself does not matter as much as what a school district does with the innovation. However, this study found that, in the case of microcomputers, the characteristics of the innovation are as important as other factors. This is due to the highly technical, complex and anxiety-producing nature of microcomputers that requires involvement at all operational levels of the school district.

This study supported the finding of Loucks and Zacchei (1983) that the microcomputer is an innovation requiring well-defined teacher training, clear direction from administrators, teacher support of the innovation and attention to institutionalization. Its implementation across a school district involves an expensive, long-term commitment. It requires the selection and purchase of materials and equipment, the training of staff to use the equipment, the maintenance of the equipment, and a plan to incorporate the equipment into the curriculum.

When comparing the five general characteristics of innovations to microcomputers, Rogers found that microcomputers are perceived to have *uncertain* relative advantage (better than what it supersedes), *neutral* compatibility (consistent with existing practices, values), *positive* trialability (able to experiment with), *positive* observability (visible to others), and *negative* complexity (difficult to understand and use) (Rogers *et al.*, 1985). The two characteristics identified by Meister that make microcomputers more difficult than other innovations to implement in a school district are that they are not self-executing and they are a complex, non-obvious innovation. They required the support of the whole multi-layered system to be implemented. Other studies show that microcomputers are the most anxiety-producing innovation among teachers of any innovation that had been studied in the past two decades (Quinsatt, 1981; McNeil, 1983; Meister, 1984). The interview and observation data from this study support those previous findings.

Level of use of the innovation
Hall and Loucks cited the level of use of an innovation as a means for determining whether the innovation was actually being implemented (1981; Hall, Loucks, Rutherford and Newlove, 1975). The data were analyzed to determine both the level and type of use of the innovation. The microcomputers were used in two settings, computer labs and classrooms. It was found that

site/setting:	lab	classroom	total
Longfellow	8	8	16
Fairview	4	18	22
Crestwood	3	12	15
total	15	38	53

Figure 5.4: Frequency of observations by site and setting.

the microcomputers were used more frequently in the classrooms than in the computer labs. The frequency of observations by site and setting is shown in Figure 5.4.

The level of use of the computer labs was at less than 50 percent as determined by the computer lab sign-up sheets maintained by the librarians. For example, 528 of the available 1137.7 lab periods (46 percent) available during the 1985–86 school year at Longfellow Middle School were used. The use of computers in individual classrooms was heaviest during October, November and February through May, suggesting that teachers used them most in the middle of each semester rather than at the beginning and ends of semesters. The use of the computer labs and computers in classrooms increased during the second semester. At the two elementary schools, computers available for classroom use were being used all of the time by March and April of 1986.

Type of use of the innovation
The type of use of the microcomputers was strongly related to the nature of the microcomputer as an innovation. The microcomputer is a general purpose device with many possible uses. Some uses are more difficult to implement in the context of a classroom than others. The data were analyzed to determine how the microcomputers were actually being used for instruction by the teachers with their students.

During the first year of implementation the microcomputers were used predominantly for computer-assisted instruction (CAI) in the elementary schools and for CAI and computer literacy in the middle schools. Other uses included programming, word processing, simulations, and data bases. The following kinds of uses were mentioned during informal interviews or seen during observations:

a) computer-assisted instruction (CAI), comprised of math, language and keyboard drills from the MECC software
b) programming with LOGO or with a drawing program
c) word-processing with the Bank Street Writer
d) computer simulations of a white water race, small business, deer population, civil war
e) use of a data base

use:	stated:	observed:
CAI	32	24
programming	8	7
word-processing	11	3
simulations	4	4
data base	5	3
produce handouts	9	4
produce IEP's	3	0

Figure 5.5: Microcomputer use by application.

f) preparation of handouts and materials by teachers
g) preparing Individualized Education Programs (IEPs) for learning disabled students

The frequency with which the above uses were stated or observed are shown in Figure 5.5.

CAI was the easiest way to bring computers into the classroom because it required the least amount of expertise on the part of teachers and the least amount of change in the classroom. The CAI programs presented drill and practice exercises of well-defined concepts with some motivational games to reward successful completion of the exercises. Generally one or two children sat at the computer in one corner of the room while the rest of the class proceeded with the regular work of the day. In this context the micro-computer was used for enrichment, remediation or reward, but it had little impact on the curriculum or the classroom.

An example of the computer used for remediation is cited below from an observation made in an eighth remedial reading classroom:

I went to Mrs. Todd's eighth grade remedial reading classroom, where she was using the Flash Spell CAI program with her students. This is a spelling game in which lists of spelling words are entered by the teacher. A student selects the assigned list, and a word is flashed on the screen for one second. The student then has to type in the word. For each missed attempt, the word will flash on the screen for half a second longer than the previous turn. At the end of twenty words, a list of the missed words appears on the screen, and the student makes a copy of them. Depending upon how many words the student spells correctly, the student is allowed a certain amount of time to play a game in which points are accrued. The points accrued are thus indirectly related to how many correct words are typed in. On the bulletin board the teacher had a display with everyone's scores and a list of students whose turn it was at the computer.

The first student to take a turn is Kelly, a restless boy who is easily distracted. He seems to be especially distracted by my presence and keeps looking to me for approval as he does each word. He wants me to notice the words he spells correctly. The drill requires a lot of concentration, and Kelly starts missing words because he doesn't pay attention to the words when they flash on the screen. He frequently makes the same mistake more than once. Occasionally he asks me for help. I try to give him a hint without interfering with his task. He soon figures out that if he just types in anything, the computer will show him the word again, so he occasionally uses that strategy to see the word again.

Kelly is very gregarious and keeps looking around to see if anyone is noticing him on the computer. His name appears on the screen when he gets a word correct, and he says, 'All right!' or he claps his hands and signals with his thumbs up. Mrs. Todd reminds Kelly not to strike the keys too hard — just to push the keys — since he becomes excited and hits them hard. He uses a one-handed hunt and peck system of typing. Once his turn came to play the game, he was impatient that the game didn't go faster.

The next student is George who needs the teacher and another student to help him get started — it has been quite a while since his last turn. The teacher chooses an easier list for him than the previous list Kelly had typed in. George also uses a one-handed hunt and peck system. He is very quiet on task. He is not distracted by me or the rest of the class. He gets all of his words correct and receives 200 seconds to play the game. A girl is assigned to help him remember the rules of the helicopter game. Kelly makes side comments and observes the computer activity rather then doing his work. George knows how to keep a key down to cause the helicopter to keep moving. He is patient and methodical in his game play. The girl cheers him on. The previous high scorer in the game is also interested in George's progress. George made an excellent score, but commented that the game was boring. I asked him why it was boring, and he told me that he didn't like to spell. However, he wanted Mrs. Todd to post his new score immediately on the bulletin board, which she did.

I chat with Mrs. Todd for a few minutes. She tells me that they have been using the computer since the beginning of the year for three days a week when they are doing individual work. She tries to keep the computer use as evenly distributed as she can with their absences. She had just started Flash Spell three weeks ago. She had not originally chosen it because she didn't want them 'playing games on the computer'. She wanted them to do 'meaningful activity' on the computer. Flash Spell had been her project for the computer class in the fall, and she was very pleased with how it was working out. (Field notes, Longfellow classroom, February 28, 1986)

An example of the computer used for enrichment is cited below from an observation made in a second grade classroom.

I went to observe Mrs. Harrison's second grade class where there were two computers being used. She had one child at each of the two computers, five children doing desk work, and about fifteen children sitting on the floor with her playing 'Doggy, doggy, who has the bone?' The children at the computers were not distracted by the game.

Lisa was working on Master Spell using a one-handed hunt and peck typing system. This program shows a sentence with a missing word and three possible choices for the spelling of the missing word. The answer selection is timed with bars going across the bottom of the screen. If the number of the correct answer is not chosen in time, there is a buzz, and the correct answer is shown. Then the student must type in the word. Lisa was concentrating very hard on the sentences and words. She frequently talked to herself 'oh, I did it wrong... let's see, where's the B', etc. She knew how to back up to correct a mistake. At the end, she was told that she had scored 'in the red'. (Since the monitor was not in color, it was hard to tell whether Lisa attached any significance to being 'in the red'.) When she was done, she knew that she had to somehow reset the computer for the next person, but she wasn't sure how to do it. She asked two other students to help her strike the three-key combination.

Next, Stephanie came to the computer for her turn. She asked the teacher if she had to reset it. The teacher told her that Lisa already reset it for her. Stephanie was very self-assured and got right down to business. Following the directions, Stephanie typed in her name, asked for instructions, read the instructions on the screen and pushed the space when done, according to the directions. When it was time for her to select a drill, the teacher told her to do #1. She had trouble finding the letters at first. She was using one-handed, hunt and peck typing. She talked to herself as she looked for the letters. She pressed the keys carefully. She often did not press the right answer in time, because she was trying to make sure that she had the right answer. She repeatedly had trouble finding the letter U. When she was finished, she asked for help resetting the computer. Again, other students helped her.

At the second computer, a boy named Kevin reset the computer by himself and prepared to use ZeeBug, a game to improve keyboard skills. There was a two-minute timer at the computer. The children were allowed to turn it three times before they must relinquish the computer to the next child. Kevin picked medium difficulty, which turned out to be too hard for him because it was testing special characters on the keyboard. At first he wasn't sure how to play the game and asked me if I knew how to do it. I explained that he had to type in the character before it collided with ZeeBug. He missed a lot of characters that he had trouble finding in time. When the game was over, he did not choose to go back to the easy level. Instead, he chose 'picture show' which allowed him to view pictures that his classmates had made and stored on the computer. Then he chose 'draw' so that he could draw his own picture. He got as far as drawing a square when his time was up. The class started getting ready to go home. He asked me if it was alright if someone else finished his picture. I said it was OK with me if it was OK with his teacher.

Jason came over to finish the picture. Jason kept working even though it was time to go home. The other children cleared their desks, and lined up at the door. Jason continued to work on the picture. Another child came over to the computer to help with the picture, rather than preparing to go home. Finally, Jason realized that he was the last one to leave. The teacher reminded him that his mother would be waiting for him so he reluctantly left the picture he had been working on. Stephan, who had to stay after school, was asked by the teacher to show me another program called Magic Carpet, which is an advanced math drill. Then he was given some other work to do at his seat.

Mrs. Harrison told me that she has just started using the computers with the second graders. She had taken the computer literacy inservice offered at the school, but had not taken the computer course. She did a precomputer workbook with her class that had work sheets about the parts of the computer and the use of the computer to familiarize them with it. Then she let them use a computer in groups with her supervising their activities. Today was the first day that she had two computers in the room to be used by individual students. Almost everyone in the room had a turn. She was very pleased with the results. She felt that they enjoyed the computers and were careful with them. (Field notes, Fairview, classroom, March 3, 1986)

An example of a teacher using the computer as a reward for good behavior and completed work is shown in the excerpt from a fourth grade class in the Fairview computer lab.

Mrs. Washington had them all sit around the tables when they entered. She asked who had finished their social studies, science and math assignments. Those who raised their hands were allowed to use the computers. The rest had to stay at the tables to catch up with their work. One boy said that he had finished, but the teacher reminded him he had math to finish. Another boy was reminded not to go because of a previous problem with another student. Students who had not 'co-operated this morning' were not allowed to use the computers. Half of the class qualified to use the computers.

The computer literacy unit for the middle school math classes was a highly-structured unit that took twelve class periods in the microcomputer lab. It was not as easy to implement as CAI in the classroom because there were many students using many computers at the same time, but it was so well-specified that the teachers knew exactly what to do each period. It had little impact on the classroom, because it was a stand-alone unit, separate from the regular curriculum, that took place in the microcomputer lab. The three excerpts below illustrate different teachers' approaches to the computer literacy unit. The first observation occurred in a sixth grade math class of twenty-one students:

> Mrs. Riesling read the instructions to the students from a lesson guide, and they followed her line by line. She told them that they were going to print out a program today. She instructed them to ... write a five-line program that printed out whatever they wanted to print out. The students proceeded to follow her instructions. Several students helped each other with typing mistakes and syntax errors. One student was reprimanded for finishing too soon and going on to the next step to RUN the program. Another student was told to type shorter lines to keep up with the rest of the class. The class was instructed to LIST their programs and then RUN them to make sure that they worked ... to remove the DOS system disks and trade them for a blank data disk ... to type SAVE and to name their program ... to remove the data disks and wait their turn at the printer. Students were given a simulation game, Survival, to play with on the computer while they waited. After three pairs of students had printed their programs, the period ended. Mrs. Riesling told the rest of the class that they would have a turn to print their programs over the next few days. (Field notes, Longfellow computer lab, February 3, 1986)

Some teachers were confident enough to tailor the lessons to the needs of their students as shown by the observation of a sixth grade learning disabled class excerpted below:

> Mrs. Lee, a learning disabled teacher, was bringing her sixth grade LD students into the computer lab for the sixth day of the twelve-day computer literacy unit. In this class Mrs. Lee had four well-be-haved boys with learning disabilities. Although Mrs. Lee had not had the computer course, she knew the correct terminology and did not hesitate to proceed. The students were eager to use the computers. She started the lesson with a ten-minute keyboard skills practice using the Friendly Computer and MasterType. MasterType was a space invaders-like game in which students had to type in letters or letter combinations to shoot down alien spacecraft or be shot down themselves. The boys seemed to enjoy it and treated it like a video game.

After ten minutes, the teacher started the rest of the lesson. The lesson was built around a White Water Canoe Race — simulation software that involved decision-making. There was a twelve-minute video film showing a real canoe race and the strategy used by the team to win the race.... Then the students were to go through the simulation to make the same decisions. There was a lot of reading involved in following the directions and setting up the supplies. The students were slow in reading and typing their responses. The boys did not necessarily follow the same strategy shown in the movie. One boy was able to get through the entire race by the end of the period. The other three finished half of the race. The teacher wrote down the status of each student so that they could resume the race the next day where they had stopped.

After the boys left, I had a short chat with Mrs. Lee. She mentioned that they were a little slower with the unit than the regular students. It would probably take her longer than twelve days to complete it. She had added the keyboard emphasis at the beginning of the period because she felt that they needed the extra practice. She showed me the rest of the lessons in the unit. (Field notes, Longfellow computer lab, March 10, 1986)

Toward the end of the school year, there was a push to complete the computer literacy unit with all of the students. The observation excerpted below illustrates that point.

The Computer Literacy unit was being taught to fourteen eighth graders who had not yet had it. They were being pulled out of PE, shop and home economics to participate in an extra offering of the unit taught by the in-school restriction teacher. They were on the third day of the unit and the first day the microcomputers are used. As they enter the class, the students ask the teacher if they will be able to use the computers today. Before they use the computers, the teacher uses a work sheet and transparency to explain the parts of the computer. The students fill in the blanks on the work sheet as the teacher names each part. Next she gives a set of instructions for the proper handling of a diskette. She gives them each a diskette and explains how to turn on the computer, one step at a time.

The first software they use is called Apple Presents Apple, a tutorial program to teach about the keyboard, use of menus, use of the shift, arrows, and return key. The students work quietly and purposefully — they all seem to be enjoying the tutorial which has a dozen different activities to choose from, including several games. The students occasionally ask each other for help ('what are we supposed to do?'). The teacher walks around, observes, and gives some helpful hints when needed. For several of the students this is the first time they have ever touched a computer, but they proceed confidently. One boy has a Commodore-128 at home, and he is able to move more quickly through the tutorial than the others.

Most students use a hunt and peck typing method with one hand — there is no evidence of typing skills among this group of students. The students are not distracted by each other, even though they are all working on different parts of the tutorial. As the end of the period approaches, the teacher gives them step-by-step instructions on how to unload and turn off the computer. The teacher was very calm and confident throughout the entire lesson. As the students are gathering up their books, the teacher tells them to save all of their work sheets and study them since they will be tested on them at the end of the twelve-day unit. When the students had left, the teacher told me this is the first time she has taught the computer literacy course, but she has no trouble with it since it is so well-specified. She can follow it, but does not always agree with it. She considers the video movies shown the first two days to be a waste of time. In her opinion, the students want to get on the computers. (Field notes, Longfellow computer lab, May 16, 1986)

The open-ended uses of microcomputers, such as programming, simulations, word processing, and data bases, required more expertise, effort, and risk-taking on the part of the teachers to implement. It was with these open-ended uses that teachers exhibited the highest levels of anxiety in both the labs and the classrooms, since they required extra effort on the part of the teacher to be integrated purposefully into the curriculum, generated the most questions from the students, and caused the most serious classroom management problems.

The excerpts below illustrate how teachers presented programming lessons in both the lab and classroom setting. The first excerpt is from the fourth grade class of Mrs. Washington, one of the key informants who was just learning LOGO in her computer course. The observation below occurred the first day she introduced LOGO programming to her students in the Fairview computer lab:

This was the first class I had observed that would be using LOGO programming. When Mrs. Washington arrived, she was apologetic at first, saying she wished she had known I was going to be there so that she could have prepared a special lesson. I told her that I just wanted to watch the children, not her. She introduced me to the children as the lady who had written the book that they had been using to learn LOGO.

She assigned the children to the eight computers in teams of two and three. Her plan was to have them experiment with color today. One child told me that he had drawn a wonderful zigzag last time by using RIGHT 45 and FORWARD 4000. He asked the teacher if they could do their own pictures today. She said that she would let them take turns typing and drawing. Another child asked if they could change the background color and she said, no, that she hadn't covered that yet.

The children were very excited and noisy — she told them that she would have to shut down the computers if they didn't quiet down. This momentarily subdued them. She commented that they were better in class when she only had one or two computers to deal with. She reminded them of the SETPC (set pen color) command and had them recite the color codes. Most of the children knew the codes by heart. She told them to experiment with the different colors.

One team began by using very large numbers which had the effect of drawing patterns on the screen — the other students noticed this and asked how to do it — soon most were drawing designs using very large numbers with the FORWARD command. Only one team of girls was trying to draw a shape on the screen. The children were very excited about the designs they were creating and turned around to look at each other's. Mrs. Washington flicked the lights, told them to clear their screens, change typists, and to draw on the screen using all of the colors. They were told not to make designs using large numbers. There was a lot of discussion and cooperation among the children about angles, distances, and color codes.

Two boys were not assigned to any team, but went from team to team asking if they needed help. Mrs. Washington explained that they were the class 'experts' who had computers at home. They helped to boot up LOGO on all of the systems. The father of one boy will be bringing in a computer to give a special talk in the near future. They seem bored after a while and act as though they would like to use the computers, too. Again the class is told to quiet down, they are getting too noisy. Two boys on one team have a disagreement about what to type next and fight over the machine. The teacher made them sit back from the machines for one minute and then allowed them to resume.

When several try to make the designs again, using large numbers with FD, she reprimands them for not using all of the colors as she instructed. When they do a shape on the screen with all of the colors, she lets them do what they want during the last few minutes. They all immediately start making the colorful designs again using the large numbers. It is time for them to go, so they all line up. One of the children asks Mrs. Washington if she can get me to autograph the book they are using in class. I agreed to do that the next time I came. (Field notes, Fairview computer lab, March 7, 1986)

An example of a teacher using programming in the classroom with first graders is shown in the excerpt below:

I visited Mrs. Lang's class to watch first graders using the computer.

There was one computer in the room, and the children were taking turns using the Friendly Computer Draw program (a LOGO-like drawing program that uses elementary programming commands). There were eight children at their seats and ten in a reading group with the teacher.

The first child was drawing a picture and knew how to move the dot and place predrawn pictures where he wanted them. The student made the mistake of putting some of his pictures too high, but resigned himself to accept them as they were since the only way to get rid of them was to erase the whole picture. He would give a heavy sigh when he realized that the picture was not exactly where he wanted it. He used two hands, one finger on each hand, and was familiar with both the keyboard and the program he was using. When he was told to stop, he knew how to save and to view his picture.

The next boy that came also knew how to use the program, but he didn't know why the color wasn't working (the computer did not have a color monitor). He asked another student about the color, but did not get a satisfactory answer. So he kept drawing in white, since that worked. The computer would beep at him if he tried to put pictures too close to the edge of the screen. He was not bothered by that — he knew to move the dot over and try again. The teacher heard the beep several times and commented, 'Honey, it doesn't work too close to the edge'. He replied, 'I'm trying to move it'.

He eventually succeeded in getting his sun drawn without a beep. He tried to get color again and still did not succeed. He was talking quietly to himself as he worked with one finger on one hand. He started putting a lot of cars in the picture, and realized he could put them on top of people. He looked at me and said that he was going to make a car run over one of the people. Then he said he was making a rush hour with cars everywhere. At that point he was told to stop, so he saved his picture, viewed it, and signed his name on the list kept beside the computer.

The third child to come was also a boy and was very young looking. He occasionally sucked his thumb while sitting at the computer. He typed in his name, but had some trouble at first finding the keys. He knew how to use the program — he started by framing his picture with a box — then drew a line across the middle of the screen like an horizon. During the first part of his session he worked very purposefully as if he had a plan for his picture in mind. Then his actions became more experimental as if he was trying to decide what to do next. Another student came over to see what he was doing and give him some advice about using the picture command. After placing a few of the predrawn pictures in his picture, he ended the session on his own by saving and viewing his picture.

When the teacher asked whose turn it was, several children said that they hadn't had a turn. When pressed by the teacher, they remembered that they had already drawn their pictures. At this point, it was time for the children to go to PE, so the computer activity ended. Miss Lang told me that she had used the computers on and off all year and that the children always wanted to use them. She had used the computer in her class as a work center, doing math and language drills, keyboard drills, and the draw program. (Field notes, Fairview classroom, May 26, 1986)

An example of a teacher using wordprocessing in the Longfellow computer lab with seventh graders is shown in the excerpt below:

I went to observe the pilot unit on the Bank Street Writer being taught by Miss Lincoln to her two language arts classes. The students had been working on the rough draft of newspaper stories. They were now to type the corrected article into the computer. She told me that she had spent the first week letting the students go through the tutorial program at their own speed. She had spent the second week having them do practice exercises from a workbook. This week they were doing two newspaper articles. Next week they would work on a narrative on the computer. Miss Lincoln described the two classes as being very bright, especially the second one. The students were having trouble with the spacing because the screen image was not the same as the printed image.

Miss Lincoln introduced me as 'the computer expert' and asked me how to solve the spacing problem. I showed the students how to hit return at the end of each paragraph and to use the tab key to indent. The keyboard skills of the class were very good. When I asked Miss Lincoln why she didn't have the students retrieve the previous version of their articles, instead of retyping them, she said that they needed the typing practice. She wasn't sure that the first class could handle doing a retrieval operation from the menu. After they finished typing, the students were told to save this new copy under a different file name and go to the computers with printers where Miss Lincoln was helping them print out the articles. There was a lot of confusion and noise since there are only two printers available. Miss Lincoln promised to print out any articles that were not printed by the end of class.

When the second class arrived, Miss Lincoln had them retrieve their previous articles and edit them, rather than retype them all over again. There was some confusion getting to the correct menu to retrieve and then getting back to the edit mode again. I again helped Miss Lincoln show them how to correct their spacing. They finished more quickly since they didn't have to retype the articles. They saved the articles and were able to print them out before the end of the period. The students helped each other retrieve and print the articles. (Field notes, Longfellow computer lab, May 1, 1986)

The next wordprocessing example occurred in an eighth grade English classroom:

I stopped in to see Mrs. White who was just starting a creative writing project with her eighth grade English class using the Bank Street Writer word processing software. Mrs. White had taken the computer class last year and used the computer with her English classes to do writing and poetry units. As a group the class was involved in writing a short story. During this visit, they were starting to develop their characters and story plot. The names of four characters had been entered into the computer. The class was divided into four groups to develop a plot. There was much lively discussion and socializing going on. The teacher had to reprimand the group a number of times and threaten to end the project if they didn't get to work. After ten minutes of group discussion, each group presented their plot ideas, and the class voted upon the best plot. A member from the group chosen came over to the computer to type in the plot outline.

With some help from me the teacher put the computer into the typing mode, and had the whole class stand around to watch the student type in the text. The girl became so nervous that she said she couldn't type, so someone else volunteered to type. The second girl was also nervous with everyone watching, but was able to type in the information. Several members of the class helped her to make corrections. The girls were more interested in the typing — the boys didn't pay attention or stood at the back of the group.

After some confusion and typing problems, the data was entered. Mrs. White had another girl save the file — the teacher walked her through the menus to perform the save. The period was just about over. The teacher asked a boy to shut down the system, because she was unsure about the proper sequence for doing so. She told me, 'I have a mental block about when to remove the disk — I'm afraid that I'll do it at the wrong time and ruin it.' I told her that as long as the red light on the disk drive was not on, it was OK to remove the disk without harm. (Field notes, Longfellow classroom, March 10, 1986)

A music teacher took her seventh grade general music students to the Longfellow computer lab to teach them how to use a data base of rock and roll music that she had developed as her project for the computer course she had taken. The observation below took place during one of these sessions:

When I came in and introduced myself to the teacher, she said that this was a bad day to observe because it was the first time that she had ever used the computers with her students. I assured her that I was not observing or evaluating her, but only interested in watching the students using the computers. The students were using a data base that the teacher had set up about rock and roll music. She was giving them questions to answer. The students were very enthusiastic, but rowdy. The teacher kept telling them to be quiet. Some of the students were able to answer the questions faster than others — they kept asking what to do next, while the others were asking what they were supposed to be doing. There was much discussion among the students about the answers to the questions.

Some of the students were trying to create a new file of their own, but they did not understand the concept of a field name as opposed to data. They were typing in data for their field names. The students seemed to know how to use the data base program to search and sort the information that was already given. They were mostly typing by one finger hunt and peck, and several were striking the keys very hard. At the end of the class, the teacher let the students remove the data base program and data disks and return them to her. (Field notes, Longfellow computer lab, May 16, 1986)

A second observation of the same teacher with one computer in her classroom was made:

Mrs. Gray had come into the computer lab to take one computer to her music classroom. I went in to observe what she was doing with it. She had told me that this was her worst seventh grade general music class. She had allowed them to go to the lab previously to use a data base on rock and roll stars. This day she was going over the whole file with them. She was trying to explain how to select and sort the data base step by step — one student was doing the typing. There were seventeen students, and it was difficult for them all to see the screen.

There were constant behavior problems. Some of them wrote on the blackboard, played at the piano, poked each other and teased each other. The teacher kept telling them to be quiet and pay attention, but they ignored her. She continued to try to explain the concept of a data base — the students tuned in and out, listening some of the time and ignoring her most of the time. Every now and then a student would notice something of interest in the file and comment on it. When the bell rang, the students ran out of the room.

After the students left I spoke to Mrs. Gray about the students. She told me that they had been more interested in the computer unit than in anything else she had done with them. The worst behavior problem in the class was the girl doing the typing. She was planning to develop several more units next year using the data base with work sheets. (Field notes, Longfellow classroom, May 19, 1986)

Another example of a teacher using a data base with students was found in a third grade classroom at Fairview:

I visited Mrs. Green's third grade class to see how they were using the computer. Mrs. Green had taken the computer class last year and was completing a unit on the fifty states. She was using the Infor-master software to build a data base with seven fields of information about each of the fifty states. The students had been assigned different states to research. They made illustrated notebooks about their states, and a few of them were giving oral reports each day about their states. The teacher was bringing one computer into the class each day to enter the data for about eight states per day into the data base.

Two girls were entering data about a state when I came into the room. One student was reading the data for a state while another typed it in. Before they saved the record, they checked the spelling and words carefully. The students knew how to correct a field of information if it was wrong. One of the two girls was in charge of entering the data into the data base. The other one was typing in the data for her state. When she was finished, the girl in charge called for the student with the next state to be entered. Several more students came up to enter the data for their state.

The teacher came over periodically to make sure they were checking their data carefully. The students doing the typing used a one-hand hunt and peck system. The girl in charge showed them how to answer the questions asked by the data base software and to hit the return key after each piece of information. Each student had to enter seven pieces of information about a state. There was a reference book beside the computer, and the children were told to verify all of their information before saving it on the data file. There was also a master list of all the states beside the computer so that the students will know who is next.

One girl did not know the date of origination for her state, and the teacher told her to look it up in the encyclopedia before coming to use the computer. The typing went very slowly, but the children seemed to derive satisfaction from seeing their data entered into the computer. There was much discussion between the children at the computer about how to enter the data and to verify the correctness of the data. They helped each other find the right keys and check the spelling. When the students are done, they will have a class data base on all fifty states which the teacher will print out and copy for each student to keep.

The overall classroom environment was very relaxed with several different activities going on at once. I chatted briefly with the teacher to compliment her on the data base unit. She stated that it was very time-consuming, but she felt it was worth it to have them use the computer as part of the unit. I left when the teacher told them to turn off the computer to listen to some more oral reports about the states. (Field notes, Fairview classroom, May 22, 1986)

Individual Concerns and Implementation

Even more important than the institutional structure and the innovation characteristics, the individual stakeholder has proven to be the key factor in implementation in previous studies (House, 1974; Berman and McLaughlin, 1976, 1978; Bass, 1978; Hall, 1981). Implementation of an innovation leading to institutionalization cannot take place unless the stakeholders involved are willing and able to change. Since the classroom teacher is the prime implementor of an educational innovation (McLaughlin and Berman, 1978), the reactions of teachers to microcomputers for instruction have proven to be especially important in their implementation (McNeil, 1983; Meister, 1984).

In general the interview and observation data revealed positive attitudes on the part of individuals at all levels of the school district toward the innovation of microcomputers for instruction, even though there were many concerns on the part of everyone involved in the implementation. Central office staff were concerned with the overall coordination, allocation of sufficient resources, and proceeding cautiously in order not to make any serious mistakes. Principals were concerned that all students had access to computers during the year. Teachers exhibited a high level of personal concern related to the complex, technical nature of the microcomputers, lack of time, and fears about their own inadequacies in coping with computers.

The SoCQ data were used in this study as an indicator of the level and stages of concern that administrators and teachers were feeling as they encountered the innovation of using computers for instruction. The seven stages of concern (numbered from 0 to 6) identified by Hall, George, and Rutherford (1979) were:

level	description
0) awareness	initial contact with an innovation with little concern or involvement with the innovation
1) informational	general awareness and desire to learn about the innovation
2) personal	individual begins to worry about the impact and demands that the innovation will make upon his/her situation and about personal inadequacy in dealing with the innovation

3) management   attention is on the process and tasks involved in using the innovation in own environment

4) consequence   attention is on the impact of the innovation on the learning environment

5) collaboration   attention is on coordination and cooperation with others

6) refocusing   attention is on exploring additional benefits and uses of the innovation as well as refinement of current use to increase effectiveness of the innovation.

The first three levels of concern were described by Martin and Heller as *self-directed*, in that they dealt with the effect of the innovation upon self. The next two levels of concern were *task-directed*, in that they dealt with the innovation as it related to a particular environment. The last two levels of concern were *impact-directed*, in that they dealt with the impact of the innovation across a set of environments, such as a school district (Martin and Heller, 1985). Individuals involved with an innovation will go through progressive stages of concern, and the stages of concern should be taken into account during the implementation process. However, the most important implication of the stages of concern of an innovation was that:

> Higher levels of concern cannot be engineered by an outside agent. Holding concerns and changing concerns is a dynamic of the individual ... there is no guarantee that arousal of higher stage concerns will follow the reduction of lower stage concerns. Providing inputs that are not stage relevant (e.g., attempting to force high level concerns) is an assured way to increase the intensity of lower stage concerns. Whether and with what speed higher level concerns develop will depend upon the person as well as the innovation and the environment context. (Hall, George and Rutherford, 1979, p. 6)

The SoCQ had been administered at the beginning and/or end of the graduate computer course taken by many of the teachers and some administrators in the school district. The individual profiles were averaged together to form the composite profiles for each group tested at the beginning of the course and for each group tested at the end of the course. There was a significant similarity among the composite profiles shown in Figures 5.6 and 5.7. The composite profiles all resembled the nonuser profile shown in Figure 5.8 and described by Hall, George and Rutherford as someone whose personal concerns about the innovation outweighed their concerns about implementing the innovation into their environment.

In all of the research that has been done to date using the SoCQ, 'the *nonuser* concerns profile stands out most clearly and consistently. Nonusers' concerns are normally highest on Stages 0, 1, and 2 and lowest on Stages 4, 5, and 6. There is some variation in the amount of intensity of these concerns ...

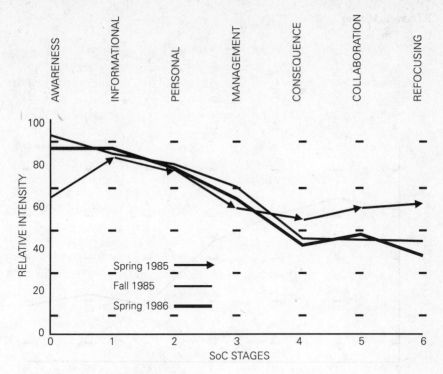

Figure 5.6: SoCQ composite pretests.

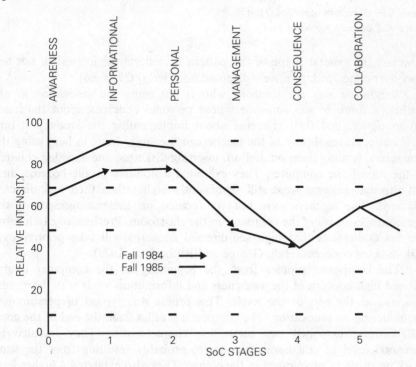

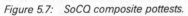

Figure 5.7: SoCQ composite pottests.

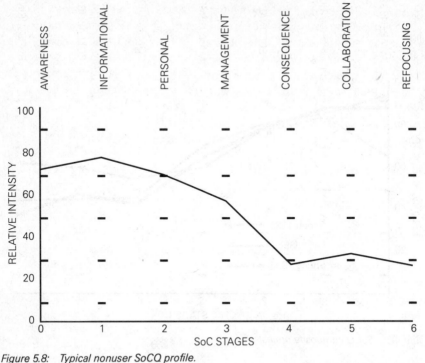

Figure 5.8: Typical nonuser SoCQ profile.
Source: Hall, George & Rutherford, 1979, p. 37

however, the general shape of the pattern ... reflects the interested, not terribly over-concerned, positively disposed nonuser' (1979, p. 36).

A nonuser was *not* someone who is not using the innovation at all. Rather, a nonuser was someone whose personal concerns about the innovation outweighed their concerns about implementing the innovation into their environment. Many of the teachers in the study were, in fact, using the computers, turning them on and off, inserting diskettes, and assisting children in the use of the computer. They exhibited a nonuser profile because their self-directed concerns were still significantly higher then their task-directed concerns. The teachers were not yet focused on the management or the consequences of using the computer in the classroom. Previous research using the SoCQ suggests that high self-directed concerns will take priority over task-directed concerns (Hall, George and Rutherford, 1979).

The composite profiles from the beginning of the computer course showed high concern at the awareness and information levels with decreasing concerns at the rest of the levels. This profile was typical of persons just encountering an innovation. The composite profiles from the end of the computer course exhibited two interesting characteristics. They revealed an increased level of collaborative concern, probably resulting from the team work on projects encouraged in the course. They also exhibited a higher level of personal concern than at the beginning of the course, reflecting the complex nature of the computer as an innovation. As the participants learned more about the computers, they became more anxious about them. These profiles were significant because they were indicators of the level and stages of concern felt by teachers and administrators throughout the district during the implementation stage of the innovation of microcomputers for instruction.

Teacher participation in the implementation process
If change is to take place in an educational setting, several previous studies have cited the importance of teacher participation in all stages of the implementation process (Berman and McLaughlin, 1976, 1978, 1979; Hall, 1981), and this has been especially true of the innovation of microcomputers (McNeil, 1983; Meister, 1984; Mojkowski, 1984; Moskowitz and Birman, 1985; Zuk and Stilwell, 1984). The data were examined for evidence of teacher participation in the implementation process.

At the district level, four teachers were included on the Computer Advisory Committee established in 1981 to develop a plan for bringing microcomputers into the schools for instruction. Their group was comprised of two business education teachers, a high school math teacher and a teacher of gifted and talented, and they helped to shape Phase I of the implementation plan to put computers into the high schools and then into the middle schools. During the 1983-84 school year, the Media Specialist met with teachers and parents of the elementary schools to gather their ideas and feelings about putting computers in the elementary schools. Both the Fairview and Crestwood principals credited their teachers with developing the proposals that caused their schools to be selected as pilot schools out of eighteen schools. 'The teachers were very enthusiastic about receiving the computers. It was at their urging and with their help that the proposal was put together and submitted to the central office' (structured interview, Crestwood Elementary, Jan. 24, 1986).

Another way that teachers participated in the implementation of an innovation was through the generation of locally-produced materials, a strategy cited by Berman and McLaughlin as one of the effective ways to achieve mutual adaptation of an innovation (1978). Once the computers were put into the schools during the 1984–85 school year, teachers were used to develop the necessary curriculum to effectively utilize the computers. During the summer of 1984 eight middle school teachers were hired to develop the computer literacy unit to be used in all math classes in the middle schools. The computer literacy unit was piloted in one school during 1984–85 and taught in all of the middle schools the following year. Similarly, a group of five elementary teachers worked with the Media Specialist during the summer of 1985 to examine all of the MECC software and correlate it with the learning objectives for each grade level, producing an Elementary Computer Software Curriculum Correlation Guide. This was distributed to all of the elementary teachers in the pilot schools during 1985–86 and would be made available to all teachers the following year. The teachers were credited in the front of each publication so that other teachers would know that the publications were produced by teachers.

There was evidence that a small cadre of 'teacher computer experts' was developing in the school district. These were teachers who had taken the computer course, were highly motivated to use the computers, and were gradually learning enough about computers to answer questions from other teachers. The Media Specialist indicated that he planned to use some of these teachers to develop and give short inservice training courses on specific topics, such as word-processing or data bases, in the schools.

Provision for staff development and follow-up support
Staff development and follow-up support were found to be general prerequisites for successful implementation of most educational innovations (Berman and McLaughlin, 1977, 1978; Berman, McLaughlin and Marsh, 1978; Fullan and Pomfret, 1977). In addition, Berman and McLaughlin cited the importance of principals as well as teachers receiving training for the innovation (1979). The data revealed that staff development for the microcomputers for instruction was an ongoing commitment in the district.

The first staff development course taught was a three-credit graduate course provided by a local university and paid for by the district for principals and other administrators during the 1983–84 school year. During the 1984–85 school year the Media Specialist ran short inservice training courses for the entire staff of each school receiving microcomputers that year. In addition, another three-credit graduate course, Utilizing Computers in the Classroom, was developed for elementary and middle school teachers. It was taught by a local university and paid for by the school district. Two sections with twenty-five to thirty participants each were offered during the spring and fall semesters of the 1984–86 school years. By June, 1986, approximately twenty administrators and 200 out of the 600 targeted teachers had completed the course. During the 1986–87 school year, additional sections of the course and a follow-on graduate computer course were planned. The Media Specialist indicated that he was also planning to develop and provide additional short inservice courses on keyboarding skills, word-processing, and data base use in the classroom.

There was also evidence that the presence of a district level microcomputer coordinator was a strongly positive factor during the implementation (*Microcomputers in the Schools*, 1983) since he was referred to in many of the interviews with administrators and teachers. He was considered the key referrent for follow-up technical support by teachers who would call him whenever they had problems with the hardware and software.

Collaboration among teachers
Implementation will not succeed where there is low morale or a feeling of isolation on the part of staff at all levels (Berman and McLaughlin, 1979). This is

particularly true of teachers using an innovation such as microcomputers (Rogers, 1985). There was evidence of some collaboration among teachers, both formally and informally. For the 220 participants, most of whom were teachers, in the graduate computer course during the 1984–86 school years, there was a formal mechanism for them to work together to learn about computers and to develop computer units for their classes. The data revealed that many of the teachers using the computers with their students were presenting the units that they had developed in teams during the course. Examples were:

a) the rock and roll data base unit used by a seventh grade music teacher;
b) the states data base unit used by a fourth grade teacher;
c) the Flash Spell unit used by a remedial reading teacher;
d) the drawing unit used by a kindergarten teacher;
e) the room arrangement unit used by a home economics teacher;
f) the creative writing unit used by an eighth grade English teacher; and
g) the introduction to computing unit used by a first grade teacher.

The composite SoCQ concerns profiles for the participants of the graduate course showed a rise in the collaboration concern among those tested at the end of the course. This indicated that collaboration had become a greater concern for them.

There was also evidence of some informal collaboration between teachers. While sitting in the computer lab at Fairview, the researcher observed the teachers discussing their lessons and problems with each other as they returned the computers to the lab at the end of the day. There was one instance in the data of a teacher presenting a computer lesson to the students of another teacher. The field notes indicated that the librarians in the elementary schools collaborated with the teachers to coordinate computer units relating to library and creative writing work. There was more collaboration among the elementary school teachers than among the middle school teachers. The middle school teachers consulted with each other regarding the computer literacy unit, but there was no other indication of collaboration among them from the data.

Incentives to innovate
Incentives have been called key factors in encouraging the implementation of microcomputer-based instruction (Winkler, Stasz, and Shavelson, 1986). Suggested incentives for teachers were merit pay (Shavelson *et al.*, 1984), release time (OTA, 1982), new job titles, reimbursement for outside courses, lending computers to teachers over holidays or summers, and subsidizing teachers to develop curriculum or courseware (OTA, 1982). Release time and lack of coercion were found to be the strongest incentives for acceptance of an innovation (Berman and McLaughlin, 1977). The most frequent incentives to use microcomputers were recognition from peers and availability of computers

after receiving training (Winkler, Stasz, and Shavelson, 1986). The incentives that were found in the data included:

a) the availability of a graduate course paid for by the school district which would enable teachers to receive graduate credit toward a higher degree or recertification,

b) voluntary use of the computers for most teachers, except the middle school math teachers (it was one of the middle school math teachers who did not like computers and did not feel comfortable with them),

c) the promise that all schools would have computers by the following year,

d) the use of teachers to develop the software guide and the computer literacy unit, and

e) recognition from peers as seen in the graduate course for computers and found in conversations with teachers who would mention other teachers considered to be especially knowledgeable about the computers.

Teacher concerns were recognized and addressed by central office and school administrators who provided ongoing staff development opportunities, encouraged teacher participation in the decision-making process, sought teacher participation in the development of materials, allowed voluntary implementation during the pilot year, and began building a technical support system. The opportunity for teachers to collaborate with each other to develop computer units during teacher training, and the availability of microcomputers after training were seen as incentives for teachers to implement the innovation in their classrooms. These strategies facilitated the implementation process during the first year and indicated an openness on the part of most administrators toward the attitudes and concerns of the teachers. The strong support for the microcomputers from the district administrators and principals created a favorable climate for implementation.

Examining Major Themes

From the data gathered from the six sources, several conflicting major themes emerged: resistance to innovation, strong grassroots support for microcomputers, fear of microcomputers, high motivation to use microcomputers, the influence of early adopter school districts, and the importance of the individual stakeholder in the implementation process.

Resistance to innovation

Resistance to innovation was evidenced at all levels of the school district. The Assistant Superintendent for Instruction was highly suspicious of educational innovation in general as he commented, 'I have had a lot of reservations about using computers in schools. I did not consider them to be the solution to all educational problems. I view the computer as a tool to save time and labor if used properly. I remember what ETV, the overhead projector and 16 mm film were supposed to do for education!' (structured interview, May 5, 1986).

As a result of reservations felt by him and others, the implementation process proceeded cautiously. Other central office staff wanted to wait for the technology 'to settle down' before jumping in too soon. For example, the Director of Vocational Education stated that they should have waited one more year before putting the microcomputers in the other three high schools. 'There were a lot of frustrations with computers during the pilot year. It takes two years for the dust to settle. Some high school teachers loved the Radio Shacks and some hated them' (structured interview, April 14, 1986). The implementation of the Apple IIe microcomputers in the eighteen other elementary schools after the pilot schools was delayed a year and rescheduled for the two-year period 1986–1988, rather than taking place during the 1985–86 school year as was originally planned.

Several supervisors expressed reservations about turning the innovation loose with teachers without the proper curriculum in place. There was the concern that teachers might use computers in an educationally inappropriate way. One supervisor was concerned that teachers would use computers to teach material beyond their grade level, thus disturbing the curriculum content for following years.

In the middle school many teachers were able to resist the innovation of microcomputers since they were not required to use them in their subject areas. Some teachers were required to use the computers, and others did so voluntarily. However, the majority of middle school teachers did not attempt to use the microcomputers in their classrooms.

In the elementary schools, however, there was strong pressure from the principals for all teachers to use the microcomputers with their students at some time during the year. At the time of the observations, most of the teachers in the two elementary schools had either used the microcomputers or were in the process of doing so. Here, resistance to innovation was in a more subtle form. In most cases, the primary teachers (grades K, 1, 2, and 3) used one or two microcomputers as an activity center in their classroom along with numerous activity centers. The upper grade teachers (grades 4, 5, and 6) most frequently used the one or two microcomputers in the classroom as an enrichment or remediation activity separate from the regular classroom work. In both cases, the teachers were simply using the microcomputer as an extension of what they were already doing in the classroom, rather than using the microcomputer as a true innovation. Only a few middle school and elementary teachers took their students to the computer lab to try wordprocessing, data bases or programming. These three activities required a change in the way the classroom was managed and a change in the way regular subjects were taught — for example, using wordprocessing as a writing tool or using a data base to organize social studies data.

Strong grassroots support for microcomputers

Throughout the data was evidence that the momentum for implementing microcomputers in the school district began as a grassroots movement. Parents pressured the School Board, the principals and the teachers through the parent-teacher organizations to get computers into the schools. As a suburban school district bordering on a high-tech metropolitan area, parental concern was expressed that their children were being left behind. Several computer enthusiasts who were teachers also pressured the principals and central office staff, and one teacher even brought his own computer into school for students to use. There were parents, central office staff, principals and teachers who felt that if the school district delayed the use of microcomputers any longer, the technology would advance beyond them.

According to one principal, once the microcomputers were in the schools, parents then lost interest in the issue. As long as they could see the microcomputers when they walked through the schools and they heard from their children that they were using the microcomputers, parents were not concerned about how the computers were being used. The visibility and use of the microcomputers satisfied parental concern, and the complex, technical nature of microcomputers acted as a barrier for their further involvement with microcomputers.

Parents occasionally still complained if they thought their child was not getting to use the microcomputers enough, according to the Assistant Superintendent for Instruction. The words of the Director of Vocational Education affirmed a broad base of support for microcomputers in instruction:

> Never in the 25 years that I have been in education have I seen everyone, including the principals, parents through the PTA's and PTO's, and the School Board, agreed upon the need for a quarter million dollar expenditure as in the case of buying the [micro] computer equipment for the schools (structured interview, April 14, 1986).

Fear of the microcomputer

The microcomputer has been described as the most anxiety-producing innovation among teachers that has been studied in the past two decades (Quinsatt, 1981; McNeil, 1983; Meister, 1984). Because the microcomputer is expensive, it is also an anxiety-producing innovation for administrators who are afraid of making the wrong decisions in selecting hardware, software, and strategies for implementation. The Assistant Superintendent for Instruction expressed fears about rapidly changing technology that would make equipment purchases obsolete. He was also afraid of making serious educational mistakes by moving too fast with microcomputers.

Teachers were afraid of the complex, technical nature of the microcomputer. They were afraid of not being able to use the software and of not being able to understand how computers work. They were afraid that their students would know more than they did about computers. They were intimidated by how expensive the computers were and were afraid that they or their students would damage them. One teacher was afraid to put a diskette in the computer or take it out for fear of ruining the diskette. She always had one of her students do it for her. Another teacher stated that the inservice course on computers was the most frightening course she had ever taken. She eventually completed the course with flying colors and became a computer enthusiast afterward, but during the course she was often on the verge of tears. Many teachers echoed the same fears about using the microcomputers for the first time.

High motivation to use microcomputers

The high motivation expressed by many to use the microcomputers was contrasted to the fears expressed by many staff members and teachers in the school district. In some cases this high motivation was expressed by those who had initially had strong fears about microcomputers, and in all cases the teachers' motivation was related to the motivation that the computers instilled in their students. Teacher comments about motivation to use microcomputers follow:

'I think the computer is a great incentive for students — they work harder to get a turn at the computer.' (remedial reading teacher)

'The children love the computer and never get tired of using it or of doing the same software over again.' (learning disabled teacher)

'It is a good experience for the students. The kids enjoy the computer and (wordprocessing) seems like real work to (the teacher), not a computer game. The students have a real satisfaction seeing their work printed out.' (language arts teacher)

'I like using the computers with these students since they are more interested in this unit than any other method I have tried.' (music teacher)

'I am very pleased with the results. The children enjoy the computers and are very careful with them.' (second grade teacher)

'The children are excited about having the computers in the room and are always eager to have their turn.' (first grade teacher)

'I am especially excited about using computers to do wordprocessing with LD (learning disabled) students since they can see and correct their spelling mistakes more readily on the screen. They get so much satisfaction from printing out their work.' (LD teacher)

In most cases the students were attentive and purposeful when working at the computer and were not distracted by activity in the room around them. Most students displayed confidence when using the computers. Typical students comments were:

'This is so excellent!'
'Right on!'
'I got it right!'
'It's my turn now.'
'Do we get to use the computers today?'

Common characteristics of the key informants

In examining the motivation of teachers to use the microcomputers, the question arose as to whether there are common characteristics that could be identified among teachers who seemed especially enthusiastic about computers. The three key informants were teachers who expressed great enthusiasm for the computers. Mrs. Burton, the Longfellow home economics teacher, said,

> 'I think that computers are the best thing to happen to add spice to the classroom … everything I do is computerized now. I'm a real computer nut!'

Mrs. Johnson, the Chapter I teacher at Crestwood, said,

> 'I generate all of my classroom materials on my home computer. I feel that the schools owe it to each child to give them the opportunity to use computers.'

Mrs. Washington, the fourth grade teacher at Fairveiw stated,

> 'The computer course makes me more nervous and uptight than any other course I have ever taken, but I am now 'hooked' on computers. I hope to do all of my own reports and writing on them now, as well as to use them with students.'

The data revealed that there were a number of common characteristics shared by the three of them. All three of them had taken or were taking a computer course by their own choice. They were all in schools where computers were available for their use, and two of them had a computer at home. All of them used the computer to help them do their own work as a teacher. The home economics teacher from Longfellow used her home computer to do all of her lesson plans, class handouts, class schedules and instructions hanging on the wall of the classroom. In addition she had used the poster-making software to make several posters for her classroom and had designed several lessons to be done on the computer. The Chapter I teacher from Crestwood used her home computer to create lessons, handouts, and posters for her students and kept her records on the computer. The fourth grade teacher from Fairview had used LOGO to make posters to decorate her classroom and had done many of her lessons on the computer as well.

All three of the key informants were not afraid to try innovative approaches with the computer that went beyond the prescribed study guides they had received from the school district. The home economics teachers was trying out units she had developed when she took the computer course and was also trying out some new home economics software and providing her reactions to the software developer. The Chapter I teacher had to adjust the grade level of most of the software to meet the special needs of her students. She also ordered additional software out of her Chapter I funds and brought back some 'shareware' from a state computer conference to try. The fourth grade teacher was teaching her students LOGO and wordprocessing at the same time that she was learning it herself in her computer course. All three of them were not afraid to admit to their students that they were learning how to use the software along with the students. All three of them relied on the expertise of some of their students who knew how to use computers to help boot the system and assist other students. Finally, all of them had the very strong conviction that all of their students should have the opportunity to use computers. This was especially true of the Chapter I teacher who felt that frequent use of computers might eventually help her students achieve some academic parity with the other students in the school.

Influence of early adopter school districts

One of the issues of interest when studying the implementation of an innovation by a majority adopter was whether there was evidence of influence from the experiences of innovators and early adopters (Hall, 1981; Rogers, 1983). Referring to the early adopters, the Assistant Superintendent for Instruction stated, 'I did not want to jump on a band wagon as many other school districts have done.' He noted that some school systems that jumped onto the computer band wagon were starting to pare down their computer expenditures. His question was always, 'What was being eliminated in order to have time for computers? I had to see a justification for the tradeoff' (structured interview, May 5, 1986).

The Computer Advisory Committee examined at least seven early adopter school districts before presenting its first recommendations to the School Board in August, 1982. The report stated, 'Fortunately, [this area] provides many opportunities for learning how computers have been and are currently being utilized in a school environment. Several school districts have been involved with instructional ... computer usage for over a decade.'

They made site visits, carried out telephone interviews, and read case studies in the literature to avoid the mistakes made by the early adopters. By reading the literature, they learned the value of approving one computer brand to be used in the district schools to insure compatibility among the schools. Many of the innovator and early adopter school districts had allowed individual schools to buy different computers, resulting in a chaotic proliferation of many brands and software packages. It became difficult for those districts to develop a standard computer curriculum. From one neighboring school district they saw the mistake of getting a 'good deal' on the wrong hardware. From another school district, they saw the value of intensive, computer-assisted instruction used to increase basic skills.

As a result of the experiences of another school district, the committee recommended against emphasizing programming in the middle and elementary schools as had been done by many innovator school districts. They also recommended against teaching the computer as a separate subject, except at the high school level, but rather to take the approach that had evolved over the previous five years to integrate the computer as a tool and a learning enhancer in other subjects. They were told that there was good software and bad software, and that a software review committee was essential to evaluate and to organize the software by grade level. From all the successful school districts came the model of a district computer coordinator needed to coordinate the computer acquisition, training and software distribution. However, the most important lesson learned from the literature about the early adopters was to establish educational goals first, then choose the software and hardware, and institute curriculum modification and teacher training while the equipment is being installed. The Assistant Superintendent of Instruction stated that he was a firm believer in curriculum first, then equipment and inservice training at the same time.

The central office staff realized from the beginning that the implementation process was multifaceted, involving curriculum changes, staff training, selection and preparation of secure facilities, equipment purchases, software distribution, and finally equipment maintenance. So they proceeded slowly, implementing the plan in stages from the high schools to the middle schools to the elementary schools.

The implementation process began in fall, 1985 and was planned to be carried out through the spring, 1988. The Assistant Superintendent for Instruction said, 'By taking our time, we hoped not to repeat the mistakes others had made. We read the literature, watched the computer market, and proceeded with great caution' (structured interview, May 5, 1986).

Importance of the individual in the implementation process
Implementation of an innovation is typically mandated from the top down and instituted from the bottom up. The individual stakeholders at all levels in the process have significant influence on the final outcome. In this study the stated attitudes and concerns of the administrators, teachers, and students were examined to determine their impact on the overall process.

The attitudes of most administrators interviewed were strongly positive toward the microcomputers, and they viewed computers as a necessary addition to the curriculum of the school district. When asked if she was in favor of acquiring the microcomputers, the Supervisor for Vocational and Special Education stated, 'Absolutely! I'm a pusher. I work hard to motivate my teachers. Some say I push too hard, but I'm twisting arms to get them all to use the computers' (structured interview, April 7, 1986). She also stated that the feedback from her teachers was positive and that she was expecting an increased enrollment as a result of using computers in the home economics curriculum. This positive response was echoed by other central office staff members.

The principals of the three schools expressed positive attitudes about having computers in their schools. The principal of Longfellow stated that he had been pushing for computers at principals' meetings for the past five years. He used computers to do his own work, and he was very 'enthusiastic' about the computers 'finally' arriving for instruction. He was personally training his secretarial staff to use the administrative computer in the office, as well as encouraging teachers to develop computer units to use in their disciplines. The principal of Fairview was 'delighted' to have the computers in her school. She was especially proud of the teachers for using the computers to produce their entire Self Study Report (required every five years for state accreditation). She felt that this experience had brought the staff closer together and made everyone more comfortable with the computers. The parents of her school were also enthusiastic about the computers and several served as computer aides. The principal of Crestwood stated that he was 'pleased' his school had been chosen to be a pilot school and credited the teachers' enthusiasm over computers as the impetus for acquiring them.

Similarly, most teachers interviewed expressed strongly positive attitudes toward the computers. Many of their attitudes were based upon their students' reactions to the computers. Two teachers admitted that they were using the computers with their students because they were required to, but that they did not personally like computers that much. All of the students observed showed enthusiasm for using the computers, except for one sixth grade remedial reading student who stated that he was bored because he hated doing spelling drills and the computer game was too slow.

Many concerns about microcomputers in instruction were expressed during the interviews and observations. The following concerns were expressed by the central office staff: insuring an equitable distribution of computer time among all students, the cost of obsolescence and maintenance of computers, having the microcomputers drive the curriculum, rather than vice versa, complexity of the overall coordination of a technological innovation, ongoing teacher training that would be needed, having sufficient staff for technical support, and having sufficient software and hardware to support the demand.

Within the schools the principals also expressed concerns about the microcomputers. Their concerns were related to: keyboarding skills — at what level and how much emphasis (Crestwood, Longfellow); increasing parental involvement (Crestwood and Fairview); all teachers and children being comfortable using the computers (Fairview); the appropriate age for children to use computers (Crestwood); acquiring more microcomputers (Fairview); maximum utilization of microcomputers (Crestwood); and evaluating the use of microcomputers (Fairview).

The librarians at each school were primarily concerned about recording the use of the software and hardware since they were responsible for maintaining circulation records. At one school the librarian was concerned about teachers using the software without properly checking it out, thereby making her circulation records for the state inaccurate.

As the primary users of computers with the children, the teachers expressed many concerns about the microcomputers. Most of the teachers interviewed had at least one concern, which was predominantly related to time, software or classroom management. The stated concerns found in the field notes were:

a) time-related concerns such as insufficient time to prepare lessons and handouts for the computer usage (7), insufficient time for each child to have a turn (5), completion of the required material in the computer literacy unit within the specified amount of time (3), and insufficient time to complete required objectives and to use the computer (1);

b) software-related concerns such as uncertainty about how to use some of the software (8), not enough appropriate software (5), inadequate documentation with some of the software (3), and not enough copies of the software for each student (3);

c) classroom management-related concerns such as maintaining discipline while in the computer lab (6), noise level of students in the computer lab (5), answering students' questions while in the computer lab (5), damage to the hardware or software by students (4), and matching the right software with the right students (4);

d) other concerns such as anxiety about being observed (5), keyboarding skills of the students (3), anxieties about the inservice computer course (3), and technical questions about the hardware (2).

The students also voiced or exhibited some concerns about the computers such as getting the correct answers (14), knowing how to use the software (10), finding the right key on the keyboard (6), finishing their task on the computer (5), getting their turn on the computer (5), making mistakes (2), and getting the highest score on a game (2).

Implementation Leading to Long-Term Institutionalization

An important question to be addressed by this study was whether the implementation would lead to long-term institutionalization of the innovation of microcomputers for instruction by the school district. If implementation is viewed as an adaptive process positioned in the center of a three-way interaction between institutional characteristics, innovation characteristics and individual concerns shown in Figure 5.9, all three factors must be working together to produce institutionalization.

It was concluded from the data that the school district exhibited the

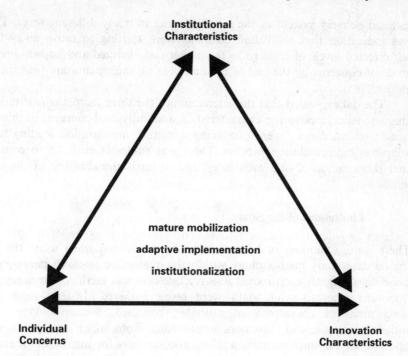

Figure 5.9:   *Context for implementation*

adaptivity to innovate described by Berman and McLaughlin as developmental (1979), in that there was evidence of lower levels of decision-making, shared responsibility, encouragement of risk-taking, sense of professionalism, high staff morale, and the presence of long-range planning (Bozeman, 1984). There was a stated commitment to continue the equipment purchases, staffing, teacher training, curriculum development and teacher participation called for by a revised implementation plan. These were the institutional characteristics that have contributed to adaptive implementation leading to institutionalization of innovations in past studies. Similarly, the innovation of microcomputers for instruction had clear goals and active principal support, was demanding and highly visible, and required specific, ongoing training. These were the innovation characteristics that have contributed to adaptive implementation leading to institutionalization of innovations in past studies.

Although the teacher concerns data revealed a high level of personal anxiety, the profiles exhibited the characteristics of positively-disposed computer users, open to becoming more active users of microcomputers for instruction. There was evidence of increasing risk-taking and experimentation on the part of teachers using the microcomputers as the first year of implementation progressed. All of the individuals interviewed stated future plans and goals for continued use of the innovation and expressed the opinion that the computers were going to become an integral part of the educational delivery system of the school district in many different ways. There was indication that individual concerns were starting to move away from self-directed levels of concern to the higher task-directed and impact-directed levels of concerns by the end of the first year of implementation (Martin and Heller, 1985).

The data revealed that the interaction of the three factors of institutional characteristics, innovation characteristics, and individual concerns of this particular school district were producing a mature mobilization leading to an adaptive implementation process. There was sufficient evidence to conclude that these factors would eventually lead to institutionalization of the innovation.

Limitations of the Study

There were a number of limitations to be considered when using the field-based case study methodology within the qualitative research paradigm. A pre-defined, tightly constructed research question was sacrificed since research questions emerged while data were being gathered. Instead there were descriptions of characteristics, attitudes, concerns, decison-making, institutional changes, and classroom interactions, from which emerged a sense about what the implementation of microcomputers for instruction meant to the school district in the study. What was sacrificed in statistical elegance was hopefully gained in insight.

The problems of external validity and reliability had to be considered before an attempt could be made to generalize from this case study. What assurance was there that the implementation of microcomputers in the school district in the study was representative of the experience of other school districts? Past research in this area (Kennedy, 1979) had shown that generalization was possible from case to case, rather than across the population, with a case study. If the characteristics of the school district being studied and its implementation process were described with great enough care, then the results could be used on a case by case basis by decision-makers in other school districts similar to the school district in the study. The power of this type of ethnographic, case study research was that the data were thick enough to be relevant to similar cases, even if they could not be generalized across the population.

A different type of generalization, the naturalistic generalization, would emerge as a result of accumulated experience. Such naturalistic generalizations would provide a way of 'knowing how things are' to guide future action in similar cases (Stake, 1978). This problem was specifically addressed by Bass in the case studies describing the implementation of alternative schools in four school districts:

> In understanding this study of alternatives, we were primarily concerned with accurately describing the implementation process in a

few districts. We felt that, by providing a qualitative sense of the factors that are important in [implementation], these case studies could help educational policy makers interested in developing educational options in other settings and suggest hypothesis for future research. (Bass, 1978, p. 17)

Another problem frequently encountered with ethnographic research involving naturalistic observation was that of the insider/outsider relationship between the researcher and the subjects studied (Merton, 1972). In this study a balance had to be maintained by the researcher between her role as an 'outside expert' and her role as an insider accepted into the school district to do observations in the classrooms. The researcher was perceived to be both an outsider and an insider — an outsider due to the researcher's position as a member of the Computer Science faculty at a local university and an insider due to the researcher's involvement in teacher education courses in the school district over a period of 18 months prior to the research. Therefore, many of the teachers and administrators already knew the researcher or had heard about the researcher prior to her presence in the schools. This enabled the researcher to be accepted into the classroom settings without being seen as a threat by the teachers. It was the researcher's responsibility to maintain her perspective as an outsider when collecting and analyzing the field data.

In addition to the insider/outsider issue, there was also the balance to be maintained between rapport/overrapport with observed subjects. A good rapport with observed subjects was necessary to insure continued access to sites; however, the researcher sometimes encountered the problem of over-rapport (Everhart, 1977). It was possible that the observed teachers would change what they are doing in their classroom so that the researcher would have something to 'see', or they would request the researcher to come at certain times to offer them suggestions or help with what they were doing. The researcher was careful to document all instances of requests for help with or advice about the microcomputers in order to describe the possible impact the researcher had on the study.

Researcher intervention
Researcher intervention was cited as a particular pitfall of ethnographic research since the researcher usually becomes closely involved with the environment under study (Everhart, 1977; Merton, 1972). Because the researcher in this study was viewed as an expert and the innovation in the study was viewed as highly technical and complex, those being studied would call upon her expertise. Since a personal rapport had been established with many of those interviewed and observed, it was difficult for the researcher to refrain from making suggestions that she knew would help them. Researcher intervention in this study was defined to be any effect that the presence of the researcher had upon the research environment.

Due to the high anxiety felt by many teachers when using the computers, some teachers were relieved to see the researcher arrive to observe and would ask her technical questions about the computers or the software. In other instances, teachers became nervous when the researcher arrived. They stated that they were just getting started on the computers, and their lessons were not well-formulated yet. They would ask for the researcher's advice about how to improve the lesson at the end of the class. In the lab settings where there were many students using many computers at the same time, the teachers would sometimes ask the researcher to help answer the students' questions. Sometimes individual students would make comments or ask the researcher questions as she sat beside the computer to observe them. The data revealed that the key informants asked the researcher for help more frequently than other teachers. This would suggest that there was a positive relationship between researcher intervention and the familiarity felt by the respondents toward the researcher.

Conclusions

Microcomputers offer the potential to greatly enhance the educational delivery system, but due to their complex technical nature, this potential has not always been realized. The prevalence of the use of CAI found in this study and in other studies suggests that educators are adapting the innovation to the delivery system, rather than adapting the delivery system to take advantage of the full potential of the microcomputer. The reason that teachers have so many problems integrating the open-ended uses of computers, such as wordprocessing, data bases, or programming, into their classrooms is that these uses require risk and real change on the part of teachers. Such uses may require the acceptance of some noise and confusion in the classroom on the part of administrators and teachers. They may also require the use of trained aides to facilitate the use of many computers by many children at the same time.

Since the institutionalization of an educational innovation takes place within the context of the local school district, the full potential of microcomputers can be realized only if all operational levels work together to adapt microcomputers into the instructional program. The centralized planning and decentralized decision-making found in this study were essential to the acceptance of the microcomputers at all operational levels.

The broad base of support for microcomputers created by public pressure, administrators, and teachers was fueled by a common sense of urgency about the expanding role of microcomputers in society. However, once the computers were in place the public was content to let the educators figure out what to do with them. The importance of the visibility of microcomputers as an innovation cannot be overemphasized. As long as parents could walk through the schools and see children using microcomputers, they were satisfied that their children were becoming computer users and very few of them questioned how the computers were being used. The visibility of microcomputers positively affected the public perception of microcomputer use in the schools, and the complexity of microcomputers negatively affected the public participation in the implementation process.

The key stakeholder in the process of implementing microcomputers for instruction in a school district was the classroom teacher. Although all of the principals expressed support for the microcomputers, it was the classroom teachers who determined whether the innovation was adopted pro forma or whether the instructional process was adapted to accommodate the innovation. Collectively and individually, they exhibited high levels of personal concern that would have to be dealt with before true adaptation could take place. The teachers who were using the computers to help them do their job better, such as create lesson plans or assignments, were the most enthusiastic users of the computers with their students. This would suggest that the best way to bring about change in the classroom with microcomputers would be to teach teachers how to use microcomputers for their own personal use, before teaching them how to use them with students.

Similarly, the teachers that had been involved in developing the computer literacy unit and the software correlation guide were also very enthusiastic about the microcomputers because they had a sense of ownership in the success of the implementation process. This reemphasizes previous findings that the more teachers are involved in the implementation process, the greater is their acceptance of the innovation, and the higher is their morale.

The importance of the role of teachers in the implementation process pointed out the need for teacher training programs on microcomputers beyond the first course. Teachers need to be offered additional courses on word-processing, modeling and data bases with an emphasis upon personal usefulness of computers, new classroom management models, training parents as computer aides, and opportunities to observe other teachers using computers with students. Teachers receiving this additional training should then participate in the development of new curriculum that calls for these open-ended uses of the microcomputers in all subject areas.

A serious concern of many educators about microcomputers in the classroom is that of equity. Many fear that microcomputers are increasing the gap between advantaged and disadvantaged students. Microcomputers effect educational equity by both exposure and *type* of exposure to computers. Previous studies have looked at equity as a combination of installed computer base and types of computer uses. They have shown that students from lower economic backgrounds are more often exposed to computer uses in which the computer controls their actions, such as drill and practice, while students from higher economic backgrounds are more often exposed to computer uses in which they are in control of the computer, such as word processing, programming, and problem solving. From this study, a different perspective on the equity issue emerges, that of teacher attitudes about whether computer use is a right or a privilege for students. Teachers and administrators who make an effort to insure that all students have equal access to computers can

	Institution:	Innovation:	Individual:
District	Broad-based support for microcomputers Broad educational goals Early adopter information Comprehensive, central planning Decentralized decision-making Size, wealth of school district	Specific goals related to microcomputers Cost of microcomputers Complexity of microcomputers Adaptability into curriculum Maintenance provided Technical support provided	Superintendent support Assistant Superintendent support Curriculum Specialist support District computer coordinator Parental support Network of enthusiasts
School	Leadership of principal School goals Decentralized decision-making School-based planning for microcomputer	School goals related to microcomputers Visibility of microcomputers Portability of microcomputers Complexity of microcomputers Availability of microcomputers Location of use – lab or classroom Technical support provided	Principal attitudes, concerns Librarian attitudes, concerns Parent aides available School-based inservice training School-based computer coordinator
Classroom	Management style of teacher Classroom goals Organization of classroom Age level of students	Teachers' goals related to microcomputers Availability of microcomputers Well-defined uses for microcomputers Appropriate software available Ease vs complexity of use Technical support provided	Teacher concerns and attitudes Sufficient training provided Collaboration with other teachers Incentives for teachers Teacher participation in curriculum development Student concerns and attitudes

Figure 5.10: Factors influencing implementation of microcomputers.

be said to view computer use as a right of the student and, by implication, to be concerned about equity.

Another important factor in the general acceptance of the microcomputers by teachers was the availability and portability of the microcomputers. Some teachers were brave enough to take their students into the lab setting, but most teachers preferred to deal with one or two microcomputers in the safety of their own classrooms. In the classroom setting teachers could set up well-defined boundaries for use of the computers by a few children at a time as opposed to many students on many computers at once. A popular misconception in the past was that the scenario of one computer for the twenty-five children in a typical classroom was a difficult classroom management problem for teachers. This study showed that, in fact, most teachers were comfortable with one or two computers and twenty-five students. They became uncomfortable with many children and many computers because they lost their feeling of control over the situation. Now that microcomputers are becoming readily available in large numbers in schools, the management of many microcomputers and the use of computer lab aides will need to be a part of future implementation plans for microcomputers in instruction.

Examining the factors that influenced the implementation of microcomputers for instruction in this majority adopter school district in relation to the three-by-three data analysis produced the factor matrix shown in Figure 5.10. Although each school district is unique, these are factors that should be considered by any school district planning for future implementation of microcomputers in instruction. The microcomputer is an educational innovation that will require ongoing mobilization, implementation and institutionalization in school districts.

Many insightful administrators have already recognized the iterative nature of implementing microcomputers for instruction and are growing apprehensive about the ongoing level of financial commitment required to accomplish an uncertain outcome. Other priorities are starting to clamor for resources once willingly allocated for microcomputers. The challenge in the next decade of using microcomputers in instruction will be to convince decision-makers in school districts to continue to supply the technical support, training, and incentives to teachers that will encourage them to move beyond their current delivery style and take advantage of the unique capabilities of the microcomputer. The challenge for researchers will be to provide the theoretical rationale and the practical models that will facilitate this higher level of implementation of microcomputers for instruction by school districts.

References

BASS, G.V. (1978) 'District policies and the implementation of change'. *A study of alternatives in American education*, Vol. I. (Rand Report R-2170/1-NIE), Santa Monica, CA: Rand Corporation.

BECKER, H.S. and GEER, B. (1957) 'Participant observation and interviewing'. *Human Organization*, 16, pp. 28–32.

BERGER, P.L. and LUCKMANN, T. (1967) *The social construction of reality*, New York: Doubleday Anchor Books.

BERMAN, P. and McLAUGHLIN, M.W. (1974) *Federal programs supporting educational change, Vol I: A model of educational change* (Rand Report R-1589/1-HEW) Santa Monica, CA: Rand Corporation.

BERMAN, P. and McLAUGHLIN, M.W. (1976) 'Implementation of educational innovation', *The Educational Forum*, 40, pp. 345–70.

BERMAN, P. and McLAUGHLIN, M.W. (1977) *Federal programs supporting educational change, Vol VII: Factors affecting implementation and continuation* (Rand Report R-1589/7-HEW) Santa Monica, CA: Rand Corporation.

BERMAN, P. and McLAUGHLIN, M.W. (1978) *Federal programs supporting educational change, Vol VIII: Implementing and sustaining innovations* (Rand Report R-1589/8-HEW), Santa Monica, CA: Rand Corporation.

BERMAN, P. and McLAUGHLIN, M.W. (1979) *An exploratory study of school district adaptation* (Rand Report R-2010-NIE), Santa Monica, CA: Rand Corporation.

BOZEMAN, W.C. (1984) 'Strategic planning for computer-based educational technology'. *Educational Technology*, 24, pp. 23–7.

DENZIN, N.K. (1978) *The research act* (2nd ed.). New York: McGraw Hill Publishing Co.

ELMORE, R.F. (1978, Spring) 'Organizational models of social program implementation'. *Public Policy*, 26, pp. 185–228.

EVERHART, R.B. (1977) 'Between stranger and friend: Some consequences of "long term" fieldwork in schools'. *American Educational Research Journal*, 14, pp. 1–15.

FIRESTONE, W.A. and HERRIOTT, R.E. (1982) 'Images of organization and the promotion of educational change'. *Research in Sociology of Education and Socialization*, 2, pp. 221–60.

GILLESPIE, G.W., JR. (1982) 'Data collection, analysis and research: A framework for organizing the fieldnote file'. Paper presented at the Midwest Sociological Society. Des Moines, Iowa.

HALL, G.E. (1981) 'Issues related to the implementation of computers in the classrooms: Where to now?' Paper presented at the NIE Conference on Issues Related to the Impementation of Computer Technology in Schools. Washington, DC: National Institute of Education.

HALL, G.E., GEORGE, A.A. and RUTHERFORD, W.L. (1979) *Measuring stages of concern about innovation: A manual for use of the SoC questionnaire,* Austin, TX: The University of Texas, Research and Development Center for Teacher Education.

HALL, G.E., LOUCKS, S.F., RUTHERFORD, W.L. and NEWLOVE, B.W. (1975) 'Levels of use of the innovation: A framework for analyzing innovation adoption', *Journal of Teacher Education*, 26, 1, pp. 52–6.

HAVELOCK, R.G. (1969) *Planning for innovation*, Ann Arbor, MI: University of Michigan, Institute for Social Research, Center of Research on Utilization of Scientific Knowledge.

HOUSE, E.R. (1974) *The politics of political innovation*, Berkeley, CA, McCutchan.

KENNEDY, M. (1979) 'Generalizing from single case studies', *Evaluation Quarterly*, 3, pp. 661–78.

LOUCKS, S.F. and ZACCHEI, D.H. (1983) 'Applying our findings to today's innovations', *Educational Leadership*, 41, pp. 28–31.

MARTIN, C.D. (1987) *School District Implementation of Microcomputers for Instruction*. Doctoral dissertation, The George Washington University, Washington, DC.

MARTIN, C.D. and HELLER, R.S. (1985) 'Analyzing teacher training in LOGO using a stages-of-concern taxonomy', *Proceedings of LOGO' 85*. Cambridge, MA: MIT Press.

McLaughlin, M.W., Berman, P. and Marsh, D. (1978) 'Staff development and school change', *Teachers College Record*, 80, pp. 69–93.

McNeil, L.M. (1983) *Learning together: Microcomputers in Crosby, Texas, schools*, Houston, TX: Rice University.

Meister, G.R. (1984) *Successful integration of microcomputers in an elementary school*, California: Stanford University, School of Education, Institute for Research on Educational Finance and Governance.

Merton, R.K. (1972) 'Insiders and outsiders: A chapter in the sociology of knowledge', *American Journal of Sociology*, 78, pp. 9–47.

Microcomputers in the schools — Implementation in special education (1983) Arlington, VA: SRA Technologies, Inc.

Miles, M.B. (Ed.) (1964) *Innovation in education*, New York: Columbia University, Teachers College, Bureau of Publications.

National Council of Teachers of Mathematics (NCTM) (1980) *An Agenda for Action*, Reston, VA.

Office of Technology Assessment (OTA) (1982) *Information technology and its impact on American education* (Summary Report), Washington, DC: Congressional Board of the 97th Congress.

Popkewitz, T.S. and Tatachnick, R.B. (Eds) (1982) *The study of schooling and field-based methodologies in educational research and evaluation*, New York: Praeger Publishing Co.

Pressman, J.L. and Wildavsky, A. (1984) *Implementation* (3rd ed.), Berkeley, CA: U. of CA Press.

Quinsaat, M.G. (1981) 'Implementing computer technology in a classroom setting: An anecdotal report of long-term use.' Paper presented at the NIE Conference on Issues Related to the Implementation of Computer Technology in Schools. Washington, DC: National Institute of Education.

Rist, R.C. (1977) 'On the relations among education research paradigms: From disdain to detente', *Anthropology and Education Quarterly*, VIII, pp. 42–9.

Rist, R.C. (1982) 'On the application of ethnographic inquiry to education: Procedures and possibilities'. *Journal of Research in Science Teaching*, 19, pp. 439–50.

Roberts, L.G. (1982) 'Case studies: Applications of information technologies in education', Office of Technology Assessment, Washington, DC: Congressional Board of the 97th Congress.

Rogers, E.M. (1983) *Diffusion of innovations* (3rd ed.), New York: The Free Press.

Rogers, E.M. *et al.* (1985) *Microcomputers in the schools: A case of decentralized diffusion*, California: Stanford University Institute for Communication Research.

Schmizzi, N.V. (1983) *Microcomputers in the schools*, Buffalo, New York: State University of New York, Buffalo College.

Sheinfold, K. *et al.* (1981) *Studies of issues related to implementation of computer technology in schools: Final report*, New York: Bank Street College of Education.

Spradley, J.P. (1979) *The ethnographic interview*, New York: Holt, Rinehart, and Winston.

Spradley, J.P. (1980) *Participant observation*, New York: Holt, Rinehart, and Winston.

Stake, R.E. (1978) 'The case study method in social inquiry', *Educational Researcher*, 7, pp. 5–8.

Webb, E.J., Campbell, D.J., Schwartz, R.D., Sechrest, L. and Grove, J.B. (1981) *Nonreactive measures in the social sciences* (2nd ed.), New Jersey: Houghton Mifflin Co.

Weick, K. (1976) 'Educational organizations as loosely coupled systems', *Administrative Science Quarterly*, 21, pp. 1–19.

Chapter 6

The Role of School-Based Computer Coordinators As Change Agents in Elementary School Programs

Neal Strudler

School districts are committing large amounts of money to teacher training, equipment, and instructional materials in the hope that implementation of instructional computing will occur. One approach to teacher training and support has been to create a new role: the school-based computer coordinator. The present study conceptualized these coordinators as change agents and analyzed their strategies, skills, and achieved outcomes.

Questionnaires and interviews were used to gather data from three computer coordinators, their supervisors, teachers, and parents. The data were analyzed case by case, and then across cases, using the framework and method of qualitative data analysis developed by Matthew Miles.

The study revealed that school-based computer coordinators use a combination of product- and client-centered strategies to facilitate computer use. These strategies include training of teachers, providing technical assistance, organizing and preparing the school's instructional computing program, and supporting and energizing the client. Effective strategies take into account the 'plight' of classroom teachers who appear burdened by existing teaching and planning responsibilities. Coordinators decrease teacher resistance by supplying materials and ideas, 'pre-booting' labs, organizing parent support, and assisting with custodial chores. They also employ the strategy of gradually 'weaning' teachers of their dependence on the coordinator.

The findings suggest that while effective coordinators must be knowledgeable about instructional computing, it is just as critical that they possess strong interpersonal and organizational skills to carry out necessary training and support functions. These skills include initiative-taking and tenacity to secure resources and 'keep the program going'. An unexpectedly important skill involves facilitating group-functioning and decision-making.

Achieved outcomes of the computer coordinators include improved teacher skills and readiness for further growth, implementation of school goals, teacher satisfaction with the program and increased feelings of self-esteem and professional growth, and greater student comfort with computers.

The present study illustrates many impediments to implementing computer-based innovations and documents coordinators' strategies and skills for overcoming these impediments. The findings of the present study are generally consistent with previous research findings on the characteristics of other types of effective change agents. The present study therefore supports the effectiveness of staffing computer coordinators as change agents at the school level.

Introduction

Purpose of the Study

The Rand Change Agent Study (Berman and McLaughlin, 1977) found that even the best innovation could not succeed with inadequately trained or uncommitted teachers. Staff development, therefore, is critical for the implementation of new programs and teaching methods. One element of effective staff development is support following initial training (Gall and Renchler, 1985). Follow-up support helps teachers to transfer newly learned teaching skills and practices into their active teaching repertoire (Joyce and Showers, 1983). The present study focused on the computer coordinator's role in facilitating the transfer of teacher training with regard to instructional computing. Specifically, the purpose of this study was to examine the role of school-based computer coordinators as change agents in elementary school programs.

A growing number of people hold the position of instructional computer coordinator at the school level (Barbour, 1986; Moursund, 1985). A recent survey in *Electronic Learning* (Barbour, 1986) yielded the following findings regarding school-based computer coordinators:

1　Job descriptions vary greatly.
2　Only twenty-one percent of the respondents actually hold the title 'computer coordinator'; the other seventy-nine percent function in that role on a *de facto* basis.
3　Eighty percent of school computer coordinators who responded fulfill their role as an additional responsibility; of the remaining 20 percent, only 4 percent fulfill their role on a full-time basis, while 16 percent function on a part-time or 'released' basis.

In a follow-up survey in *Electronic Learning*, McGinty (1987) reported that 33 percent of the school level coordinators are now functioning in that role on a full-time basis. McGinty maintains that this shift seems to involve a redefinition of computer coordinators' jobs, and he characterizes this shift as the biggest change in the profession over the past year. McGinty stated that job descriptions of school-level coordinators still vary greatly. The 1987 survey yielded the following:

1 Over 90 percent of the school-level coordinators are responsible for teaching students.
2 Over 80 percent are responsible for evaluating software and making recommendations for purchase.
3 Over 70 percent are responsible for evaluating and recommending hardware, maintaining the school's equipment, purchasing software, training other teachers and teaching programming to students.

The present study attempted to provide a detailed description of the computer coordinator's role. It focused on the emerging group of coordinators who have been provided released time to facilitate computer implementation in the schools.

A recent study of school improvement found that the successful implementation of innovative programs is dependent upon the intervention of key personnel involved in various *change agent* roles (Huberman and Crandall, 1982). A change agent is defined as an assistance person whose role includes responsibility for initiating or facilitating change. In the present study, school computer coordinators were conceptualized as this type of change agent, hired on a part-time basis to provide a variety of services on a school level.

This emerging role is being given increased attention because of a shift in the approach to school improvement. Whereas the post-Sputnik school reform campaign tended to rely on centralized curriculum changes, current efforts focus on school-based change. With this change there has been a corresponding shift in change agent roles from disseminator of curriculum ideas and materials to process consultant or trainer (Beaton, 1985). Whereas the former role emphasized implementing change through the spread of 'packaged' programs, the latter role involves attending to the process and training needs of local school personnel.

While change agents are widely used in current school improvement programs, little is known about their functions, the strategies they employ, the specific skills most crucial for their success, or how to train for such skills (Fullan, 1981; Louis, 1981; Miles *et al.*, 1986a). The *Patterns of Successful Assistance* study (Miles *et al.*, 1986a) focused on these concerns in its two-year investigation of seventeen change agents working in three urban school improvement programs. Miles (1984) developed a list of strategies that change agents use, skills they need, and outcomes they intend to effect. Lists of strategies, skills, and outcomes, shown in Appendix A, were adapted from Miles' work and used in the present study to investigate the role of computer coordinators.

Research Questions

This study investigated the activities of school-based computer coordinators in their effort to facilitate change in their schools. In particular, it set out to answer the following questions:

1 What is the situational and historical context in which computer coordinators do their work?
2 What is the range of strategies used by computer coordinators?
3 What skills do they need in that role?
4 What are the intended and actual accomplishments resulting from the computer coordinators's work?
5 What rewards and frustrations do computer coordinators experience?

In the process of analyzing the data, I became increasingly aware that the coordinators continually faced obstacles to implementing their program. I conceptualized these obstacles as 'impediments'. The data were analyzed to determine specific impediments. The results of this analysis are included in this report since these results help in interpreting the findings relating to the other research questions.

Method

Research Design
Questionnaire, interview, and observation procedures were used in this exploratory case study of three school-level computer coordinators carrying out a change agent role. The data were gathered from multiple sources. Responses of the coordinators to particular questions were checked against responses to similar questions by other informants, namely, their supervisors (principals and the district computer coordinator) and clients (the teachers and parents in their school). Observation of representative activities and examination of relevant documents provided an additional check on the validity of the coordinators' responses.

Sample
In 1984, the Eugene, Oregon District 4J Computer Council recognized the need for a uniform approach to computer education at the elementary level. In June of that year, a group of teachers, under the direction of the District Computer Coordinator, began developing a program that would focus on integrating the computer into the established curriculum and on providing articulation between grade levels. The program was piloted during the 1984–85 school year. The pilot study was evaluated (Ames, Gilberstad, Sky and Strudler, 1985), and the program was deemed feasible contingent upon continued district support for computer resources and staff development. The evaluators recommended that part-time 'computer persons' be designated to coordinate training, maintenance, and scheduling at the school level.

During the 1984–85 school year, only one of Eugene's twenty-four elementary schools employed a released-time computer coordinator (defined as any coordinator who is assigned .10 FTE (full time equivalent) or greater for computer-related responsibilities). By the following school year, nine elementary schools had opted for released coordinators. The present study examined the situational and historical reasons for this trend.

At the time this study was conducted, Eugene School District 4J had nine elementary schools with released-time computer coordinators. A sample of three of these schools was selected for this study because their coordinators were identified as having brought about a high degree of implementation of instructional computing. The identification process involved consulting with the district computer coordinator, the district evaluation specialist, and the Educational Service District curriculum/staff development specialist, and by personal observations of computer implementation in the schools. Additionally, consideration was given to choosing coordinators who vary with regard to critical variables, namely: (1) technical expertise in computing, (2) role expectations of computer coordinators by supervisors, teachers, and themselves, (3) previous teaching experience in the particular school, and (4) available resources. In this report, the three coordinators are designated as Tom at East School, Sue at Central School, and Karen at West School.

Data collection instruments

Semi-structured interviews and a questionnaire were adapted from those used in the studies of school improvement coordinators by Miles and colleagues (1986a) and of staff development specialists by Beaton (1985). A form of the questionnaire was given to each coordinator to assess his or her strategies and skills, and achieved outcomes. Another questionnaire, almost identical, asked each supervisor to prepare a similar profile of each coordinator.

Four interview schedules pertaining to the role and qualities of the computer coordinators were administered. Informants included the coordinators (interviewed twice), their supervisors (principals, district administrators), and their clients (teachers and parents). Fifty-two interviews were conducted, ranging from twenty-five minutes to more than two hours in length. Further data were gathered by direct observation of instruction and staff meetings and by analysis of planning documents. The data were collected over a ten-week period of time.

Data analysis

All fifity-two interviews were tape-recorded, and selected segments were transcribed. Field notes and interview data were coded for analysis according to the list of variables adapted from Miles (see Appendix A). A second coder was employed and the coding of skills and outcomes was checked for inter-rater reliability. Addenda to the initial coding definitions were created and codes were modified until a reliability rating of 87 percent was achieved for both variables (skills and outcomes), coded together. Strategies were not tested for coding reliability. Rather, strategies were treated as a high inference variable, allowing greater latitude for interpretation by the author.

Results

Presentation of Findings

Results of the data analysis are reported in this section. A description of the district context precedes the three cases studied. Each case includes a description of the school context and computer program (research question 1), followed by a description of the rewards and frustrations experienced by the coordinators (research question 5). These results are presented case by case to help the reader get a 'flavor' of each of the individual cases.

Following these case by case descriptions are a presentation of the impediments to integration of computer into the curriculum along with the strategies, skills and outcomes used by the coordinators and the outcomes they achieved (research questions 2–4). These sections describe the coordinators collectively rather than case by case. The descriptions and analyses are based on interview data and confirmed, where possible, by observation and document study. For a detailed account of the strategies, skills, and outcomes of the individual coordinators, see Strudler (1987).

District Context and Program Overview

The study was conducted in the Eugene Public Schools, a medium- to large-sized district of over 1000 teachers and approximately 17,500 students (K-12). The district is home of the University of Oregon and shares with two other local districts the provision of education to a northwestern regional center of 150,000 people. The district serves about 8000 elementary school children in its twenty-four elementary schools. By the end of the 1985–86 school year, there were approximately 1000 computers used in K-5 programs. Many of the schools have had computers in place for several years.

In 1984, the District Computer Council recognized the need for a uniform approach to computer education at the elementary level. In June of that year a group of six teachers, under the direction of the district computer coordinator, began developing a program that would focus on integrating the computer into the established curriculum and on providing articulation across grade levels. The proposed program was to emphasize 'tool applications for microcomputers; applications which could be integrated into the existing curriculum, yet which would extend teaching/learning in ways that capitalize on the computer's unique attributes'. From these broad goals, curriculum 'strands' were subsequently developed for graphics, keyboarding, word processing, and problem solving.

While this concept of computer integration has received much recent support, there are very few comprehensive models for actually implementing such a plan. Until recently, most curricula have promoted computer education as a discipline taught separately from traditional subjects. Further, a majority of the computer resources were allocated to the secondary schools. Thus, this district's plan for systematic implementation of computers in elementary schools offers some far-reaching alternatives to what has been done in the past.

The program, consisting of three completed strands (graphics, keyboarding, and word processing) was piloted during the 1984–85 school year. The pilot study was evaluated (Ames, Gilberstad, Sky and Strudler, 1985), and the program was deemed feasible, contingent upon continued district support for computer resources and staff development. The evaluators recommended that part-time 'computer persons' be designated to coordinate training, maintenance, and scheduling at the school level. Without such services, the evaluators concluded that implementation of the program would be difficult.

The computer education program was initially planned to be phased in over a three-year period. The district provided software and training as an incentive for schools to participate voluntarily. It was projected that all schools would implement the program by the end of the three years. This model for district-wide implementation, however, was contingent upon continued funding at the district level. Due to budgetary constraints, adequate monies were not allocated and the three-year timeline was abandoned.

Presently, the choice of whether or not to implement the program is made at the school level. The district coordinator, John, explained that the building-based funding is a 'real significant fact'. While John implied that this funding model makes it difficult to implement district-wide programs, he does see value in allowing each school to appropriate its own expenditures. He commented, 'I hate it and I love it all at once. But it's a given in this district'.

John has modeled at the district level the strategies that he recommends for school-level implementation. He has coordinated an active network of computer representatives throughout the district and has instituted a district-wide computer council that sets policies and goals for computer use. In schools where no 'computer person' has emerged, John sought teacher representatives and worked with building principals. Further, he encouraged teachers and administrators to share ideas and curriculum materials, and solicited the support of district principals regarding the allocation of monies at the school level for software and staff development. Overall, his style is active but facilitative. His approach has been to encourage and support voluntary computer implementation and staff development.

In District 45, the decision to employ a released coordinator is made at the school level. Each school is allocated a specified FTE for various specialists (media, physical education, music, art, etc.), depending upon the school's enrollment. From the allotted FTE, building principals may provide for a released-time computer coordinator. As one coordinator explained, 'The district isn't willing to pay for it. So it has to come out of the school, and making those kinds of decisions is real hard'.

Teachers and administrators generally felt supported by the district office regarding increased computer use in the schools. They almost unanimously expressed positive regard for the work of the district coordinator. Almost as unanimously, however, coordinators and administrators felt that their computer programs were not adequately funded by the district.

The district coordinator characterized the problem of inadequate funding as 'inevitable' and stated that the district is doing well relative to other districts. He explained that 'sometimes it's a blessing that we don't have as much money as I wish because the lack of money can also temper mistakes' (i.e., budget constraints can limit the imprudent expenditure of funds for equipment and programs). On the other hand, he added that 'for us to really institutionalize computers and make them part of the fabric of school is going to require more than the two to five year crescendo and decline [that characterizes other change efforts in schools].'

CASE #1: TOM'S WORK AT EAST SCHOOL

Informants Used for this Study

Each quotation used will acknowledge one of the following informants as the source:

Computer Coordinator:	Tom
Supervisors:	John (District Computer Coordinator)
	Laura (Principal)
Clients:	10 teachers
	2 parents

School Context

East School is a medium-sized school of 400 students and twenty-six full-time and part-time teachers. It serves a community of middle to upper middle income families in the rolling hills along the outskirts of Eugene. The school is divided into five quads, each of which shares a common building and a 'mini-school' identity. One of the quads has formally obtained the designation as an alternative school, one of several alternative elementary programs in Eugene. The alternative quad maintains a distinct identity apart from the overall school program, but participates in many school-wide endeavors including the computer program.

East's faculty characterize the 'flavor' of their school as caring, active, professional, and innovative. They believe that parents, teachers, and the school's administration have high expectations for student achievement. Community members appear pleased with East's educational program. The school is closed to transfers from students outside of East's attendance area — evidence of its public approval.

One by-product of East's high standards, however, appears to be a demanding, and for some, stressful work situation. One teacher explained, 'It [teaching at East] requires some energy'. She continued, 'We have a highly energetic principal. She expects a lot, and some people have trouble keeping up with her.'

Another teacher stated that 'a lot of people put pressure on themselves'. But added, 'There is a lot to do.'

Program Background

Computer use at East began with the purchase of some Commodore PET computers about five years ago. In the 1983–84 school year, East had two Commodore 64's and six PET computers. The computers were kept in each quad and were periodically moved from classroom to classroom. Several teachers were interested in using the computers, and a computer committee was organized to formulate school-wide goals.

East's principal, Laura, recalled that in 1983, her first year at that school:

> One or two quads would make fairly good use of them [the computers] and some of the others would admit that it just sits there. They really didn't use it much because they didn't seem to know how to work them into the program. They didn't have the time; they didn't have the expertise. So in some quads it was used; in others it was not.

During the 1983–84 school year, East's staff recognized the need for some guidance and direction with using the computers. One teacher explained the mood of the faculty:

> There was a consensus that we needed to do something in this area [instructional computing]. Of course the Eugene district office was pushing this idea and we thought the wave of the future would be with computers, and they [students] needed some computer literacy. To what degree that was going to come about, I don't think any teacher really knew. But we knew that it was part of the future and if you wanted to be able to deal with that successfully, you need to start at the early ages. And so the consensus was fairly easy to form.

The East faculty recognized the need to have someone coordinate the computer program. One teacher echoed the sentiments of the staff: 'We realized that that's the only way teachers would use it [computers] because teachers are overloaded as it is and we don't have the time.'

Laura had a similar assessment of the situation and acted to meet those needs. She stated:

> One of the things that I began to take a look at was to see if it would be possible if we had staffing to bring in a part-time computer

specialist who could then begin to work with staff in developing their expertise in computers. If you had someone on-site who could assist them instead of saying to go take a class in the evening.... Later, I took it to the staff to say, 'Here we have some additional staffing. You know, this is a choice that we have.' And there were some different — some people had some other ideas for the use of the funding. We could've used it to increase the music program. We could've used it to hire a resource teacher. And there were some people who thought perhaps we should do some of these things. But it was at a staff meeting, we did agree that we would try it [hiring a part-time computer coordinator] for one year if we had the funding.

The necessary FTE was available, and Laura sought to hire the first released-coordinator in the district. According to John, the district coordinator, Laura asked him to recommend someone and John suggested Tom. Tom was subsequently hired for a half-time appointment for the 1984–85 school year.

During his first year, Tom set up a computer lab in one of the quads and worked to secure more computers. He wrote a grant proposal and was awarded twelve PET computers that the district office amassed from schools that no longer wanted them. Also, he assisted with fund-raising jogathons that enabled the school to buy several Apple systems. Laura also allocated funds for hardware, software, and staff development, and teachers recognized her as being supportive of the program. Tom's appointment was renewed for the next school year with a .6 FTE. By the end of the 1985–86 school year, East's lab consisted of eighteen PETS, two Commodore 64's, and eight Apple II computers.

Program Overview

The two main goals of the computer program at East are to get students using computers in their studies and to train the classroom teachers so that they become comfortable in incorporating computers into their instructional program. Thus, Tom was hired to organize the program, teach the students, and teach the teachers. Originally, East's goal was to have a computer person and a computer lab only for one or two years. The East computer plan of May 1986, however, states that the computer room should remain for the foreseeable future, space permitting. The status of the lab, as well as the coordinator position, is reassessed annually.

Major areas of focus for computer use include graphics and problem solving in all grades, as well as keyboarding and word processing in grades 3–5. Classes are scheduled into the computer lab on a rotating basis. Each class attends for a one-week block during every three-week cycle. Teachers accompany their class to the lab. While Tom has the primary responsibility for planning and implementing the lessons, teachers are encouraged to get involved and participate. Generally, Tom introduces the programs and skills during the days that he functions in his coordinator role (Monday through Wednesday). Teachers then are responsible for supervising their class in the lab on Thursday and Friday, the days that Tom is not there. During those times, Tom leaves detailed plans that direct student learning activities, and trained parent volunteers are present to assist.

The 1985–86 computer plan includes the following staff responsibilities:

1 Computer Coordinator
   a Support and encourage students and staff in their use of computers.
   b Help integrate computers into the curriculum.
   c Plan and implement an academic program in line with the district computer curriculum.
   d Plan and/or provide inservice for staff.
   e Provide training and scheduling for volunteers.
   f Provide teachers with off-computer lessons [ie., preparatory and follow-up lessons away from the computer] to use with their students in the classroom to assure that the lab time is well spent.
2 Teachers
   a Take classes to lab at scheduled times.
   b Take advantage of inservice opportunities.
   c Take responsibility for proper handling of hardware and software by students.
   d Follow established procedures for leaving the lab for the next class and shutting it down.
   e Teach off-computer lessons (especially keyboarding) in the classroom prior to and after sessions in the lab.
   f Give feedback to computer coordinator and computer committee members.
3 Computer Committee
   a Assure continuation of a strong computer program.
   b Make recommendations to staff regarding major decisions
   c Approve all hardware and software purchases.
   d Review, evaluate, and rewrite the building computer plan in the spring of 1985–86, and thereafter as often as necessary.
   e Accept feedback from staff and advise the computer coordinator.

Personal Background of Coordinator

Tom graduated from college with a degree in history and elementary education after spending four years in the Marines as a radar technician. He began his teaching career in the Teacher Corps Program, and was hired in

1973 as a third- and fourth-grade teacher in Maine. Two years later, he enrolled in graduate school in guidance and counseling. Upon completing that program, Tom worked at the junior high level where he was assigned to deal with the school's major discipline problems. This role led to what he characterized as a 'burnout experience'. As a result, he left the teaching profession for two years. Eventually, however, Tom relocated to the Northwest and resumed teaching at the primary level.

Tom got interested in computers in 1981. He explained that he was really dissatisfied with teaching facts, and he saw computers as a means of broadening the scope of what students can learn in school. He began to participate in computer-related workshops and eventually was hired to work at a teacher resource center on a part-time basis. In that position, Tom worked closely with John, who was then director of the resource center. Subsequently, John recommended Tom for the newly created coordinator position at East for the 1984–85 school year.

Rewards and Frustrations

I would look for someone [for the coordinator role] who sees a problem as a challenge rather than seeing it as a frustration. Because nothing has been neat and clean. Everything has been murky and muddy and has had to be clarified as I went along. That's one of the things I really like to do is to get the challenge of a problem that seems like it's almost impossible.... I like to clarify murk! (Tom)

The above statement provides a good perspective from which to examine the rewards and frustrations of Tom's role. Tom views his coordinator responsibilities as going well beyond the short-term goals of getting students and teachers more comfortable with the technology. He believes that computers can open up new avenues in education (e.g., increased opportunities for problem solving and higher order thinking) and he envisions himself as a 'change agent' towards those ends. But while the general goal is clear, the necessary steps and strategies can be 'murky and muddy', similar to any innovation in its formative stages. Tom recognizes this situation and embraces the challenge.

The *rewards* that Tom has experienced are many. He is pleased with the progress that the teachers have made in their attitudes and skills. He maintained that most teachers are staying with their class in the lab and bringing their class to the lab on Thursdays and Fridays. He reflected on the teachers' progress and assessed that two teachers are not really interested and one is still afraid. 'I guess the rest of them are all really involved, and when I think about it, that's a really good percentage. Hmm, revelation! [laughs] Joy!'

Also, Tom feels good about some of the other outcomes. He recognized

that students have expanded their skills, specifically mentioning their improved keyboarding. Also, he cited the equal involvement of both girls and boys
(this was one of his goals) and the fact that East does not have a 'computer
elite'. Tom added that 'kids have ideas of the usefulness of computers in
varied situations' and are 'becoming independent'.

Tom also expressed satisfaction with the development of a 'framework'
for the program. He stated that the plan for the lab for next year is 'firm' and
the plan for implementation of the program is 'relatively fixed'. He elaborated
that he would use the same schedule as this year and expand upon the curriculum that he has created. The curriculum, he explained, will integrate with
class work and have a developed scope and sequence that avoids repeating
programs on different levels. Tom projected that next year the 'teachers will
have more and more ownership of the lab'.

As previously described, Tom feels as though the computer program is
becoming institutionalized. He mentioned how the program has evolved and
is pleased that teachers, parents, and students have come to expect and value
what his program offers.

One area of *frustration* for Tom involves the rapidly changing world of
computers in education. When asked about his strategies for getting from
point A (current situation) to point B (future goals), he offered a detailed
explanation:

> The problem is that point B is pretty fuzzy and has been shifting
> around, so it's been hard to pin down. Point B originally was work
> yourself out of a job; get the teachers so that they're completely
> comfortable with the computers — they know all the systems, all the
> stuff, and they're just ready to go however the set up is — whether
> the computers are in the classroom or in the lab. Then the teachers
> will just plug right into it because they'll be so literate and have
> everything all square in their minds about how to use computers.
> Point B, that always sounds good. It sounded great to me when they
> hired me. That whole idea, I figured I can do, no problem. But it's
> gotten more and more elusive. As you get closer to it, it gets fuzzy
> and some parts of it seem way out of reach. [For example], the com-
> puter technology changing the way it is, and the changes in software,
> and the sheer amount of knowledge that's necessary to keep on top
> of it, or even on the bottom of it. It's so much that I don't feel liter-
> ate and on top of things, much less getting a whole staff of people,
> who have had less experience with computers than I have, on top of
> things and literate. I feel pretty frustrated sometimes setting myself
> up as the person who's going to be able to do that.

Tom explained his strategy for dealing with this frustration:

> That point B has sort of been replaced by showing progress each
> year in a defined way towards that elusive goal, not necessarily say-

ing, though, that in two years you can leave it. [I'm] hoping maybe along the way that things will be crystallized and a lot more clear in everybody's mind. And I don't feel like I'm inadequate because I'm not on top of that stuff. I don't think that anybody is right now. I think that everybody has shifting views of the computer as an educational tool and I don't think it lessens what we're doing. But I do think that it makes such a defined goal almost impossible.

Tom's recognition of the enormity of the task of computer integration perhaps tempers his patience with resistant teachers. He expressed confidence that when a framework for teaching with computers crystallizes, teachers will be more willing to get involved. Thus, Tom does not appear overly frustrated with teachers who do not fulfill their responsibilities concerning the program (i.e., working with the students in the lab, bringing their class in on his off-days). While he did express frustration with the lack of progress and the negative modeling that resistant teachers present to their students, he appears quite accepting and patient. Tom seems calm in the knowledge that the program will evolve in due time.

CASE #2: SUE'S WORK AT CENTRAL SCHOOL

Informants Used for this Study

Each quotation used in this section will acknowledge one of the following informants as the source:

Computer Coordinator:	Sue
Supervisor:	John (District Computer Coordinator)
	Nora (Principal)
	Peter (Assistant Principal)
Clients:	12 teachers
	2 parents

School Context

Central School is a medium to large-sized school of 450 students and twenty-seven full-time and part-time teachers. It serves one of Eugene's lower socio-economic communities along the outskirts of the city. Central is one of only three schools in Eugene with sufficient enrollment to warrant an assistant principal.

Central's faculty characterize the 'flavor' of their school as professional, innovative, hardworking, exciting, and cooperative. Teacher informants almost unanimously expressed satisfaction with their school's program and work environment. Both of Central's administrators were new to their roles in the 1985–86 school year. Nora had previously served as the school's assistant principal, and Peter was in his first year at Central.

Program Background

Computer use at Central began in 1980 when the TAG program acquired a Commodore PET computer. The following year Central obtained two more Commodores, and Sue emerged as a leading advocate of computer use. She wrote a booklet about basic computer operating instructions and began to help teachers who sought programs that would provide drill and practice in basic academic skills.

In 1983 Central bought two Apple systems. Subsequently the school sponsored a triathlon and other fund-raising events to increase the school's computer resources. By May of 1986, Central owned fifteen Apple II's, two Commodore 64's, and two Commodore PETs. All informants agreed that Sue was the driving force that fueled the growth of Central's computer program.

During the 1984–85 school year, Sue got involved in the district's pilot program and became one of the writers of the elementary computer curriculum. Teachers from Central volunteered, and six were chosen to participate in the study in the spring of 1985. Other teachers at Central also wanted to get involved and asked Sue if she would help train them as well. At that time, Sue was a full-time physical education instructor and performed her *de facto* coordinator role in addition to her teaching responsibilities. Sue recalled the situation:

> I was concerned about the kind of job I was doing there [in P.E.]. My administrator was concerned that I was doing too much; that I wasn't able to give the time to P.E. or to myself because I was starting to have frequent absences. And it was because I was highly stressed. I was jumpy, I was nervous, I was defensive — which is not a normal style for me to be — crabby to kids, crabby to teachers. And I soon realized what was doing it and just cut back. I said, 'I can't anymore and I won't. It's ruining my health'.

Teachers questioned whether Sue would perform that role if she were allocated time to do so. Nora explained:

> It was sort of an awareness on the part of the staff that there was a need because they [the teachers] were progressing only so fast. And the part of Sue — that 'I can't take on any more and carry on a full time PE load.' And so the decision then came that 'we need you [Sue] half-time, and can we work that out?' — which we were able to do.

Teachers confirmed this assessment. One teacher stated that it was the 'general consensus of opinion' that Sue be given a released-time appointment. She reported that 'there were very few dissenting, if any, that I can remember. I think they [the teachers] all felt "Yeah, let's try it".

Sue was given a half-time appointment for the 1985–86 school year and proceeded to organize Central's expanding computer lab. Sue continued conducting inservices for teachers and parent volunteers. In December of that year, she submitted a proposal with John, the district coordinator, to Sunburst Communications, a leading publisher of instructional software. She proposed that Central School and Sunburst form a partnership in which, together, they would develop a 'national model showing "real life" classroom use and integration of computers' into the math, language arts, and problem solving curricula. Sunburst accepted the proposal, and the Central faculty reaped the benefits of large quantities of software and teacher inservices provided by Sunburst staff. Further, the 'Sunburst connection' appears to have boosted the teachers' enthusiasm regarding instructional computer use at Central School.

Another important factor in Central's computer program has been the presence of administrative support. Sue commented:

> I've been through three administrators since I started this [working with computers]. And one said, 'Go ahead, though I don't have the slightest idea what you're working on. I know you're a good teacher so as long as it doesn't take away from what you're doing, [it's O.K.].' And the other one said, 'Yeah, I think I see some value and I will support you in what you're trying to do, but I don't know enough about it to help you.' And then the one I have now is saying, 'Yes, I will clear the way for you. I will help make things happen for you. I will support you.' And really, all three administrators helped because of the lack of a negative attitude toward computing. They were interested — they may not have been very knowledgeable, but they were interested and supportive through each development, and each in their own way helped facilitate getting [us] to where we are right now.

Program Overview

Major areas of focus include graphics and problem solving in all grades, as well as keyboarding and word processing in the upper grades. Teachers sign up to bring classes into the computer lab and are encouraged to do so for blocks of two or three weeks at a time. Teachers are responsible for planning the instructional activities and for implementing the lessons in the lab. Sue is available to do demonstration lessons and to help teachers as they become familiar with the various programs. While Sue will help with the teaching of students, she sees teacher training as her primary responsibility. Trained parent volunteers are present in the lab to assist teachers with getting the lab ready for use and helping individual students.

Goals for the 1985–86 school year as stated in the Central computer plan include:

1 Begin implementation of the district computer curriculum.
2 Incorporate activities that extend the computer curriculum to

enhance other subject areas (data base in science, social studies, etc.) or use as a utility to help students produce a school newsletter.

3   Have all classroom teachers (K-5) work with computer teacher and P.I.L.'s (acronym for 'partners in learning' which is Central's name for parent computer lab volunteers) to teach computer curriculum to students in their class.

4   Develop a library of teacher utility programs and help teachers begin to utilize them in their class preparation.

A major focus for Central's computer program involves teacher inservice training. Teachers are required to attend an initial one and one-half hour orientation and subsequent monthly sessions. In addition, optional inservices are planned to introduce various programs and other topics of interest. Released time is provided from school staff development funds for formal inservice sessions. A total of forty-three days inservice time for computers was allocated to be shared among the Central faculty.

Nora described Sue's role:

Sue's whole philosophy is 'I'm there to assist you, I'm not there to do the teaching'. And that's been the philosophy from the beginning. So the teachers know that they're the ones who are going to do whatever it is with the kids. Sue will help with technical problems, will help giving suggestions if the teacher has a problem, but basically it's up to the teacher to teach the lesson....

The 1985–86 computer plan includes the following staff responsibilities:

1   Computer Teacher
   a.   Support and encourage students and staff in their use of computers.
   b.   Plan and implement with Central staff an academic program in line with the district computer curriculum.
   c.   Help integrate computers into the curriculum.
   d.   Plan and/or provide inservices for staff.
   e.   Provide training and scheduling for volunteers.
   f.   Oversee lab supervision.

2   Teachers
   a.   Attend required inservices throughout the year.
   b.   Take classes to lab at scheduled times.
   c.   Be responsible for proper handling of hardware and software when supervising children in the lab.
   d.   Follow established procedures for leaving the lab for the next class and shutting it down.
   e.   Teach off-computer lessons in the classroom to assure that time spent in the lab is well used.
   f.   Work with computer teacher and P.I.L.'s to teach computer curriculum.

g. Give feedback to computer teacher and computer committee members.

3 Computer Committee
a. Assure continuation of a strong computer program.
b. Make recommendations to staff regarding major decisions about computers at Central.
c. Approve all hardware and software purchases.
d. Accept feedback from staff and advise the computer teacher.
e. Review and evaluate the building computer plan in the spring of 1986 and thereafter as often as necessary.

While a large majority of the staff expressed support for Sue's role as teacher trainer and not instructor of students, some did express their disapproval. One teacher stated that while Sue does a good job of coordinating, he believes that the coordinator should be more of a computer teacher. He said:

> We don't need another administrator. We've got two administrators here already, and if we're buying a third administrator, then I think we're selling the kids short. I think that the coordinator ought to spend some kid time.... I guess what I'm saying is some people aren't, as I understand it, and this is all hearsay, getting as much of her time as they would like.

The teacher described Sue's style and priorities as 'administratively oriented' and maintained that 'some would prefer more help with booting programs and running the class'. The teacher continued, 'This is one reason for stress in this building. It's one more thing that's difficult to handle'.

Another teacher raised similar objections regarding Sue's role at Central. She stated that if the district values computers in the curriculum, there should be a computer specialist as in music or physical education. She said:

> I'm not sure I see it in the same way she does. I think that at the level we're working at now that she can't just be the trainer of staff. She's going to have to still do some of the introduction of the programs with the kids to get them started. Once they get started, I think the teachers can handle it. But if the kids are going to be doing it in the way she wants it done and in the way that I think is good for the school, I think she has to [do more teaching of students].

Personal Background of Coordinator

After graduating from college with a degree in physical education, Sue became a Peace Corps volunteer in Venezuela. The project was a joint effort with the Teacher Corps, a federal program that trained teachers to work in low income areas. After receiving a master's degree in physical education in the first year, Sue spent the following two years supervising physical education teachers in Venezuela.

After her Peace Corps experience, Sue returned to Eugene where she was hired as a physical education specialist. She has worked in that role for twelve years and is currently a half-time P.E. teacher. While her major responsibility in that role is to teach children, Sue has conducted workshops for teachers at Central on the physical education needs of elementary students. She commented that her role as a P.E. specialist helped prepare her for her computer coordinator role. She explained that her work in P.E. helped establish her, 'at least in the eyes of these people [the Central faculty], as a person ... who's willing to teach all ages, everybody'.

Sue got interested in computers around 1980. She enrolled in a series of free programming classes sponsored by Radio Shack and subsequently participated in inservices and university classes on educational computing.

Rewards and Frustrations

For Sue, the major *rewards* of her role appear to be rooted in the satisfaction of seeing her vision of educational computing translated into a viable school-wide program. Sue appears to be experiencing the rewards of a proud parent whose child is growing up. When asked how she thought her work has impacted the program, she replied:

I think a great deal. I know — when a new teacher comes into the lab ... [for] the first time — how heavily they lean on me. And as they acquire the skill they need, they go forward like a child learning to walk. And I know how many of them have come to me and said 'We wouldn't have done it if we had not had you to ask questions, if you had not been as patient as you were with my dumb questions, and if you weren't there to support me, and to tell me that I could do it, and set things up for me initially, and hold my hand'. I think many — a large percentage, like 90 percent of our teachers — would not [have persevered in the lab] had I not been here to do that [provide assistance and support].

Sue expressed being pleased with the teachers' enthusiasm for participating in the program and expanding their computer use. She cited a 'new sense of pride on the part of the teachers ...' that goes beyond the computer lab and the technology. Sue appears proud of the progress that teachers have made, and recognizes their readiness for continued growth. Further, Sunburst Communications has made a commitment to continue its relationship with Central School, thus guaranteeing more software and training. Overall, Sue is very optimistic that the program will continue to expand, and that teachers will find more effective ways to enhance the curriculum with computer applications.

Sue did experience some *frustration* in her work at Central. She recalled the frustration when she began functioning as a released-time coordinator: 'I had an empty room that had to be remodeled. So I had to learn about wiring systems...', getting materials, and funding sources. For Sue, the big challenge was learning how to arrange for services (i.e., electricity, plumbing, carpentry, carpeting), as well as how to 'expedite the process with the downtown bureaucracy'.

Sue continued:

> I learned by experience, trial and error, making a lot of mistakes, making myself real obnoxious to a whole lot of people downtown saying, 'I need this, I need it now, if you've got it I'll come and get it. What does it take to get it ordered now?' [I learned by] going through a lot of red tape downtown — they were in a stage of transition too. They were trying to straighten out some procedural problems they were having and so I just had to be real obnoxious and real persistent with them.

Sue's ambitious timeline for implementing the program may have also been a source of frustration for her. Nora explained some of the adjustments that Sue had to make in her work with teachers:

> She's had to be adaptable to the different levels of teacher eptness [sic] or ineptness [said laughing], confidence. And that can be really frustrating when you're not used to it because she always ran her own program. She didn't have to work with someone else with the development of that program [physical education]. And suddenly with this [instructional computing], she was working with all teachers — some very capable, some not so capable. So she had to adjust how she presented the material — the manner, the speed, and all of that to meet their individual needs. And I think that ... it was frustrating at times.

While Sue thought that she could have worked herself out of a job by the end of the 1985–86 school year, she has adjusted her schedule. She expressed hope that she could accomplish this goal by the end of the following school year. She did add, however, that she's 'not sure if it is realistic'. Apparently, Sue has developed a greater understanding of the difficulty of realizing her goal of working herself out of a job. She did not report feeling frustrated about her adjusted timeline.

Sue's greatest frustration with the current status of the program appears to involve her desire to have the quality of instruction in the lab monitored. As Nora pointed out, Sue 'still gets frustrated when she sees that there are some people [teachers] who aren't using the lab correctly'. Sue, however, plans to take steps to improve this situation. She commented, 'I think I need to do a ... better job of communicating procedures, whether it's in the lab or [whether it involves the] use of the computer [in the classroom]'. Further, she would like for the computer committee and the school's administration to take necessary steps to ensure quality instruction with computers. While she does not see herself being a 'teacher policing other teachers', she does have some definite proposals to monitor the quality of instruction with computers.

CASE #3: KAREN'S WORK AT WEST SCHOOL

Informants Used for this Study

Each quotation used in this section will acknowledge one of the following informants as the source:

Computer Coordinator: Karen
Judy (District Computer TOSA-Teacher on Special Assignment)
Supervisor: Glenn (Principal)
Clients: 12 teachers
2 parents

School Context

West School is a medium-sized school of 375 students and twenty-seven full-time and part-time teachers. It serves a community of middle income families along the outskirts of Eugene.

West's faculty characterize the 'flavor' of their school as cooperative, open, friendly, hard-working, and professional. Teacher informants almost unanimously expressed satisfaction with their school's program and congenial work environment. The building principal, Glenn, appears to encourage open communication and a 'team concept' among staff members.

Program Background

West School acquired its first computers in 1982 when a few teachers expressed an interest. At the beginning of the 1983–84 school year, West had one Commodore-64, one PET, and one VIC-20 computer. During that year, Judy, then a new second-grade teacher at West, and another teacher, helped stimulate further interest among teachers and parents. Fund-raising activities were organized, and West's computer committee began to meet.

In the following school year, the West faculty made computers a building goal for that year. The program was awarded an $8000 grant from the district to expand West's computer resources. Judy was active in writing the proposal. In addition, $6000 was raised from a jogathon that was strongly supported by parents. As a result of these fund-raising efforts, West was able to buy 14 computers and a large quantity of software. This enabled West to establish a lab of twelve Apple IIc's, with some Commodore computers dispersed for use in individual classrooms. Ten computers were placed on movable carts for easy transport to the classrooms.

In February of 1985, six West teachers became involved in the district's pilot computer curriculum study. Again Judy, one of the curriculum writers and trainers for the district, was a major force in making this happen at West. The computer committee continued to function and was responsible for managing the software inventory and hardware, organizing the parent volunteer program, annually reviewing the building plan, and scheduling the lab. Also, parents continued to support computer use at West, both in fund-raising and in providing lab assistance before, during, and after school.

In the following year, Glenn and the staff recognized a need to hire a released-time coordinator for the program. According to Glenn, West adopted the position that all teachers should be 'sort of their own expert' without relying on one expert in the building. He explained, however, that 'it was just getting out of hand with all the software and trying to keep track ... and keeping machines up to date. It was just not possible for everyone to know everything'.

One of the more experienced computer-using teachers noted, 'We have more software here than just about any school in the district — more programs, with less people knowing what's on each disk than just about anywhere'.

When an extra .2 FTE became available after the beginning of school, Karen, a half-time kindergarten teacher, was hired for the job. Glenn had been hoping for a .4 allotment, but explained that 'when the kids showed up, there weren't enough tenths'.

Despite Karen's lack of extensive computer experience, Glenn reported choosing her because she had the time to do the job and the organizational skills that he felt were necessary. While Judy might have been a more logical choice, Glenn stated that Judy did not have the time when the FTE allotment became available. Judy was given a half-time appointment at the beginning of the school year as the district TOSA (Teacher on Special Assignment) for computers. In addition, she held a half-time position as a second grade teacher.

Karen began functioning as the computer coordinator in the middle of November. Both she, Glenn, and the staff agreed to consolidate her .2 appointment (one day a week for the school year) into a .4 appointment for less time (until spring break).

West became involved in a National Science Foundation (NSF) grant during Karen's tenure as coordinator. The grant, procured by a University of Oregon professor, was designed to formulate a model for integrating computer tools (database, spreadsheet, graphics) into the curriculum. It involved four classroom teachers in grades 3–5, Karen, and Glenn, and included extensive training for the participants. Judy got the initial information regarding the grant. Karen then went to a preliminary meeting, presented details to teachers, wrote up a proposal (with input from Judy), and secured West's participation in the grant.

Glenn has been seen by West's faculty as a strong supporter of the computer program. He was a member of the school's computer committee through 1984–85, and is a member of the district's computer council. Teachers recognize the allocation of staff development funds and the available computer resources as evidence of his support. Glenn has urged teachers to participate in the computer program but has not mandated participation.

In the 1984–85 school year, the West staff made a commitment to computers by making it a major building goal to increase computer use. This was not the case the following year. Karen stated that 'people went in different directions.' She explained:

> It got kind of dropped this year. And I know that a lot of teachers are feeling that they want to go back and make .... another building goal for computer education — which I think would be real valid for our school.

Program Overview

Karen recalled that when she began her position, 'It was a mess'. She explained that 'for me, I couldn't see how to even begin. I think that was one of the problems, you know. It was so overwhelming I didn't even know where to begin and I didn't even know what questions to ask'. Eventually, Karen recognized that her first priorities would be to schedule classes and decide what to teach. She conducted a needs assessment and eventually decided to focus on the district graphics and keyboarding strands. In addition, individual teachers implemented some of the applications (e.g., database programs, MECC Graph) encountered in the NSF training.

Because of the limited time Karen had to perform her role, she chose to concentrate on grades 3–5 and suggested that primary teachers get priority next year. Thus, upper grade teachers were scheduled to bring their classes into the lab on a regular basis. Karen introduced the lessons during the first sessions and then encouraged teachers to take more responsibility for the teaching. West's long-term goal, according to Karen, was to 'integrate the computer into what we're already teaching'. She added, though, that 'we realized that we couldn't do that this year. So we started at a place to make the teachers computer literate by teaching the strands'.

Karen assessed that close to 100 percent of West's faculty favors integration of computers into the curriculum. Apparently, though, teachers disagree on what Karen's role should be towards accomplishing that goal. While many appear satisfied to get some guidance and then do it themselves, some teachers would prefer to have a 'computer teacher' instructing students. One teacher explained, 'They [the teachers] wanted someone to take over that room — to clean it up — to teach classes.... They don't want to be in there with their kids'.

Another teacher supported this contention by describing that the computer coordinator's job is to 'teach students, to give lessons — not to be the librarian for the computer program'.

One teacher challenged the merit of the stated goals of computer integration. 'You see', he explained:

They always want to justify everything by integrating it into the total curriculum. I mean that's the way they do everything and, I've taught for twenty-eight years. I mean I've really been around this block a couple of times. And that's the way they always justify something that's new — it's going to be a part of the total curriculum. It's going to improve the whole [with emphasis] ball of wax, you see. Well, be that as it may, [laughs] it raises questions in my mind.

In addition to scheduling classes, modeling lessons, and conducting inservice training, Karen spent much time trying to organize the materials in the lab and set up a system for keeping them in order. Also, she helped coordinate the parent volunteer program that staffed the lab before school. A parent confirmed that the parent volunteers didn't start supervising the lab until after Christmas time. When asked why, she replied that parents were ready, but no one contacted them and organized a program until Karen finally did. In the previous year, one of the members of the computer committee was responsible for working with parent volunteers.

The lab was reported to be in steady use during Karen's tenure, but lab use dropped off after her time allotment expired. Karen worked under much stress, which was compounded by some personal problems that she encountered during this time. Karen became very ill and missed several weeks of work due to her illness. Glenn commented:

The job was almost overwhelming because there was too much to do and the problems with the computer program are so involved, that I think she was somewhat frustrated by not being able to do the usual 110 percent job that she does. There were just so many things that needed to be done. I don't think there was enough time in the day for her to get them all finished.

When assessing the current status of the program, one experienced computer-using teacher stated:

Our computer program in the building is not a program. I mean it's just some people going in [the lab] at different times. And it's too bad. So I'm not saying it's [because of] Karen. What I'm saying is that we don't have a coordinated effort in this building and we need it ... Karen did a lot of preparation and stuff in getting the computer room going and everything. So she's been very busy. But we haven't seen it in the classroom as such. And that's where it needs to be.

Others made similar assertions. Glenn attributed some of the lack of
organization to a lack of consistent leadership in the program. He explained
that for one thing, Judy has done less for the program at West since becoming TOSA. He commented:

> I don't think we have a leader right now.... Maybe I see that as one
> of the problems that we have. We don't have that person. I think
> Judy is, and has been the impetus for a lot of things, but I don't call
> her a leader in the sense that there hasn't been enough of the little
> details taken care of. You know I think she's gotten a lot of people
> thinking about computers and doing with [i.e., using] computers, but
> there's all sorts of loose ends that need to be tied together. And
> someone's got to do that and I don't think she has.

Thus, Glenn felt that a large part of Karen's job was to 'tie together' the
'loose ends' of the program. 'You see,' he continued:

> My goal was to get a lot of this stuff organized, to get this software
> thing worked out. I think we've got a lot of software that's junk and
> we've got a lot of software that's good, and you know, we don't have
> enough copies of it and that kind of stuff. And the teachers wanted
> time in the lab with someone. They wanted someone to schedule it.
> They wanted someone to be right there with their kids all the time.
> So there's a lot of pressure to take her [Karen] away from organizing
> the materials.

The district coordinator reflected on this situation. 'Judy is probably part
of the problem now', he admitted. 'With Judy sort of being there and sort of
not, it must make it real diffuse in that building. Who's driving here? Where
is the vision?'

Karen added that 'my gut feeling is that it [lack of organized growth]
may certainly be due to the fact that we have not had a consistent computer
coordinator'.

Personal Background of Coordinator

Karen graduated from the University of Oregon with a B.A. degree in
elementary education. She then went on to teach a total of eight years — two
years in the second grade and six years in kindergarten. Karen has been
teaching at West School for five years.

Karen got involved with computers through an introductory workshop
in BASIC programming at a local science center. She followed that experience with a second workshop in BASIC, and then in 1985, she became a participant in the district's elementary computer curriculum pilot study. Unlike
Tom and Sue, Karen was a teacher/participant in that study — not one of
the curriculum writers and organizers. Karen stated that while she was devel-

oping an interest in computers at that time, she considered herself to be a novice computer-user. She recalled that Judy approached her and said, 'Karen, we've got this pilot program [and] I want you to do it'. Karen admitted that she wasn't aware of the commitment of time and energy that she was about to make.

After the pilot study, Karen attended a summer conference, participated in a keyboarding workshop, took a class on databases in education, and took part in the NSF training on integrating computer applications into the curriculum.

Rewards and Frustrations

We got a lot of things accomplished, [but] it's hard for me to start a job and not get it finished. (Karen)

For Karen, the major *rewards* of her role resulted from her 'getting teachers in [the lab] who wouldn't have done it on their own.' Lab use by teachers increased during the time she coordinated the program, and individual teachers improved in their comfort and skills with computers. Further detail regarding these accomplishments can be found in the Outcomes section of this report.

The rewards that Karen experienced, however, were accompanied by many *frustrations*. One source of frustration concerns Karen's background and experience in computing — her entry characteristics for the position. She began her role with limited expertise in educational computing and no experience with West's computer committee, the program's decision-making body. A second source of frustration involved the program itself, its lack of organization, direction, and progress toward long-term growth. The third source of frustration is related to the other two. With limited experience and much to do, Karen was allotted a brief amount of time (.2 FTE) to 'tie up the loose ends' of the program. In the following section, I will explore each of these factors in an attempt to illuminate some of the difficulties that Karen faced in performing her role.

It seems clear that Karen's *limited experience* with using computers at West created an extra hardship for her in her role. As was previously described, Karen mentioned that at the outset, she 'couldn't see how to even begin'. She stated that she 'came in this year not knowing very much', and that 'being on the committee last year would've helped a lot'. Judy commented that upon assuming her role, Karen 'did not have an idea of the scope of the job'.

Informants reported that Karen worked hard to compensate for her lack of familiarity with some areas of educational computing. One teacher explained:

She had to put a lot more into the job than say Judy would have if Judy would have been here. Because Judy already had that background knowledge that I don't think Karen had. And I think Karen worked really hard at it to prepare herself — which I think really bogged her down.

Another teacher added:

What Karen was doing was very stressful ... and it didn't help that she came in with no computer background. You can imagine the stress ... Oh don't you remember, when you just started working with computers, that anxiety that that machine contributes to your life by doing nothing when you want it to [do something]? How impatient you get when people come, want it yesterday and want it now?... She's an administrative personality type, meaning she wanted to get it [i.e., details of the program] on paper — organized in an administrative fashion. She wasn't the type of person to walk in and flip disks around ... She's an administrative person and that was her approach to the job. And she did a very good job. And you know, she doesn't still have a lot of expertise — of course she gained so much.

Several teachers mentioned that Karen functioned fine in her role without being an 'expert'. Teachers cited having confidence in Karen's thorough preparation and her knowledge of the programs being presented. An experienced computer-using teacher commented that 'Karen presented things to us that we didn't know. I mean, Karen has been open, she's been objective, she's been learning'. In fact, one teacher remarked:

In some ways, until people are more comfortable, a person like Karen is almost better than someone who is a real expert, because they may not understand ... about a teacher who doesn't know how to put the disk in.

Karen stated, however, that it would have helped in some instances to have been perceived as more of an expert. While some authority appears to come with the role, some teachers seemed less patient with Karen than they might have been with a 'higher status expert'. She remarked:

I mean there were times when just because I said something — even though I didn't know what I was talking about — but just by saying it, sometimes people have the attitude, 'Oh, she's the computer coordinator, O.K.' But then there were other times when the fact that I wasn't an expert, or the fact that, 'You know Karen, [hits table], you don't have this done now, and I want it now! And you know you don't have anything else to do ...' That got in the way.

A former computer committee member commented about Karen's lack of experience with West's program and how that affected her approach to the role:

> It was hard for her to know where to go or who to talk to sometimes because she hadn't been working at it that long. I think it was a burnout style. She listed a lot of things that had been done, some of which you wouldn't think of [doing], that did get done. [But] I'm not sure if her focus was best for us.

Karen found the *program's lack of organization and direction* to be a source of frustration. She quickly realized that West's school plan, 'has a lot of holes in it', and it was a formidable task to 'tie up the program's loose ends'. As was previously described, Judy had previously been a major force in expanding West's computer resources and establishing a foundation from which to build. According to Glenn, however, Judy did not continue to provide the leadership to move the program ahead. Karen admitted that the lack of consistent leadership may be the reason for the program's lack of organized growth. She commented that West's program is in its 'infancy stage now. I think our hardware and our software greatly exceeds our ability, and interest, and feeling of comfort in teaching [with computers]'.

Whereas the faculty chose computer education as a building goal in 1984–85, they did not continue their commitment (as a faculty) to that goal during the following year. Karen stated that she thought 'a great majority [of the teachers] wanted somebody just to take the kids.' Several teachers confirmed this attitude. One remarked, 'We are so bogged down with curriculum and we continue to be, that I just felt like, you know, "Jeez, they're asking us to do one more thing. When are we going to do it?"' Another teacher elaborated on her lack of commitment to schoolwide integration of computers:

> I don't think all teachers need to teach the computer to their students. I really like the idea of a computer specialist because it's like — all of us don't teach PE, all of us don't teach music — we don't all have the expertise in those fields. And I feel like it's just kind of a hit and miss, disjointed thing if everybody's trying to do it and are not even comfortable with it. You know, I think it's kind of like being the jack of all trades and the master of none.... I think there has to be someone who really knows what they're doing and is interested. You know, I just feel like we all don't sing. Because that's part of our curriculum doesn't mean that we all can do it, and do it well. So I feel the same way about computers and the role of the computer coordinator.

Thus, much of the framework needed for the program to grow was not in place. Teachers were open to some form of expanded computer use at West, but many were not committed to the goal of schoolwide integration.

Furthermore, there was not an adequate system for keeping the lab organized and operating smoothly. Parent volunteers had previously performed some of these responsibilities, but as of December, volunteers had not as yet been organized. The computer committee had experienced an abrupt change of personnel, with Judy being the only faculty committee member from the previous year. A parent, who had been active in the program, recalled how the program functioned during the 1984–85 school year:

> It was very vague, in a way, because you had your computer committee, but it was hard for me to figure out who was in control of what. Like Sally was doing the back-to-back computer introduction with the kids, Linda was … pretty much taking care of the computer lab, Judy was sort of in control of your other things. So if I had a question, I sort of had to scrounge around and try to figure out who was going to answer it. And often times, I'd leave a note or talk to Judy and she'd say, 'Well, I'll get back to you'. And it would be a while. So I found myself just pretty much — if it was a question about a teacher, who was coming in, when — I would pretty much have to go and find out myself.

With the change in personnel in the 1985–86 committee, the parent explained that 'what we did, I felt, was to start from scratch all over again'. She stated that the parent volunteers didn't get organized and explained that 'it could be because I was kind of waiting for someone else to do it. The other thing was, … at the beginning of the year, we did not have a computer coordinator.' When Karen was finally appointed to that position, she became 'in charge of a lot, and everyone seemed to expect her [with emphasis] to do everything'. The parent concluded that the lab didn't get rolling because she didn't push, and she felt that 'the teachers didn't care'.

Karen's frustration with the enormity of her task was compounded by the *limited time* she had to perform her role. She stated that 'there's so much [to the job] because the technology is really ahead of what teachers know and feel comfortable with'. As was previously mentioned, Karen got frustrated trying to break the problem of organizing the program into manageable parts. She explained that as she untangled the problems, she would constantly uncover other matters that required attention. A parent remarked:

> Just watching her, [I could see that] she felt really pressured. She felt like she had a million things to do, and she was not getting very much, or getting enough of it done…. Every time I talked to her she was like, 'Ahhhhhhh'. You know, a pile of papers this high….

Glenn confirmed that the 'problems of the computer program are so involved … [that] I don't think there was enough time in the day to get them finished'. He continued, 'I think that she had envisioned really getting the whole thing straightened out and moving smoothly', but added, 'I don't think it's the kind of job where you can get a lot done quickly'.

Karen was confronted with several major decisions, such as establishing priorities for her role, deciding what to teach, and organizing the lab and a schedule for its use. While some suggested that Karen might have involved a broader base of teachers in making these decisions, Karen often found teachers hesitant to get involved. In view of the time constraints of her appointment, Karen sometimes found it necessary to make decisions quicker than she might have liked in order to move the program along.

Karen acknowledged the disjointed state of the program and concluded that there is a need for consistent, expert leadership:

> I think it's [getting West's computer program together] obviously going to take more than one year, and I think it's going to take somebody who's got a little more computer expertise and more than just my 4 tenths position [for half the year]. It's going to take somebody who's here for at least 5 tenths of the day and here for more than just one year. I think it's going to take two or three years.

Impediments to the Integration of Computers into the Curriculum

Despite the groundswell of enthusiasm for computer use in schools, there are a number of impediments to integrating this technology into the curriculum. In order to be effective, coordinators must apply specific strategies and skills to overcome such obstacles. The following discussion of impediments, therefore, is offered to help explain the strategies and skills that were examined in this study.

While the district is supportive of the goals of computer integration, many informants cited the *district's lack of additional budgetary support* to implement the innovation. Individual schools that are interested in expanding their computer use must rely largely on existing district allocations for staff development and support personnel. Schools wanting a released computer coordinator must 'find the tenths' necessary to staff the position. While district funds have been budgeted for hardware and software, many school-level personnel consider the funding to be inadequate for computers to have a significant impact on school programs.

As described in the three cases, teachers embraced the challenge of increased computer use with varying attitudes. Within the range of reactions, however, there are a few recurring themes which involve impediments to computer integration. First, teachers expressed feeling *burdened* with their present teaching and planning responsibilities. Many teachers alluded to having to work an ever-expanding curriculum into their school day. Therefore, even teachers who are comfortable with the new technology are concerned about having new demands placed on their time and energy. For those who are not comfortable, the resistance to 'one more thing' tends to be that much greater.

The phrase '*add-on*' was often used to describe how many teachers viewed current plans for classroom teachers to integrate computers. While most accepted the concept of integration *in theory*, the current *realities* (the 'fit' of existing software into the curriculum, limited resources, teachers' lack of familiarity and comfort with the technology, etc.) contribute to what many teachers view as a 'computer-expanded' curriculum. They explained that the added computer-based curriculum only partially supplants what is being taught in the existing curriculum. The rest, they maintain, is an 'add-on'. Many teachers do not see how current computer-based curriculum materials and the plans for implementation will enable them to teach more, better, or faster. In short, many do not see how computers will help them to do their job better.

Teachers' *previous experiences with other educational innovations* impose further obstacles toward their present computer use. The more the participants have had negative experiences with previous innovations, the more cynical or apathetic they tend to be regarding current change efforts (Fullan, 1982).

Also, teachers mentioned the *competing demands of other school improvement programs*. While computer education was given top priority at some point in each of the schools, many teachers cited being involved in programs aimed at other aspects of their professional growth (e.g., teaching strategies, ITIP, working with 'at-risk' students). In addition, all of these improvement efforts must compete with the 'ordinary demands of keeping school running' (Miles *et al.*, 1985).

While teachers involved in the present study supported expanded computer use in their schools, some were not convinced that computers should be integrated by all classroom teachers. Many teachers preferred hiring a *computer specialist* who would be responsible for teaching computer-related topics to students, much as art and music specialists do in their respective areas. Proponents of this approach were resistant to the expectation that all teachers acquire the expertise necessary to teach with computers.

Strategies Used by Computer Coordinators

The strategies that the coordinators gradually evolved can be viewed as efforts to overcome the existing impediments that inhibit implementation. Also, implicit in these strategies is the assumption that a majority of teachers are open to greater computer use, but not truly committed to the innovation. Figure 6.1 illustrates the spectrum of teachers' attitudes toward using computers. The model, which was suggested by John (the district coordinator), uses his estimated percentages. Depicted on the left side are the truly resistant teachers who want nothing to do with computers. On the far right are the 'computer zealots', teachers who will figure out ways to teach with computers

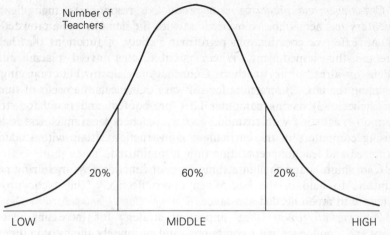

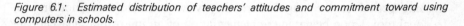

Figure 6.1: Estimated distribution of teachers' attitudes and commitment toward using computers in schools.

despite existing obstacles. The majority of the teachers, however, remain in the middle group: those open, but not truly committed to increased computer use.

The three coordinators in the present study use a variety of common strategies that help overcome the impediments to increased computer use and facilitate teachers' movement to the right (in Figure 6.1), toward greater comfort and commitment. The key strategies discussed in this section are organized into four clusters: (1) resource-adding, (2) organizing and preparing, (3) training, and (4) collaborative problem solving.

Resource-adding addresses a major impediment to implementation — insufficient computer resources. This strategy is critical due to the need to supplement district funding for computer hardware and software. While this strategy is used in the work of other change agents (Beaton, 1985; Miles *et al.*, 1986a), it appears especially critical for computer coordinators. Coordinators pursue this strategy by seeking grants from outside sources and soliciting monies from their school's budget for equipment, software, and staff development. Successful resource-adding does a great deal to enhance the program's credibility with teachers. They are much more resistant to allocating instructional time to computer-based activities if the quantities of hardware and software are inadequate to meet the needs of their students. Also, successful resource-adding contributes to the credibility of the coordinator with teachers. And as Rogers (1983) found, credibility is positively associated with change agent success.

Organizing and preparing is a productive response to the 'plight' of elementary teachers who are overloaded with the demands of a crowded curriculum. Effective coordinators perform a variety of functions that help to overcome this impediment. Where possible, they avoid placing further burdens on already busy teachers. Coordinators help by: (1) organizing and scheduling the lab, (2) screening for software that meets the needs of students and teachers, (3) having computer labs 'pre-booted' and ready for student use, and (4) assisting with custodial chores. Teachers seem much less resistant to using computers in the curriculum if instructional time with students is maximized and teacher preparation time is minimized.

Coordinators can facilitate some support functions by organizing parent volunteers to help in the lab. When done effectively, this tactic provides teachers with much needed assistance.

Training of groups is an important strategy for increasing teachers' facility and confidence with computers, and ultimately their commitment to integration. Training helps to move teachers through an awkward transitional learning period to the stage where they view computers as another professional tool. Upon beginning implementation of an innovation, teachers are initially concerned about how it will affect them personally (Hall, 1976). Will they feel incompetent in trying to teach with computers? Does the integration of computers into the curriculum threaten their self-concepts as professionals? Effective training helps to overcome such concerns that serve as impediments to implementation of the innovation.

A subsequent level of teacher concern involves how the innovation will impact students (Hall, 1976). This explains teachers' preference for training sessions targeted for teachers of specific grade-level or interest areas. This approach appeals to the teachers' 'practicality ethic', that is, their belief that new practices and methods should be practical in meeting the needs of their students (Doyle and Ponder, 1978). Teachers also stated a preference for friendly, but structured sessions that consist of brief demonstrations and ample time for practice.

Although none of the coordinators employed a formal *coaching* component, their training program was based upon being available to provide *follow-up support* on an individual basis. While much of the support involved giving *technical assistance*, all three coordinators used strategies that provided for the affective needs of their clients. All coordinators were non-evaluative and non-judgmental, and *supportive emotionally* — approaches that contribute to the building of trust and rapport. Previous studies of effective change agents (Beaton, 1985; Miles *et al.*, 1986a; Miles *et al.*, 1986b) confirm the importance of providing non-judgmental support to establish a safe environment that facilitates change and growth.

Energizing and motivating the client appear critical to the training process. As was previously emphasized, teachers have a great many demands placed upon them, and they often need a 'pat on the back' or an 'encouraging word' to get them to cope with a stressful learning situation. *Demonstrating and modeling* serves to energize and motivate teachers. By being in a position to observe effective teaching with computers, teachers become encouraged that they can do it, too.

Collaborative problem solving is a noteworthy strategy that helps teachers and the coordinator to integrate the new technology into the school program. Similar to other change agents (Beaton, 1985; Miles *et al.*, 1986a; Miles *et al.*, 1986b), computer coordinators work collaboratively with individual teachers to effect change in the content and delivery of instruction. In addition, however, successful coordinators work collaboratively with small groups of teachers (usually grouped by grade level) and their school's policy-making body — the computer committee. This strategy of collaboration appears especially important for establishing teacher ownership of the program. Teachers emphasized that effective coordinators listen to what they have to say and involve them in making decisions about the program. Teachers expressed being less resistant to change when they can influence the 'fit' between their other curricular responsibilities and the computer program. This is consistent with the findings of the Rand Study (Berman and McLaughlin, 1978), which suggested that involving teachers facilitates commitment as well as more informed decision-making.

Coordinators enhance the strategy of collaboration by emphasizing their *homophyly* (similarities of beliefs, experience, etc.) with clients (Louis, 1981; Rogers and Shoemaker, 1971). They tend to play down their computer expertise and resist being called 'the expert'. Rather, they prefer to be seen as 'just another teacher who knows something about using computers in schools'. While teachers may welcome the advice of experts, many are resistant to an expert 'coming in and telling them how to teach'. Perhaps this resistance is due to the great discrepancies that exist between 'ivory tower' theories of education and the many impediments that make it difficult to translate those theories into daily practice. At any rate, by collaborating and de-emphasizing their expertise, coordinators seek to minimize teacher resistance.

Skills Used by Computer Coordinators

Skills are the tools with which coordinators carry out their strategies for expanding computer use. While various strategies are critical for overcoming impediments to implementation of instructional computing, coordinator skills are needed to actually facilitate change. A description of each skill, as used by each coordinator, is presented in the case studies (Strudler, 1987). In this section, I will offer a brief overview of the skills used across the three cases and highlight a few key points.

The findings suggest that while effective coordinators must be knowledgeable about instructional computing, it is just as critical that they possess strong interpersonal and organizational skills to carry out necessary training and support functions. Nearly all informants expressed that interpersonal skills for coordinators are more important than their knowledge of computing. Like any good teacher, coordinators rely on interpersonal skills to convey the 'subject matter' in a clear and patient manner, and to motivate people to learn. Teachers appear especially resistant to 'computer experts' who 'know, but can't teach'. Of course, coordinators who are truly effective are strong in both areas of expertise. The need for coordinators to possess a combination of interpersonal and technical skills is consistent with findings regarding other change agents (Beaton, 1985; Miles *et al.*, 1986a, 1986b; Rogers, 1983).

Table 6.1 provides a summary of five different approaches to quantifying skills used by coordinators. The number in each column represents the percentage of mentions of each skill out of the total for that approach (column). For example, the second column consists of the total mentions of a particular skill throughout all of the interviews across the three cases. *Technical expertise*, then, comprised 11.3 percent of all skills mentioned throughout the interviews. The actual frequency was sixty-three, and the total mention of all skills coded was 556. The percent derived is therefore 63/556, or 11.3 percent.

Percentages were used to assign an equal weight to each skill category and thereby standardize the reporting. Also, using percentages allowed for a straightforward way to compute an average score (in the last column).

The third column represents the percentage of responses to interview questions asking about the coordinator's *strengths* or *main contributions* to the program (out of the total responses citing strengths or main contributions). The fourth column lists percentages of skills mentioned as being involved in *critical incidents*, that is, incidents in which the coordinator was identified as being especially helpful. The fifth column lists how supervisors and coordinators ranked the importance of various skills on their questionnaires. The percentage given was derived by weighting informants' responses and then computing a total. The higher the percentage, the higher the average rank of that skill.

The sixth column lists the percentage of times that each skill was *recommended* by informants as critical for selecting school computer coordinators. The final column shows the *average percentage* derived from the adjacent five columns. Skills are listed by the total average, from highest to lowest.

Readers should be cautioned about placing too much emphasis on the summary statistics. They were provided to supplement, not substitute for, the detailed descriptions of skills in the case studies (Strudler, 1987). In presenting findings for their research project, Miles and his colleagues offered similar warnings. They stressed, 'The important thing is to draw clear meaning from the three cases, in answer to our research questions' (Miles *et al.*, 1986b). When viewed in perspective, the data in Table 1 are a useful supplement to the descriptions of skills and offer a framework for discussion.

Readers also should resist the convenience of merely referring to the composite average column. Much meaning can be derived by analyzing disparities in the various columns. For example, while *group functioning* is

Table 6.1: *Perentage of times that each change agent skill was mentioned in interviews*

Change Agent Skill	Total Mentioned	Strength Contrib	Critical Incident	Quest Rankings	Recs for Selection	Total Average
Technical Expertise	11.3	9.6	21.2	7.3	23.4	14.6
Admin/Organization	10.3	14.4	3.8	3.8	13.8	9.2
Providing Support	10.1	8.7	17.5	6.7	1.1	8.8
Resource Bringing	7.4	8.7	11.2	4.3	2.1	6.7
Collaboration	8.3	3.8	11.2	2.2	7.4	6.6
Training & Workshops	7.4	8.7	7.5	5.4	3.2	6.4
Interpersonal Ease	4.5	4.8	2.5	9.4	10.6	6.4
Diagnosing Indiv or Org	5.9	3.8	6.2	10.8	3.2	6.0
Initiative/tenacity	5.8	9.6	0.0	6.5	7.4	5.9
Communication	5.9	5.8	3.8	6.2	7.4	5.8
Knowledge of EI Curric	3.4	6.7	3.8	4.0	6.4	4.9
Master Teacher	2.9	3.8	5.0	3.5	6.4	4.3
Demonstration/Modeling	2.2	1.9	0.0	8.3	4.3	3.3
Trust/Rapport Building	3.4	5.8	0.0	5.6	0.0	3.0
Managing/Controlling	4.0	1.0	1.2	3.0	2.1	2.3
Group Functioning	1.6	0.0	0.0	8.1	1.1	2.1
Confidence-Building	2.2	1.0	1.2	5.1	0.0	1.9
Independence-Building	2.0	0.0	3.8	*	0.0	1.1
Use of Humor	0.5	1.9	0.0	*	0.0	5.0
Confrontation	0.7	0.0	0.0	0.0	0.0	0.1
Conflict Mediation	0.4	0.0	0.0	0.0	0.0	0.1
Total	100.0	100.0	100.0	100.0	100.0	100.0

* Skill was not included on questionnaire

listed in the bottom third of the skills, it received a high rating on the questionnaire and very low ratings in the other categories. The questionnaire, it should be noted, was completed only by supervisors and coordinators. Thus, the imbalance in scores reflects the fact that while teachers are not aware of the value of this skill, coordinators and supervisors are.

Technical expertise was cited as the single most important skill used by coordinators. If various interpersonal skills were grouped together, however, the *interpersonal skills cluster* would rank at the top of the list of skills. It should be stressed that technical expertise was defined in this study as 'knowledge of hardware and software involved in instructional computing'. As one principal commented, 'You [coordinators] don't have to know how to change circuit boards and know all the 'ins and outs' of the insides of computers ...' John confirmed that a coordinator does not need an extensive background in academic computer science.

Rather, coordinators need a solid command of microcomputer operations including basic care and maintenance, saving and printing files, using peripherals, and general troubleshooting. In addition, effective coordinators possess a broad knowledge of software, including how to troubleshoot when problems arise with particular programs. While coordinators emphasize to teachers that they 'don't have all the answers', it appears critical that they have the knowledge to help solve most technical problems and minimize undue stress. Sometimes, learning to use computers can be extremely frustrating — enough to induce some people to avoid further use. In such cases, simple technical help can be far more effective than hours of well-intentioned nurturing and support. Teachers, as learners, need to feel successful, and technical expertise can often contribute to such success. When compared with Tom and Sue, it seems clear that Karen's deficiencies in this area hampered her effectiveness. One teacher stated that a computer coordinator should be able to:

> diagnose a problem instantly, rather than by trial and error, [and] know exactly what to do to get the kid back on track.... Most of us don't have that expertise, and I want someone who does.... [Karen] herself will admit that she's not an expert. In other words, it's trial and error for her when the program won't run for some reason. Why it's 'guess and by golly' for her too.

While it seems unreasonable to expect coordinators to 'instantly diagnose' all problems, a coordinator loses *credibility* if he or she frequently has difficulty in troubleshooting. Consistent with previous research on change agents (Beaton, 1985; Miles *et al.*, 1986a; Rogers, 1983), knowledge, competence, and experience are critical for change agents to establish credibility. Interestingly, over 21 percent of the critical incidents cited (incidents when coordinators were especially helpful to teachers) involved coordinators' use of technical expertise. Also significant is the fact that technical expertise comprised over 23 percent of recommendations for the selection of coordinators, further confirmation of the importance of this skill.

Technical expertise also appears important because of the developing nature of the innovation. Coordinators must keep abreast of advances in hardware and software and facilitate decisions concerning how these advances might enhance the achievement of curricular goals. In the case of computers in education, the innovation is difficult to tie into a 'neat curriculum package'. The field is changing rapidly and will continue to do so. Computer coordinators therefore must have the technical expertise to keep up with these changes.

Interpersonal skills, which include support, collaboration, interpersonal ease, communication, and trust and rapport building, are clearly critical for change agents to establish and maintain positive working relationships with teachers. This finding is consistent across the three cases, as well as with previous research on change agent activities.

The coordinators also need interpersonal skills to reduce the discomfort of a threatening learning situation for teachers. The fact remains that while computer expertise is desirable for elementary teachers, it is not yet a fundamental skill. The current payoff in terms of opportunities for student learning does not warrant mandating computer use where teacher commitment is not in place. It makes better sense to provide opportunities for teachers and encourage their participation. To carry out this strategy, interpersonal skills are clearly needed to facilitate teacher involvement and promote commitment.

Balance of skills. Apart from the mere possession of the necessary skills, coordinators need a delicate sense of timing and balance in their use. Though it involves a difficult balance, effective coordinators seem to combine being patient and 'low key' with being active and systematic. As Beaton (1985) suggested for staff development specialists, coordinators must balance process-oriented interpersonal skills with task-oriented training and organizational skills.

One difficult balance to achieve involves the inevitable conflict between overcoming teacher resistance to computers and facilitating teacher independence. Basically, the more a coordinator does to make things easy for teachers (e.g., choosing materials, planning lessons, teaching the lessons, always being there to 'bail people out', etc.), the less stress and resistance there tends to be. On the other hand, the more a coordinator provides such help, the more the teachers tend to be dependent on that 'helping hand'.

John alluded to this conflict in a parable that contrasted the approaches of Tom and Sue:

> It's like you have two nests of little birds. And in the one nest the daddy bird [referring to Tom] says, 'Don't worry, I'll fly you forever. I'll take you anywhere we need to go, and I'll do a nice job of it. And you'll love me.' And they do. And he does [a nice job]. And in the other nest, the mommy bird [referring to Sue] says, 'I'm going to teach you to fly. And you're going to fall on your butts at times. And other times you won't. And it's going to be fun, and crazy, and overtaxing. And you've got to trust me. But someday you'll be able to fly, and if I'm not around anymore, it won't matter much.'

Thus, the question arises regarding how helpful to be. While John clearly endorses the second strategy, it may not work with all teachers in all settings. Ambitious plans for getting teachers to independently fly on their own can result in increased teacher competence. It may also create, however, greater teacher resistance. Tom insists that a developed curriculum and framework for implementation needs to be in place before teachers at East should be expected to commit themselves to a computer-based curriculum. Meanwhile, his approach is to gradually draw teachers in. In any event, effective coordinators judiciously analyze and *diagnose individuals and organizations.* They consider the comfort level and commitment of the individual staff members and the school as a whole in choosing a preferred timeline and approach for computer implementation.

Table 6.2: Frequency and percentage of outcomes effected by computer coordinators

Outcomes	Frequency Mention	Percent Mention	Quest. Ranking	Percent Ranking	Total Average
Capacity Building	26	17.1%	56	29.3%	23.2%
Implementation of Program	36	23.7%	40	20.9%	22.3%
Satisfaction with Program	25	16.4%	26	13.6%	15.0%
Student Impact	28	18.4%	7	3.7%	11.0%
Use of Specific Products	11	7.2%	19	9.9%	8.6%
School Climate Change	9	5.9%	12	6.3%	6.1%
Organizational Change	12	7.9%	8	4.2%	6.0%
Institutionalization	3	2.0%	12	6.3%	4.1%
Short-Run Success	2	1.3%	6	3.1%	2.2%
Positive Relationships	0	0.0%	5	2.6%	1.3%
Total	52	100.0%	191	100.0%	100.0%

Outcomes Effected by Computer Coordinators

Table 6.2 shows the most frequently cited outcomes in the present study. The second column lists the frequency that particular outcomes were mentioned, and the third column shows the percentage of the total outcomes that particular outcomes were mentioned (e.g., for capacity building $26/152 = 17.1$ percent). The fourth column lists the weighted rankings from the questionnaires given to coordinators and supervisors. (See the explanation of the weighted rankings for skills in Table 6.1.) The fifth column shows the percentage for these rankings. The last column displays the average of the two percentages (from the third and fifth columns). Outcomes are arranged by the total average, from highest to lowest.

In each case, informants reported *capacity-building*, which is improvement in the capability or skills of teachers, as a prominent outcome. Other high ranking outcomes include *implementation of the program* and client *satisfaction with the program*. Also, the programs clearly had impact on the students regarding their comfort and confidence in operating computers. Interestingly, *student impact* ranked as the second most noteworthy outcome, according to the frequency of mention. Coordinators and supervisors, however, did not rate this outcome high on their questionnaires. One explanation for this difference might be that the coordinators and supervisors placed a higher priority on the training of teachers. Also, they might have regarded student impact as pertaining to gains in academic skills, and therefore did not consider increased 'computer literacy' as part of this outcome. Also, they might have sensed that the present study was focusing on teachers as the primary clients of the coordinators.

Discussion

Integration: Is It Worth It?

Most educators recognize a clear trend toward greater computer use in schools (Reed and Sauter, 1987). Furthermore, most would predict that computers will one day become an everyday tool in all aspects of the curriculum. The question then becomes how to implement this innovation, and on what timeline. It seems clear that computer education in the schools can be most efficiently implemented at present through specialized classes taught by qualified computer teachers. Such an approach requires minor curriculum reform and minimal teacher training. In a sense, though, this implementation strategy is a 'quick fix'. While it addresses the immediate computer literacy needs of students, it does little to bring the majority of teachers, as well as school programs in general, into the information age.

Proponents of computer integration foresee a gradual transition toward using computers in all aspects of the curriculum. They stress the need for teacher training and curriculum reform. While this approach involves a significantly greater change than does computer specialization, the long-term payoff appears far greater. School districts, then, must establish priorities regarding computer implementation. District administrators should consider both the costs and benefits of computer integration and plan accordingly.

Impediments in Perspective: The Need for Teacher Commitment

In the Rand Change Agent Study, Berman and McLaughlin (1977) found that teacher commitment to an innovation has the most consistently positive relationship with project outcomes. The authors explained that project success is unlikely unless teachers want to work hard to make it happen. Factors that lead to teacher commitment include the innovation's quality, need, and clarity (Fullan, 1982).

In the current case of integrating computers into the curriculum, all of these factors have been questioned. Teachers agree that computer-based applications are improving, but the quality of many programs and their 'fit' into the curriculum still leave much to be desired. While the need for increased computer use throughout the curriculum is well supported for schools of the future (Moursund, 1986; Reed and Sauter, 1987), the immediate need is not quite so clear. Also, while the Eugene District has provided a framework for integrating computers (i.e., the district curriculum strands), and has made steps to clarify the goals and means of implementation, the large goal of integration is still perceived by some as undeveloped and 'fuzzy'.

Overall, many teachers are not yet convinced that the current implementation of computer applications can effect a significant difference in student learning. Nor are many teachers convinced that computer education should be the top priority in their program for professional growth and school improvement. Most teachers, however, do recognize the need for teachers and students alike to begin making the *transition* toward more meaningful use of computers in schools.

The Eugene district provides a framework for such a transition. It stipulates that all elementary teachers should be trained and able to integrate computers into the curriculum. As stated, however, there are a great many *impediments* to implementing such a plan. The strategies used by effective coordinators to overcome these impediments, then, are critical for program success. A discussion of such strategies follows.

Effectiveness of Larger Strategy of Using Computer Coordinators

Most teachers today have jumped on the computer bandwagon to some degree. Only the most resistant teachers have managed not to take part in some of the inservice offerings available. Such workshops, however, appear to be 'loosely coupled' to subsequent practice. Little follow-up occurs and only a small percentage of teachers are able to effectively transfer into classroom practice what they have learned in workshops and university classes.

Another approach to integrating computers in education might involve the centralized research and development of major curriculum reform. This strategy would clearly help provide a framework for implementing a computer-based curriculum. Such centralized efforts and 'teacher proof' curriculum projects, however, are currently not highly regarded. While some excellent materials have been developed, most have not been effectively implemented at the school level.

A current trend in school improvement focuses on school-based change rather than centralized curriculum reform. Consistent with this trend, computer coordinators serve as on-site staff developers and help mold the innovation to 'fit' a school's educational program. In addition to dealing with curriculum issues, coordinators provide a variety of training and support functions that lead to implementation of computers in their schools. Therefore, the 'game plan' of hiring computer coordinators appears to be a very good one. Although the plan is costly, it seems to hold true that 'you get what you pay for'. Effective coordinators can bring about significant changes at the school level.

Suggested Guidelines for Implementation of Coordinator Role

Time needed
Two elements of time required must be considered: the full-time equivalent (FTE) allotted for the position, and the number of years projected for the

appointment. It appears that a .5 FTE is adequate for coordinators in medium to large-sized elementary schools. If less time is allocated, role expectations should be adjusted. As was clearly illustrated in one of the case studies, ambitious plans and limited time for implementation leads to frustration.

Supervisors and coordinators stated that coordinators should be allocated a minimum of two to three years to perform their role. Of course, this recommendation is dependent upon the extent of the school's goals regarding computer use. The concurrent goals of teacher independence and computer integration involve significant changes in practice, and therefore require much time to accomplish.

As was learned in all of the cases, it is difficult for a coordinator to 'work herself out of a job'. Tom, in the conclusion of his second year in his role, has made much progress in establishing a framework for computer use and getting teachers comfortable with computers. Teachers at East, however, were far from being independent of his services. Teachers at Central appeared to be further along toward independence. After implementing an ambitious program with teachers in her first year as released coordinator, Sue had hoped to be able to phase out her job after one more year (by the end of the 1986–87 school year). While Sue recognized that this goal was possible, she did expect that teachers would continue to need support in organizing the lab, selecting software, and keeping abreast of advances in the field.

One possible way to phase out reliance on a coordinator might be to use a 'multiplier mode' to spread the innovation. This strategy consists of asking teachers to lead workshops, demonstrate their work to others, act as mentors, serve as a cadre, and begin to act like teacher specialists (Miles *et al.*, 1986b). While such an approach may not eliminate the need for a coordinator, it may help decrease the needed FTE for the role.

Need for long-term planning

Each school examined in the present study demonstrated a commitment to computer education in staffing the coordinator position. The role of the coordinator, however, is but one factor of many that needs to be considered in establishing a long-term building plan. If the school's plan involves integration on a large scale, it appears critical that teachers assume ownership of the plan and commit themselves to carrying it out. Coordinators can facilitate teacher ownership and commitment by working through the school's computer committee. Sue's work at Central attests to the effectiveness of this strategy. The computer committee appears to be a critical component of establishing and implementing a long-term plan for computer use.

Selection and training of coordinators

Prospective coordinators should possess a good balance of technical, interpersonal, and organizational skills. 'People skills' appear to be more difficult to teach and learn, and therefore people chosen as coordinators should already be strong in such skills.

It appears to be an advantage to choose coordinators from the school's existing staff. With trust and rapport already in place, the coordinator can 'move the program along' at a more accelerated pace than could an 'out of staff' person. Out-of-staff coordinators, therefore, have a greater need for strong interpersonal skills in order to work effectively with new colleagues.

Training should be considered to facilitate coordinator effectiveness. While coordinators would benefit from participating in a general forum in which they can share concerns, training sessions for targeted needs would also be helpful. As Miles and his colleagues (1986b) recommended for change agents in their study, computer coordinators would benefit from training in organizational change. Such training might involve specific strategies and skills in working with the school as an organization, including strategies for working with computer committees and parent volunteer programs. Other topics for training might involve issues and techniques related to current hardware and software.

Implications for Educational Policy Makers

Computer education has been a much publicized, high profile innovation. It is estimated that in the spring of 1987, there were close to two million computers in elementary and secondary schools across the country. Consistent with other innovations, however, inadequate funds have been allocated to support the implementation of computers in schools. Teachers have not been adequately trained, and computer-based curricula are still in their infancy.

The present study illustrates how difficult it is to effect significant educational change. It involved three schools that have been active in implementing and expanding computer use. Yet there are many impediments to full-scale implementation of this innovation. Computer coordinators use a variety of strategies and skills to help overcome these impediments in order to effect meaningful change. It appears that without the implementation support that coordinators provide, instructional computer use is unlikely to fulfill its promise as an educational innovation.

The findings of this study are consistent with the findings of other studies on educational change. The present study supports the effectiveness of staffing change agents to work with teachers at the school level.

Limitations of the Study

Five limitations of the present study seem noteworthy. The first limitation of the study was the small size of the sample examined. The present study examined the work of three computer coordinators in elementary schools in one school district. Therefore, the present findings are not readily general-izable to other coordinators working at various school settings in different locations.

The second limitation was the nature of the sample. To discover effective coordinator behaviors, the present study examined coordinators in schools where a high degree of implementation was reported. Thus the present sample lacked the inclusion of ineffective coordinators with which to contrast effective skills, strategies, and outcomes.

The third limitation was the method of data collection. Data were gath-ered primarily by interviewing teachers, coordinators, supervisors, and par-ents involved in each school's program. While relevant documents were examined and classroom observations conducted, a majority of the data were based on informants' perceptions of the program. Implementation effects (e.g., improved computer skills of teachers and students), for example, were based on informants' perceptions of such effects rather than on the use of measures involving direct observation.

The fourth limitation was the lack of precision in the coding system used to measure strategies, skills, and outcomes. Multiple codes can often apply to many of the effective behaviors and outcomes. For example, in helping a teacher who 'gets stuck' using a particular program, the coordinator might use a combination of skills including: providing support, trust and rapport-building; confidence-building; independence-building; communication; dia-gnosing individuals; and interpersonal ease. Therefore, it was necessary to create addenda to the coding system in order to increase coding reliability. The fact remains, however, that many actions do involve multiple codes. The codes given in the present study, therefore, represent a systematic approxi-mation of the variables being examined.

The fifth limitation was the method of data analysis used in the present study. While steps were taken to establish inter-rater reliability, the fact remains that the author individually selected what interview data to tran-scribe. Further, after the data was coded, the author chose what 'chunks' of data to use in the text of this report. While various steps were taken to in-crease the validity of the findings (e.g., using multiple measures, cross-checking findings across multiple sources, having informants read drafts of the cases to check for accuracy), the method of data analysis and reporting was reliant on the interpretations of the author.

Recommendations for Further Study

Results and limitations of the present study suggest six directions for future research:

1   The present study yielded rich descriptions of the work of elementary school-based computer coordinators in one district. The study should

be replicated and extended at different settings, including at middle school and high school programs. In addition, larger samples might be used to increase the generalizability of the findings.

2   Much can be learned from comparing and contrasting effective coordinators and programs with less effective coordinators and programs. Such a comparison would help to further identify effective strategies and skills needed by computer coordinators. In addition, by studying less effective programs, we can learn more about the impediments to computer integration and strategies that might be used to overcome such impediments.

3   Further studies of change agent behaviors should use measures involving direct observation of implementation effects rather than continuing to rely on informants' perceptions of such effects. The addition of observation measures would increase the validity of future studies and enable more valid comparisons of findings across cases and studies.

4   We need to examine the cost-effectiveness of the school-based coordinator model. How does the effectiveness of this approach compare to other approaches such as the allocation of funds for the research and development of a computer-based curriculum, or a more traditional inservice model?

5   While the coding system used in the present study offers a valuable framework from which to examine coordinators' work, it is somewhat 'clumsy' in the amount of overlap that exists in like skills and strategies. A more streamlined coding system, perhaps made up of clusters of strategies or skills, would facilitate easier comparisons and clearer reporting of findings.

6   The present study suggests that computer coordinators can increase their effectiveness by participating in training that involves particular strategies and skills. Therefore, training modules should be developed, implemented, and evaluated with coordinators. Such modules might include strategies for: (1) organizational change (including working with school computer committees), (2) overcoming teacher resistance and building teacher independence, (3) resource-adding (e.g., grant writing), (4) working with parent volunteers, and (5) implementing a computer-based curriculum.

Appendix A

Variables Used in the Study

Strategies Used by Change Agents

A *strategy* is defined as a carefully planned method of translating theory and assumptions into action in order to achieve a goal. A total of fifteen strategies were used to categorize the approaches employed by the coordinators. The list was based on the system developed by Miles (1984) and modified by Beaton (1985). They were defined as follows:

Providing technical assistance: helping individuals develop competence in specific techniques.

Resource-linking: a dissemination process that involves transmitting ideas from outside researchers and trainers and building them into a teacher's repertoire of skills through on-going training; or introducing clients with needs to resource people.

Solution-giving: providing innovation or other products of research as solutions to the perceived needs of others; often initiated without negotiation.

Training of groups: running workshops and courses to teach understandings and skills.

Coaching of individuals: training and teaching one-to-one using clinical observation and conferences in the teacher's classroom.

Organizing, preparing: planning, researching, and preparing for the operation of the computer program.

Demonstrating, modeling: demonstrating skills or techniques to assist understanding and to serve as a model for the learners to copy.

Energizing, motivating: initiating awareness and involvement; building confidence and a willingness to improve; establishing a rationale for the techniques being taught.

Supporting the client emotionally: relaxing tension and dispelling fear; reassuring and stressing positives with sensitivity and empathy; stroking of client.

Developing a support structure: creating a network or procedure for the support of clients, involving their teaching peers, their supervisors, or both. Creates a mechanism for support.

Supported planning: assisting clients through the planning process.

Collaborative problem solving: shared involvement with clients in the problem-solving process.

Resource-adding: supplying materials and ideas to clients.

Monitoring, evaluating: judging the effectiveness of a teacher's performance in order to stimulate change.

Controlling client action: exercise of power, albeit expert power used with client consent, to direct the actions of clients.

Skills Used by Change Agents

Skills are defined as requisite knowledge or ability, or special qualifications to perform the tasks involved in the role. The focus in analyzing the data is on attributes and capabilities of the change agent expressed with a qualitative description by informants; e.g., the trainer does this well (or poorly). Skills can be seen as generic tools, and thus may be applicable in many different strategies.

The classification of skills is based on the revised system of Miles and colleagues (1986a). They subdivided the skills into general skills and specific skills. The twenty-one skills used in this study are defined (in abbreviated form) as follows:

General Skills

Interpersonal ease: relating simply and directly to others.

Communication: ability to listen, talk, and write.

Group functioning: understanding group dynamics, able to facilitate team work.

Training/doing workshops: direct instruction, teaching adults in a systematic way.

Master Teacher: wide educational experience, able to impart skills to others.

Knowledge of elementary curriculum: knowledge of elementary school subject matter.

Technical expertise in educational computing: knowledge of hardware and software involved in instructional computing

Administrative/organizational: defining and structuring work, activities, time.

Specific Skills

Initiative-taking/tenacity: starting or pushing activities, moving directly toward action.

Resource-bringing: locating and providing information, materials, practices, equipment useful to clients.

Trust/rapport-building: developing a sense of safety, openness, reduced threat on part of clients; good relationship-building.

Support: providing nurturant relationship.

Confidence-building: strengthening client's sense of efficacy.

Confrontation: direct expression of negative information without generating negative effect.

Conflict mediation: resolving or improving situations where multiple incompatible interests are in play.

Collaboration: creating relationships where influence is mutually shared toward decisions regarding the program.

Humor: Use of humor to aid work with clients.

Diagnosing individuals/organizations: forming a valid picture of the needs/problems of an individual client or a school as an organization.

Managing/controlling: orchestrating the improvement process; coordinating activities, time and people; direct influence on others.

Demonstration: modeling new behavior in classrooms or meetings.

Independence-building: Getting people to do it themselves.

Outcomes of the Change Agent Activities

Outcomes in this study are considered to be any effect on teachers, students, administrators, or schools that results from the interventions of the change agents. The outcomes, based on the classification of Miles (1984), form a hierarchy in that outcomes that come later on the list are considered more difficult to attain. If two or more codes applied to a particular incident being coded, precedence was given to the highest outcome in the hierarchy. Abbreviated definitions of the ten outcomes follow:

Short run success: small achievements made that enable other achievements.

Use of specific products: teachers use products or materials that they hadn't previously used.

Positive relationships: client satisfaction with positive relationship with the change agent.

Satisfaction with the program: positive attitudes of individual teachers and administrators toward the program.

Implementation of program: the extent to which the formal program is being carried out.

School climate change: feelings, norms, or sentiments have changed.

Organizational change: changes in the structure or procedures of the school.

Student impact: students have a favorable attitude to the new teaching method, or have changed behavior in some way, or have changed in achievement.

Capacity building: improved capability or skills of teachers.

Institutionalization: program features, structures, and procedures are built into the school.

Biblography

AMES, C., GILBERSTAD, N., SKY, N. and STRUDLER, N. (1985) *Eugene school district 4J elementary computer program pilot study evaluation*, unpublished manuscript, School District 4J, Eugene.

BARBOUR, A. (1986) 'Electronic learning's first annual computer coordinator survey,' *Electronic Learning*, 55, pp. 35–8.

BEATON, C. (1985) *Identifying change agent strategies, skills, and outcomes: the case of district-based staff development specialists*, unpublished doctoral dissertation, University of Oregon.

BERMAN, P. and MCLAUGHLIN, M. (1977) *Federal programs supporting educational change, Vol. VIII, Implementing and sustaining innovations*, Santa Monica, Calif.: Rand Corporation.

BERMAN, P. and MCLAUGHLIN, M. (1978) *Federal program supporting educational change, Vol. VII, Factors affecting implementation and continuation*, Santa Monica, Calif.: Rand Corporation.

DOYLE, W. and PONDER, G.A. (1977–78) 'The practicality ethic in teacher decision-making.' *Interchange, 8,* 3, pp. 1–12.

FULLAN, M. (1981) 'School district and school personnel in knowledge utilization', in LEHMING, R. and KANE, E.M. (Eds) '*Improving schools: Using what we know*, Beverly Hills, CA: Sage (pp. 212–252).

FULLAN, M. (1981) *The meaning of educational change*, New York: Teachers College Press.

GALL, M. and RENCHLER, R.S. (1985) *Effective staff development for teachers: A research-based model*, Eugene, OR: ERIC, Clearinghouse on Educational Management, College of Education, University of Oregon.

HALL, G.E. (1976) 'The study of individual teacher and professor concerns about innovations', *The Journal of Teacher Education, 27,* 1, pp. 22–3.

HUBERMAN, M. and CRANDALL, D. *People, policies, and practices: Examining the chain of school improvement, Vol. IX*, Andover, Mass.: The Network, Inc,: 1982.

JOYCE, B. and SHOWERS, B. (1983) *Power in staff development through research on training*, Alexandria, VA: Association for Supervision and Curriculum Development.

LOUIS, K.S. (1981) 'External agents and knowledge utilization: Dimensions for analysis and action', in LEHMING, R. and KANE, M. (Eds) *Improving school: Using what we know*. Beverly Hills, CA: Sage. (pp. 168–211).

MCGINTY, T. (1987) 'Electronic learning's second annual computer coordinator survey: Growing pains — A portrait of an emerging profession', *Electronic Learning*, 6, 5, pp. 18–23, 48.

MILES, M.B. (1984) *The role of the change agent in the school improvement process*. Abstract of paper presented at the annual meeting of the American Educational Research Association, New Orleans.

MILES, M.B., SAXL, E.R. and LIEBERMAN, A. (1985) *New York City teacher centers consortium evaluation report: 1984–85.*

MILES, M.B., SAXL, E.R. and Lieberman, A. (1986a) 'Key skills of educational "change agents": an empirical view', *Curriculum Inquiry.*

MILES, M.B., SAXL, E.R. and LIEBERMAN, A. and JAMES, J. (1986b) *New York City teacher centers consortium evaluation report: 1985–86.*

MOURSUND, D. (1985) *The computer coordinator,* Eugene, OR: International Council for Computers in Education.

MOURSUND, D. (1986) 'The future of computers in instruction', *Proceedings of Extending the Human Mind: Computers in Education Annual Conference.* Eugene, OR: Center for Advanced Technology in Education, University of Oregon, (pp. 107–121).

REED, S. and SAUTER, R.C. (1987) 'Visions of the 1990's: What experts predict for educational technology in the next decade'. *Electronic Learning,* 6, 8, pp. 18–23.

ROGER, E.M. (1983) *Diffusion of innovations* (3rd ed.) New York: Free Press

ROGERS, E.M. and SHOEMAKER, F.F. (1971) *Communications of innovations: A cross cultural approach,* New York: Free Press.

ROSENBLUM, S. and LOUIS, K. *Stability and change: Innovation in an educational context,* Cambridge, Mass.: ABT Associates.

STRUDLER, N.B. (1987) *The role of school-based computer coordinators as change agents in elementary school programs.* Unpulished doctoral dissertation, University of Oregon.

IV

Naturalist Research on CAL in the United Kingdom

Introduction

The final report, 'Just a Few Machines Bleeping away in a Corner: A Review of Naturalistic Studies of Computers into Education in the UK,' by John Beynon, is a comprehensive look at the scope and significance of naturalistic research on computers in education in the United Kingdom. The author admits that there are only a very few naturalistic studies of instructional computing in the UK that are available at the present time. However, one of these is the monumental UNCAL (Understanding Computer Aided Learning) project from the early 1970s from which much can still be learned about conducting field-based naturalistic evaluation of large CAL projects and about the essential nature of interactivity in human learning (Kemmis, Atkin and Wright, 1977).

According to Beynon: 'Research to date has primarily been of a distant, schedule-based kind, reifying the technology and heavily technicist as opposed to educationist.' Beynon describes the ongoing debate, similar to that in the United States, between a '... hugely enthusiastic advocacy ... and an equally spirited dismissal of alleged benefits.... What is immediately noticeable ... is the conspicuous lack of classroom-based data to substantiate the various claims and counter charges.' So it seems that while our contemporaries in the UK may temporarily lack the diversity of naturalistic studies evidenced by our first volume of case studies on computer aided learning, their perspective on the substantive and methodological issues involved reveals an intellectual maturity and practical determination.

Beynon concludes with a caveat that the purpose of an ethnography of school computer use should be to ascertain whether the use of existing educational practices concerning microcomputers is '... wise, accessible to all, and used in democratic and beneficial ways'. He points out a noteworthy objective for us all on BOTH sides of the Atlantic Ocean.

Reference

KEMMIS, S., ATKIN, R., and WRIGHT, E. (1977) *How do students learn? Working papers on the UNCAL evaluation studies,* (Occasional publications no. 5), Centre for Applied Research in Education, University of East Anglia, Norwich: UK.

Chapter 7

'Just a Few Machines Bleeping Away in the Corner': A Review of Naturalistic Studies of Computers into Education in the UK

John Beynon

Introduction

When I was asked to write this paper I was happy to accept, but with one reservation: I was not able to do what the editors originally requested, namely a critical overview of 'naturalistic studies' of microcomputers in the classroom (hereafter referred to as IT/Education) in the United Kingdom. The reason was simple: even if an expanded definition of 'naturalistic studies' was adopted, the fact remained there had been precious few of any quality or scale. Although there is a huge UK literature on computers/teaching/learning, the vast bulk of it can be located in what I elsewhere (Beynon, 1989) term the Cognitive Psychology/Artificial Intelligence paradigm, an interdisciplinary framework of Computational and Developmental research which, it is hoped, will result in new computer-based environments to foster intellectual development. At the centre is the computational metaphor for the mind and the familiar Cognitive Science endeavour of constructing models of mental processes. Moreover, the debate about the introduction of computers into UK classrooms is ever in danger of polarizing into those writers who mount a hugely enthusiastic advocacy (a mixture of people drawn from the New Technology industries, business and commerce, educational technologists, academics and 'missionary' teachers, often Mathematicians) and an equally spirited dismissal of the alleged benefits (by academics and teachers who argue that computers could deskill teachers, impoverish pedagogy, and warp subject sub-cultures and values). What is immediately noticeable in this 'debate' (if it can be termed that!) is the conspicuous absence of classroom-based data to substantiate the various claims and counter-charges. At the centre of this paper, then, is a plea for ethnographers to adopt a higher profile in I.T./Education than they have to date; and, also, for teachers to become more skilled observers and evaluators of their own deployment of, and pupil responses to, microcomputing. Research to date has predominately been of a distanced, schedule-based kind, reifying the technology and heavily 'technicist' as opposed to educationalist, and has ignored the contribution that Educational Ethnography has made to our understanding of classroom processes. In a paper (1989) Hugh Mackay and I attempt to account for the failure of the Sociology of Education in the UK to address IT/Education, either in terms of policy, implementation or effects. We point to the new technology's potential to revolutionize and transform schools and schooling; call for qualitative research to focus on pupil-machine interaction; and for sociologists to reformulate the Sociology of Technology, of which IT/Education would be an important aspect. In writing that paper we became acutely aware of the absence of fieldwork-orientated IT/Education research/evaluation and found ourselves repeatedly having to refer outside the UK for instances: for example, to the USA (Turkle, 1984) and Canada (Olson and Eaton, 1986; Olson, 1988; and Hawes *et al.*, 1988).

Although classroom ethnographers have not figured prominently in the debates surrounding microcomputers into classrooms, there are some promising signs that the situation is about to change. If by 'naturalistic studies' is meant research that employs, with various degrees of rigour, fieldwork data gathering mechanisms (for example, participant and non-participant observation, and formal and informal interviewing), then the outlook begins to look brighter, as the following examples illustrate: Jackson (1987) on English teaching and the new technology; Wright (1987) on teacher's views on technology in two primary schools; Medway (1988) on the Technical and Vocational Education Initiative (TVEI) and its implications for English teaching (and further reports referring to the same project by Barnes *et al.*, 1987; Medway and Yeoman, 1988; and Busher *et al.*, 1987); Hughes *et al.* (1987) on pupils' perceptions of computers; and Mackay's (forthcoming) work on definitions of computer literacy in secondary schools. Equally positive are some of the small-scale case studies undertaken by teachers and reported in the UK/USA Final Report of the Micro-Electronic Project (1987). One looks, also, to the Economic and Social Research Council (ESRC)-sponsored Computers Into Classrooms project (started in October, 1988) — to employ fieldwork procedures and, thereby, help redress the quantitative and positivist bias to current research.

Structure of this Paper

I have referred to the scarcity of naturalistic research into IT/Education in the UK but there are, of course, a small number of notable exceptions to which I shall now turn. In *Section 1* I first contextualize them by providing an overview of Naturalistic Studies in the UK by identifying the two principal strands and their defining characteristics. In *Section 2* I focus specifically on

IT/Education and on five 'naturalistic' studies, namely the UNCAL project in the late 1970s; the DTI evaluation, papers from which are now beginning to appear; a recent Micros Into Primary Schools Project; an IT/Education implementation study in a secondary school; and, finally, a study of gender-differentiated usage of computers in secondary schools. By relating their contents in some detail I hope to provide American readers with a good idea both of the extent to which classrooms in the UK have been 'technologized' and of the main contemporary debates.

SECTION 1

Naturalistic Research in the UK—An Overview

To talk about 'naturalistic research' in the UK context is, as Atkinson and Delamont (1980) make clear, to refer to something different from that found in America. If the American and Canadian tradition is predominantly anthropological, then the UK one is sociological in orientation and inspired by the Chicago School of Mead, Blumer, Becker and Goffman. In the UK, two principal modes of naturalistic enquiry have come into prominence over the past decade and a half, namely:

— Educational Ethnography, drawing heavily on Symbolic Interactionism, which has now established itself as a force to be reckoned with in UK research;
— the 'illuminative evaluation' work associated with the Centre For Applied Research Into Education (CARE) at the University of East Anglia, Norwich, and which has been a highly influential role model in the furtherance of evaluative and 'action' research.

I shall now briefly portray each.

Educational Ethnography in the UK

The application of ethnography to school and classroom processes was pioneered in the UK in the late 1960s, most notably by David Hargreaves (1967 and 1972) and Colin Lacey (1970). Their work was influential in developing amongst like-minded Sociologists a commitment to an 'anthropology of classrooms' which did not manipulate, control or eliminate variables, but concentrated on subjective processes. Furthermore, they noted the already well-developed and productive tradition of classroom observation across the Atlantic. Previous classroom studies heavily relied on standardized measures to rate teacher-pupil interaction, with the school viewed through management and organizational theory. Educational Ethnography, it was hoped, would correct some of the assumptions made by 'black box' researchers who took internal school processes largely for granted. The shift of research emphasis was from what schooling does (for example, the 'political arithmetic' of inequality of opportunity) to how it is done, from product back to process, backed up by renewed attention to Meadian and Schutzian philosophy. This led economic/reproduction theorists of education to accuse ethnographers of treating classrooms as if they were outside society and for ignoring external factors: micro-level research, it was often implied, was atheoretical and unsystematic, exhibiting gross empiricism and paying undue attention to 'negotiation'. The recurrent criticisms made of the Symbolic Interactionist/Ethnography model were that:

— it failed to move beyond observable forms and simplified the interactive process;
— it attributed too much autonomy to the actor, whereas determining influences governing actions may reside outside the individual; may not be directly visible; and may not even impinge on daily consciousness;
— it did not produce conceptual generalizations and theoretical explanations beyond the particular.

Others argued that if only the micro- and macro-level approaches to research could somehow be linked their respective shortcomings would be countered. A number of writers have subsequently attempted this (for example, Hargreaves, 1978 and 1979; Woods, 1979, 1980a and 1980b; Pollard, 1979, 1980, 1982 and 1985), whilst others have suggested that it is both proper and desirable that there should be multiple sociologies of the classroom (for example, Delamont, 1978 and 1983). Beyond this there are still fundamental problems in linking micro- and macro-level work: what is to be brought together and can links be made in terms of theory, method, data, or all three (Meyenn, 1980)? Neither can the micro be taken as a simple or partial reflection of the macro, but the danger of a clumsy lumping together remains.

Meanwhile, David Hargreaves (1978) argued that the task was not to link but articulate theory at each level. Hammersley (1980), in calling for ethnographers to operate at the macro level, brought into play Glaser and Strauss' (1967) distinction between 'the formal' (abstract and theoretical) and 'the substantive' (accounts and theories referring to the internal working of a particular setting) to map out four complementary modes of research, namely the 'micro-formal', 'macro-formal', 'micro-substantive', and 'macro-substantive' (Figure 7.1). Interactionists must not simply assert the existence of structural links, but demonstrate them.

However, in spite of the many reservations towards ethnography, including those of researchers claming a more 'scientific' stance, it seems that at the end of the day it alone can provide the wealth of real-life, processual data to

	Formal	Substantive
Macro	For example: Marxian types of socio-historical development Parsons on the Social System	For example: Marx and Weber on Capitalism Bernstein on open and closed forms of schooling
Micro	For example: Goffman on interaction rituals Sacks on conversational organization	For example: Hargreaves, Lacey and Ball on subcultural differentiation and polarization Woods on adaptational modes

Figure 7.1:   Modes of research

complement (and sometimes correct) abstract theorizing and, also, generate new theory.

Although Woods (1983), for example, opined that the 'micro situation can only be understood properly if it is realized that there are sinews and filaments in it that reach out into the wider world', he applauded the attention to concepts which involved both micro and macro elements (for example, 'strategy'); and called for an extension of the range of approaches and fresh developments in theory and teamwork research. Since the early 1980s interest in Educational Ethnography has grown and the flow of high quality classroom-based ethnographies, as well as guides to field procedures, has continued unabated both in this country and America.

The CARE Evaluators

The CARE model of evaluation is one that remains close to the common-sense knowledge of the practitioners and the milieu in which they work. The objective is not to pursue a theoretical but a practical understanding of a situation, an understanding which is valid for them. The worth of a school project is accorded by its participating teachers, therefore, rather than by academics. The justification is that only such applied research can result in 'practical theories' to guide practical actions and, thereby, break down traditional barriers between the evaluators, participants and the wider world. A distinction is thus drawn between a research as opposed to an evaluation approach, the latter being seen to contact directly with the setting it studies as it conveys, rather than explains, multiple interpretations of that setting. Such 'condensed fieldwork' is founded on practitioner values, is descriptive, makes no recommendations, refrains from researcher interpretation and attempts to protect participants from the possible adverse consequences of the research. The emphasis is firmly upon understanding rather than the application of any previous 'findings' as it avoids 'contaminating' or obscuring data with interpretations or theories. Indeed, the process of 'illumination' is aptly termed as it is meant to assist participants to develop insights into their work and to carry this process on after the evaluator has left the scene. It works in a Democratic (as opposed to an Autocratic or Bureaucratic) mode in that it claims to provide a better basis for taking decisions, that is, by the close examination and discussion of instances of action and their key constituents. In the process it raises the issue of who research is for and whose interests it should serve. It is a model which places teachers at the centre as interpreters of constraints, mediators of conflicts and generators of ideas and solutions. Meanwhile, the role of the researcher is akin to that of a broker in that s/he is involved in the exchange of information between groups who require information of each other. S/he strives to be neutral and refuses to work for sectional interests but for the wider benefit of all. S/he negotiates which areas s/he will study as opposed to impressing them upon the situation, so that what finally emerges is not the researcher's understanding but the subjects'. Indeed, s/he takes care not to smuggle his/her own values into the enterprise as s/he collects definitions. Neither is s/he a 'change agent' as much as an explorer of participants' actions, interpretations and concepts. Evaluation is based on a set of developing principles rather than an adherence to any grand theory, and is an innovative form of data gathering and a radical attempt to create a new tradition of research rather than another form of academic theorizing.

However, it is the debate concerning the ethics of fieldwork and evaluation engaged in by CARE workers throughout the 1970s which is one of their most enduring contributions. Against the evaluator as 'honest broker' of information is the argument that s/he, nevertheless, has responsibilities to a wider audience, namely the general public. Although participants have a right to privacy, where their activities impinge on public interests then they forfeit that right. Indeed, democratic evaluation can itself become manipulative in that in the politics of access/confidentiality and negotiation/release all the power can too readily reside in the evaluator's hands. S/he can so easily override participants' might of control for the sake of securing release. Furthermore, the 'right to privacy' and the public's 'right to know' cannot always be made to fit. Indeed, tension between the ethics of access and release are most evident in those instances where some participants have more scope than others for editing out 'discreditable' aspects of a report.

In spite of the undoubted value of such a debate the 'illuminative evaluators' have, nevertheless, been heavily criticized on a number of counts. For Goodson (1977), for example, evaluation fails because:

— there is too great a reliance on participants' taken-for-granted perceptions, which may pass uncontested;

— the research model is ahistorical and does not pay enough attention to how settings (and people) are the products of previous decisions, policies and experiences;

— it is too locked into the personal and private nature of the evaluator's perceptions and reasoning.

Similary, for Barton and Lawn (1981) evaluative reports have been too elective, subjective and free wheeling, often based on insufficient data. They criticize the methodology for being conservative in that the evaluators do not challenge or interject new questions, findings or theories into the world of the practitioner perspective. Neither need participants' accounts always be consistent with his/her actions, and perceptions can be inconsistent and change in a short space of time. However, perhaps the most serious charge against the CARE case study evaluators is made by Atkinson and Delamont (1981), who accuse them of not taking ethnographic methods seriously and, as a consequence, producing one-off cameos of particular locations which cannot be accumulated and related together in any meaningful or coherent manner. The results of such case study research is doomed to remain unreconcilable and idiosyncratic. By turning away from interpretive methods they deny the power of ethnography to generate analytical concepts which facilitates comparison across settings and leads to formal concepts and theoretical insights. In spite of the debates on the ethics of data gathering and release they believe that evaluation fieldwork has not been carried out with the necessary care and systematic rigour, each report remaining trapped inside the straitjacket of each setting. Like Barton and Lawn they call for evaluation to take cognizance of structural factors beyond the participants' arena. Analysis is too readily traded-in for naive portrayal and yet, ironically, it is the former that is likely to be more helpful to participants.

SECTION 2: THE PROJECTS

CARE has been linked to IT/Education evaluation for over a decade, notably through the evaluation of the National Development Project into Computer Assisted Learning in the late 1970s, and recently by the evaluation of the Department of Trade and Industry's Micros Into Schools initiative. I shall only briefly comment on the first, more fully on the second given its contemporary relevance.

UNCAL
This is perhaps best remembered for its attempt to obtain critical purchase on CAL's contribution to the curriculum at different levels of demand; and then to draw up a typology of student-computer interactions so that some initial sense could be made of them using observational data. It was a four year

evaluation project (MacDonald, 1977 a and b; Kemmis, 1977) which established four major principles of procedure:

— independence (in that it set itself to be independent of its sponsors);
— confidentiality of data;
— negotiation of access and release of data with those evaluated;
— a non-recommendatory stance, with data collected largely through unconstructed interviews and observations of circumstances, actions and consequences.

The significant shift was that the UNCAL Project turned its back on tests of student attainment and focused instead on what happened when students used CAL, which was defined in terms of four curricular paradigms:

— Instructional CAL, involving drill, practice and tutorial activities;
— Revelatory CAL, utilizing simulations and 'trial-and-error' exercises;
— Conjectural CAL, relating to the creation of 'new' knowledge;
— Emancipatory CAL, encompassing activities that free individuals from routine, time-consuming tasks.

Furthermore, a five-fold typology of student-CAL interactions was developed, as follows:

— Recognition tasks, involving 'yes-or-no' types of response;
— Recall tasks, typically requiring 'fill-in-the-blank' kinds of responses;
— Reconstructive understanding tasks, usually of the 'multiple-choice' variety;
— Global reconstructive tasks, calling for open-ended responses and analytic, synthetic and creative solutions;
— Constructive understanding tasks, demanding even more open-ended and original responses.

Whilst these types may be too narrowly task-orientated and rigid to describe the range of individual and group responses and spin-off activities occasioned by the best practices in contemporary IT/Education, they have yet yet to be picked-up, tasted, extended and re-defined by UK researchers. They still constitute a good starting point, albeit approaching the interactions more from the nature of the technology's demands than that of pupils' actual sense-making and responses.

DTI's Micros Into Schools evaluation
The evaluation team, commissioned by the Department of Trade and Industry (DTI) in 1987, was again led by Barry MacDonald (1988) and consisted of Bridget Somekh, John Sohostak and Catherine Beattie. The brief was a retrospective evaluation of the DTI's Micros Into Schools Support Scheme, 1981 – 1984, and to make recommendations for future action. To do this they:

— reviewed the relevant literature;

— surveyed by questionnaire a wide sample of knowledgeable users and key informants;
— undertook field-based 'mini-case studies' of contemporary IT/Education practices in three local education authorities.

This evaluation (Somekh, 1988) deserves close scrutiny not only for the clarity of its recommendations but also because it provides the most up-to-date picture of IT/Education implementation in the UK at the present time. The limitations are honestly laid out at the outset, namely time constraints which meant that the literature review was not exhaustive and the survey 'was neither piloted nor validated by the standard procedures for constructing questionnaires'. More importantly, the sample was 'based largely on personal knowledge of the relevant community by the evaluators' and only 66 per cent completed the questionnaire. No claims are made for representativeness across the country, therefore, and the mini-case studies are presented as 'impressionistic accounts, lacking the authority of fully negotiated inter-subjective agreement'. Yet the convergence of conclusions across the separate strands of the evaluation allowed the team to claim with confidence that the findings and recommendations would be likely to 'command widespread support in the educational community'.

The conclusion was that the DTI intervention had been decisive in promoting computer awareness; however, when judged in purely educational terms, some policy decisions had been ill-advised, with little time for teachers to prepare, especially given the inadequacy of the in-service traning provision. Moreover, software was typically 'educationally retrogressive' and few teachers were aware of the full capabilities of the hardware: as a result often ineffective use was made of micros. The scheme had been too rushed and would have been better if based upon adequate research insights. Furthermore, although the IT/Education literature has consistently advocated exciting uses to develop open-ended enquiry learning, in practice usage has been generally pedestrian and dominated by drill and practice. However, the evaluation reported different overall pictures in primary and secondary schools. The former are presented as generally engaging in better micro usage, although there is a continuing need for more resources. The organization of the day into extended periods of time with one teacher, and the lack of pressure from examination syllabuses, has encouraged group collaboration and cross-curricular work. The primary environment, being more flexible, has made it easier for teachers to experiment and fit the computer into the curriculum, unhindered by rigid timetables and subject boundaries. Conversely, the tighter organization and management of secondary schools has obstructed the use of micros for cross-curricular work. As a result, computers in secondary schools have been used primarily in examinable subjects (Computer and Business Studies, for instance) so that only some pupils (and some teachers) have had ready access to them. Whereas, in general, children are well-disposed towards computers, teachers in UK schools are less favourably inclined, either because they feel incompetent, or because the available facilities are inadequate, or because they are not yet convinced of their educational potential. Nevertheless, the evaluation stresses that the long-term implications of IT/Education on curriculum, pedagogy and school organization and management are likely to be radical and states that:

> Too little is still known about the effect on children's minds of the experience of growing up in a computer-based society. In short, we need to have a variety of models for the new 'electronic classrooms' and their relationship to society which will take us into the 21st Century.

The evaluation concludes that 'in 1988 it is clear that a beachhead in [UK] schools has been established, but no more'. As a consequence there is no room for complacency but an urgent need for:

— more and better machines and vastly improved educational deployment;
— more in-service training and research-based curriculum development projects which centre on the use of sophisticated packages;
— the development of flexibility of response to varied computer environments given that the rapid pace of technological change makes it impossible to predict with any certainty the skill demands of even the near future.

Finally, the evaluation made some interesting points about girls and computers to which I shall refer later.

Micros into Primary Schools project and related projects
In 1985 researchers based at King's college, London, undertook case studies in six Inner London Education Authority (ILEA) primary schools to identify factors that promote or inhibit the uptake of Information Technology; and, also, to examine classroom attitudes arising from uptake. Data was gathered through interviews with sixty-five teachers and six heads, and sixty-two hours of activities were observed (Hall and Rhodes, 1988). As a result recommendations were made regarding: (i) the use of microcomputers by young children; (ii) teacher intervention; (iii) Teacher Education; and (iv) general policy for the promotion of IT/Education.

The project followed a three-year pilot scheme in ILEA from 1981 to 1983 which had examined the introduction of micros into teaching in twenty-two schools, some of which had, by 1985, established regular use. Amongst the most interesting points made by the 1988 investigation (excluding references to gender-differentiated usage to which I shall turn later) were:

— whilst children were observed capably organizing themselves when working with the micro it was noted that a small number of children were gaining superior knowledge of the micro in comparison to their peers. Hall and Rhodes comment that teachers must try to involve all children to a similar extent in micro activities and avoid encouraging 'individual experts';

— children working in pairs were more successful than in groups or individually, but the pairing of children of disparate abilities tended to be less successful and required a high degree of teacher intervention to be beneficial;

— children were observed to maintain concentration over longer periods than might have been expected when working on the same topic with different media. Teachers need to check that concentration is being maintained and that the activity remains educationally relevant as opposed to being merely an 'occupying activity';

— valuable task-oriented social activity frequently occurs when children engage in micro activity together, even in the absence of teacher input;

— word-processing programmes are particularly beneficial to the furtherance of literacy, allowing pupils to concentrate on content and encouraging interaction between writing, talking, reading and experience skills. Indeed, the editing and printing facilities are highly motivating and aid the production of texts which can be a valuable addition to classroom reading resources;

— teacher intervention in micro activities of primary age children is necessary to encourage children to employ to the full the potential of much software;

— few teachers thought that the use of a micro had significantly influenced their curriculum, teaching style, or relationship with children, and only 40 per cent (16) thought there had been a noticeably positive effect on children's learning;

— several factors were indentified that inhibited micro usage, amongst these: lack of appropriate training; access problems; dissatisfaction with software; and lack of convincing evidence that there are, in fact, educational benefits;

— the opportunity for some children to use a micro but not others should be avoided. It is best for the overall responsibility for computers to be entrusted to one member of staff;

— it is important that both technical and educational aspects of microcomputers in primary schools are addressed in pre-service and in-service courses. Moreover, there is an urgent need for more research into the educational benefits of microcomputers and the best ways for teachers to use them. (A previous study on training primary school teachers to use computers effectively had been carried out from 1985–1987 by Cox and Rhodes in twelve Inner London Education Authority schools and eight Inset courses. This indicated that short courses alone were inadequate to meet teachers' training needs.)

John Beynon

The Barnaby Comprehensive study
There have been few studies to date on the implementation of micros in schools. An exception is that by Bliss, Chandra and Cox (1986), who examined the introduction of computers into Barnaby Comprehensive, 1982–1984, through an analysis at the levels of teachers, departments and school. They conclude that although the general attitude of staff was positive, more than half had serious misgivings. They felt the change in their role occasioned by computers was unfavourable, and they perceived their traditional role as 'importers of knowledge' was threatened.

Amongst the advantages mentioned were that micros were:

— motivational tools promoting individual learning;
— statistical tools offering dynamic visual displays;
— a means for reforming learning through the visual medium.

Amongst the reservations itemized were:

— the quality of software and the danger of encouraging solely game-playing;
— difficulties of access and infrequency of use;
— the problem of brighter pupils overusing computers and the less able losing out.

Seven types of teacher relationship with IT/Education were identified, namely: the favourable; critical; worried; unfavourable; antagonistic; indifferent; and uninitiated. However, the projects's main value lies in stressing the importance of the social atmosphere of the school into which computers are introduced.

Girls and computing
The obstacles encountered by girls and women teachers are referred to in two of the projects detailed above. In their Microcomputers Into Primary Schools Project, Hall and Rhodes record that:

— the child computer 'experts' encountered in classes did not include any girls. Teachers must avoid the reinforcing the emergence of such 'superior' male pupils by involving all pupils in using micros;
— more male teachers attend courses and make use of microcomputers, but female teachers must be given the opportunity to become more involved and so redress what is an unbalanced role model being presented to children;
— there is a need to monitor whether girls are receiving the same range of opportunities to use the micro as boys.

Similarly, the CARE-based study reports that:

There is clearly still a need to ensure that girls are encouraged to use micros and shown positive models of women teachers using them effectively. There is no evidence that girls are hesitant in using micros in the early years of the Primary School, but they often begin to be hesitant towards the end of the Junior School.

This problem is compounded by the fact that many pupils find their experience of computing discontinued when they arrive in the secondary school, and this may be a greater long-term handicap to girls than to boys.

In the same vein Lorraine Culley's (1986 and 1988) research is highly significant in that not only does it look at ways in which in UK secondary schools computing may become a masculine activity, but argues that:

> ... in girls-only schools there is no shortage of enthusiasm for computing; that Computer Studies is a popular option; and that Computer Clubs thrive. Since outside social influences are unlikely to be radically different for girls attending single-sex schools, the processes involved in the organization of teaching with and about computers in a co-educational setting must be significant.

She acknowledges that the practices of schools and teachers are not the sole factors involved in gender stereotyping, which carries the weight of wider social forces. Computing in secondary schools is essentially a masculine domain and thus recreates existing social and gender relations, attitudes and assumptions. It is massively associated with male staff; mathematical concepts and departments; fits in neatly with the gender differentiation of subject/option choices; and, as a result, plays relatively little part in girls' hopes for the future, whereas it is central to those of many boys. Since home computing is dominated by fathers and sons, girls are less familiar and confident with computers and boys assume this lack of interest and incompetence is part of 'being a girl'.

Amongst her suggestions to counter gender-based bias in computing are:

— a breaking of the link between Mathematics and Computer Studies and a monitoring, from a gender standpoint, of option organization and choices;
— the elimination of Mathematical and Technological bias from Computer Awareness courses;
— that more female teachers should become involved with computers — across the curriculum;
— an examination of the subtle processes of gender differentiation and a countering of boys' domination through the introduction of alternative teaching strategies;
— single sex classes in computing/Computer Studies, with gender itself on the agenda of Information Technology and Inset Courses.

Conclusion

In the opening section I attempted brief critical portraits of the two most no-table naturalistic paradigms to have emerged in the UK in the 1970s and 1980s, namely the Ethnographic and the Illuminative Evaluative. In the sec-ond section I summarized in some detail for American readers, who may be unfamiliar with the work, some of the issues to have emerged from recent 'naturalistic' (defined broadly) studies of aspects of IT/Education in the UK. My choice and acount is a personal one, but it can be said with some justification that both CARE and the Educational Computing Unit of King's College, London, already have a considerable track record in monitoring the impact of microcomputers on schools. None of the five studies (including Culley's) can be described as 'ethnographic' even though each, in part, employs observation. I am not, of course, implying they should be criticized for this: on the contrary, they are eclectic in the methods employed and make no attempt to locate themselves in Symbolic Interactionism or Interpretive Sociology. What I am saying, however, is that in my view there is an urgent need for ethnographers (employing the accepted canons of participant/non-participant observation; formal/informal interviewing; grounded theory; life histories; and a concern for the systematic collection and analysis of data) to study IT/Education in primary and secondary classrooms. It needs to be studied in a 'bottom-up' manner as opposed to the 'down-loading' of prefor-mulated questionnaires, surveys and other quantitative, mostly narrowly psychometric, devices (Beynon, 1985). In short, it is time to open up research options in the way they have been expanded through the emergence of Class-room Studies (e.g., Hammersley, 1986a and 1986b) throughout the 1980s. In-deed, in the circumstances the five studies described ought to be regarded as remarkable for employing 'naturalistic' methods at all, a point underlined by recent surveys of current and projected enterprises (notably by Govier, 1988; Lewis, 1988; and Morrison, 1988).

If there is a need for ethnographic data, there is also an urgency: at the moment, in spite of the considerable research effort, there is nevertheless a gaping ignorance as to how teachers and pupils *actually use* microcomputers and what the latent and manifest effects are for teaching and learning. As Richards (1987) puts it, given the scale and speed of IT/Education implemen-tation educationalists really must become better informed of 'the most fruitful uses to which these powerful tools can be put and of the kinds of capabilities and attitudes children need to acquire if they are to interact profita-bly with them'. It is my view that for this to happen naturalistic studies of IT/Education in the UK will have to become more vigorously ethnographic. The project currently underway in the University of Western Ontario points the way and one hopes that British researchers will take note. Neither is this a call for yet another academic exercise: on the contrary, ethnography can speak to teachers in a strong, classroom-related way. For Hargreaves (1978), for example, it has at least four immediately useful capacities, namely:

— the 'appreciative', or insights into actors' rationality;
— the 'reflexive', as it acts as a guard against ineffective policy implementations;
— the 'designatory', or the development of an appropriate conceptual discourse;
— the 'corrective', as it corrects bland assumption or simplifications.

I noted earlier the apparent complacency of the Sociology of Education in the UK towards IT/Education. One eminent representative recently commented to me that it was his belief that in ten years time the whole thing would be forgotten as dead as the 'teaching machines' of the 1950s and early 1960s. 'Technology will never revolutionize education', he said. 'All it will ever be is just a few machines bleeping away in a corner.' He may well prove to be correct (although I personally doubt it), but he had to admit that his scenario was every bit as much crystal-gazing as that by Meighan and Reid (1982), who forecast computers will change the very functions and purposes of schools. But, in any case he surely misses the point: we need to know how they are impacting on teachers, pupils and curriculum *now* and, even more importantly, how we can ascertain that what they have to offer is wise, accessible to all, and used in democratic and beneficial ways. This is not going to be achieved by researchers (or teachers) turning their backs on them. Neither, in my opinion, is it going to be achieved by the limited, narrowly prescribed 'scientific' methodology that has attached itself hitherto to IT/Education. Educational Ethnography — with its emphasis upon situated actions, meanings, interpretations and processual detail — can lead to new insights and lines of enquiry. Only with the emergence of micro-substantive and micro-formal theories will a fuller understanding follow of what the 'technologization' of education actually in practice entails.

Acknowledgment

I am grateful to Karen Harris for typing this article at short notice.

Bibliography

ATKINSON, P. and DELAMONT, S. (1980) 'The two traditions in educational ethnography', *British Journal of Sociology of Education,* 1, 2.

ATKINSON, P. and DELAMONT, S. (1981) 'Evaluating Educational Innovations'. Paper to SFAA Conference, Edinburgh.

BARNES, D. *et al.* (1987) 'The TVEI Curriculum, 14–16: An Interim Report'. Available from MSC, Moorfoot, Sheffield S1 4PQ.

BARTON, L. and LAWN, M. (1981) 'Back inside the whale: A curriculum case study', *Interchange.*

BEYNON, J. (1985) *Initial Encounters in a Secondary School: Sussing, mucking and coping,* Falmer Press.

BEYNON, J. (1989) *Towards A New Paradigm of I.T./Education.* Available from Communication Studies, The Polytechnic of Wales, Treforest, Mid Glamorgan, CF37 1DL.

BEYNON, J., and MACKAY, H. (1989) 'Information technology into education: Towards a critical perspective', *Journal of Education Policy.*

BLISS, J., CHANDRA, P. and COX, M. (1986) 'The introduction of computers into a school', *Computer Education,* 10, 1.

BUSHER, H. *et al.* (1987) 'TVEI in Practice: Three Case Studies', TVEI Developments No. 4: available from TVEI A (3), 4th Floor, 236 Grays Inn Road, London.

DELAMONT, S. (1978) 'Sociology and the classroom,' in BARTON, L. and MEIGHAN, R. (Eds) *Sociology Interpretations of Schooling and Classrooms,* Nafferton, Driffield.

DELAMONT, S. (1983) *Interaction in the Classroom,* Methuen, London.

GLASER, B. and STRAUSS, A. (1967) *The Discovery of Grounded Therory,* Wiedenfeld and Nicholson.

GOODSON, I. (1977) 'Evaluation and evolution', in NORRIS, N. (Ed.) *Theory in Practice,* The Safari Project, CARE, University of East Anglia, Norwich.

GOVIER, H. (1988) *Microcomputers in Primary Education: A Survey of Recent Research,* ESRC, 160 Great Portland Street, London, W1N 6BA.

HALL, J. and RHODES, V. (1988) *Microcomputers in Primary Schools: Some Observations and Recommendations for Good Practice.* Available from The Educational Computing Unit, Centre For Educational Studies, King's College, London.

HAMMERSLEY, M. (1980) 'Classroom ethnography', *Educational Analysis,* 2, 2.

HAMMERSLEY, M. (Ed.) (1986a) *Controversies in Classroom Research,* Open University Press.

HAMMERSLEY, M. (Ed.) (1986b) *Case Studies in Classroom Research,* Open University Press.

HARGREAVES, A. (1978) 'Towards a theory of classroom strategies', in BARTON, L. and MEIGHAN, R. (Eds) *Sociological Interpretations of Schooling and Classrooms,* Nafferton.

HARGREAVES, A. (1979) 'Strategies, decision-making and control: Interaction in a middle school classroom', in EGGLESTON, J. (Ed.) *Teacher Decision Making in the Classroom,* Routledge and Kegan Paul.

HARGREAVES, D. (1967) *Social Relations in a Secondary School,* Routledge and Kegan Paul.

HARGREAVES, D. (1972) *Interpersonal Relations and Education,* Routledge and Kegan Paul.

HARGREAVES, D. (1978) 'Whatever happened to S.I.?', BARTON, L. and MEIGHAN, R. (Eds.) *Sociological Interpretations of Schooling and Classrooms,* Nafferton.

HAWES, D. *et al.* (1988) *Schools, Computers and Learning Project,* Ontario Ministry of Education.

HODGES, A. (1984) *Alan Turing: The Enigma,* Unwin.

HUGHES, M. *et al.* (1987) 'Children's ideas about computers', in RUTKOWSKA, J.C. and CROOK, C. *Computers, Cognition and Development,* Wiley, Chichester.

JACKSON, V. (1987) 'English teaching and the new technology', *Educational Review,* 39, 2.

LACEY, C. (1970) *Hightown Grammar,* Manchester University Press.

LEWIS, R. (1988) 'I.T. in Education Research Programme, 1988–93', Occasional Paper Inter/1/88, Available from the Department of Psychology, University of Lancaster, LA1 4YF.

MACDONALD, B. (1977a) 'The educational evaluation of NDPCAL', *British Journal of Educational Technology,* 8, 3, October.

MACDONALD, B. *et al.* (1977b) *The Programme at Two: An UNCAL Companion to Two Years On,* CARE, The University of East Anglia, Norwich.

MEDWAY, P. and YEOMAN, D. (1988) 'Technology Projects In The Fifth Year'. Available from the TVEI Unit, Room 5/11, 236 Grays Inn Road, London WC1X 8HL.

MEIGHAN, R. and REID, W. (1982) 'How will the New Technology change the curriculum?' *Journal of Curriculum Studies*, 14, 4.

MEYENN, R. (1980) 'School girls' peer groups', in WOODS, P. (Ed.) *Teacher Strategies*, Croom Helm.

MORRISON, A. (1988) 'I.T. In Primary Schools: a research review for the Scottish Education Department', Occasional Paper, ITE/30/88, ESRC, 160 Great Portland Street, London, W1N 6BA.

OLSON, J. (1988) *Schoolworlds — Microworlds: Computers and the Culture of the Classroom,* Pergamon Press.

OLSON, J. and EATON, S. (1986) *Case Studies of Microcomputers in the Classroom,* Toronto, Ministry of Education.

POLLARD, A. (1979) 'Negotiating deviance', in BARTON, L. and MEIGHAN, R. (Ed.) *Schools, Pupils and Deviance*, Nafferton.

POLLARD, A. (1980) 'Teacher interests and changing situations of survival threat', in WOODS, P. (Ed.) *Teacher Strategies*, Croom Helm.

POLLARD, A. (1982) 'A model of coping strategies', *British Journal of Sociology of Education*, March.

POLLARD, A. (1985) *The Social World of the Primary School*, Holt, Rinehart and Winston,

RICHARDS, C. (1987) 'Primary education in England: An analysis of some recent issues and developments', in DELAMONT, S. (Ed.) *The Primary School Teacher*, Falmer Press.

SOMEKH, B. (1988) 'Micro reflections'. Paper delivered to BERA Symposium on IT/Education, University of East Anglia, September.

TURKLE, S. (1984) *The Second Self*, Granada.

WOODS, P. (1979) *The Divided School*, Routledge and Kegan Paul

WOODS, P. (Ed.) (1980a) *Teacher Strategies,* Groom Helm.

WOODS, P. (Ed.) (1980b) *Pupil Strategies*, Croom Helm.

WOODS, P. (1983) *Sociology and the School*, Routledge and Kegan Paul.

WRIGHT, A. (1987) 'The process of microtechnological innovation in two primary schools', *Educational Review*, 39, 2.

Notes on Contributors

John Beynon is Reader and course Tutor of the BA in Communication Studies and MA in Communication, Culture and Society at the Polytechnic of Wales. A former comprehensive school teacher and journalist, he has published extensively in the areas of classroom interaction and ethnographic methodology, notably *Initial Encounters* (Falmer Press, 1985) and *Be a Man!* (Routledge and Kegan Paul, forthcoming. His work in computers in education has culminated in three volumes, *Understanding Technology in Education*, (1991) edited with Hughie Mackay and Michael Young, and *Technological Literacy and Curriculum*, (1991) and *Computers into Classrooms* (1992) edited with Hughie Mackay, all published by Falmer Press.

Robert L. Blomeyer, Jr. is presently a faculty member in the Curriculum and Instruction Department in the College of Education at Oregon State University. Before OSU he was an assistant professor in the Curriculum and Instruction Department at the University of Houston specializing in research and teaching concerning microcomputer applications and computer literacy for teachers. He has recently participated in a strategic planning symposium organized jointly by the Czechoslovakian Foreign Ministry and WACRA (*Czechoslovakia in Transition: Developing Strategic Initiatives with Case Study Methodologies*, October 7–12, 1990). Dr Blomeyer and other symposium participants will contribute to developing specific educational projects to aid Czechoslovakia and other new European democracies in transition to the global market economy.

Daniel McLaughlin is Assistant Professor of Multicultural Education and Curriculum in the Graduate School of Education at the University of Utah. Before moving into higher education, he spent thirteen years a teacher and an administrator in community-controlled schools on the Navajo reservation. He has been editor of the *Journal of Navajo Education* since 1988. His most recent article is 'The Sociolinguistics of Navajo Literacy', *Anthropology and*

Education Quarterly (1989). His forthcoming book entitled *When Literacy Empowers: An Ethnography of English and Navajo Print* is to be published by the University of New Mexico Press in 1991.

C. Dianne Martin is Assistant Professor in the Department of Electrical Engineering and Computer Science at The George Washington University, Washington, DC. She has been invited three times to the Soviet Union as a computer specialist to present seminars on computers in education. Her current research interests include use of hypermedia to collect, analyze and report on qualitative research, school district implementation of micro-computers for instruction, and ethics and social impact education in computer science. Her recent publications include *Bits 'n Bytes About Computing: A Computer Literacy Primer* (Heller and Martin, 1982) and LOGOWORLDS (1983) published by Computer Science Press, 'School District Implementation of Microcomputers for Instruction', *Journal of Research on Computers in Education*, (Winter, 1988) and 'Professional Codes of Conduct and Computer Ethics Education' (Martin and Martin), *Social Science Computer Review*, Spring, 1990.

Paul A. Pohland is Professor of Educational Administration in the College of Education at the University of New Mexico in Albuquerque, New Mexico. He received his PhD in 1970 from Washington University in St. Louis. His doctoral dissertation entitled *An Inter-organizational Analysis*, is an alter-native intepretation of data gathered during the 1968–9 research leading to publication of 'Educational Technology and the Rural Highlands' by Smith and Pohland in *AERA Monograph Series on Curriculum Evaluation, Number Seven, Four Evaluation Examples: Anthropological, Economic, Narrative and Portrayal*, R. Stake (ed.) 1974. Professor Pohland continues to be a signifi-cant influence on case research in educational administration. He is the coordinator of the New Mexico Principals' Center and has been editor for *New Mexico Case Records in School Administration* (New Mexico Principals' Center 1988, 1989 and 1990) and contributor to many other publications.

Ray C. Rist is Director of Operations in the General Government Division, United States General Accounting Office. His extensive knowledge of evaluation design principles has helped construct the proper analytical framework for GAO jobs as diverse as reviews of defense programs to education and employment work. His work in the areas of program evaluation and policy analysis spans nearly 20 years and has involved him in countless studies at the local, state, national, and international levels. His 14 books have been published by, among others, Harvard University Press, MIT Press, Columbia University Press and Klett-Cotta Press of Stuttgart, Germany. His most recent books are *Policy Studies Review Annual, Vol. 8* (Transaction Books, 1986) and *Finding Work: Cross-National Perspectives on Employment and Training Policy* (Falmer Press, 1987).

Louis M. Smith is Professor of Education at Washington University in St. Louis, Missouri. He is a contributor to and continuing influence on naturalistic and case study research as a tool for understanding education. His recent publications include *Educational Innovations: Then and Now* (1986), *The Fate of an Innovative School* (1987), and *Innovation and Change in Schooling: History, Politics, and Agency* (1988).

Bernadine Stake is a Professor in the Curriculum and Instruction Department, University of Illinois. In addition to teaching, she has considerable experience in program evaluation. She was Co-Director of two national project evaluations on gender equity, the 'Evaluation of a National Sex Equity Demonstration Project' in Florida and the 'Non-Sexist Teacher Education Project' in Washington, DC. Stake is involved in making interactive videotapes of classroom children learning science and mathematics through critical thinking and problem-solving. She is also active in her community, where she has served on the Urbana City Council for 16 years.

Neal Strudler is Assistant Professor in the Department of Instructional and Curricular Studies, University of Nevada, Las Vegas. He began his career as a classroom teacher, before becoming assistant principal working on a large scale evaluation of a proposed computer curriculum in the Eugene, Oregon public schools. Strudler has been the Editor of books and courseware for the International Society for Technology in Education since 1987. He is currently a professor and program coordinator of the technology in education program at the University of Nevada. In that role, he is teaching both graduate and undergraduate classes designed to help teachers integrate technology into their instruction. He views himself as a change agent helping to prepare more change agents. He has written many articles, most recently 'Software Review of AppleWorks 3.0' (Dec. 1988) and 'Teaching Thinking Skills with Data-bases' (Jan 1989) in *The Computing Teacher*.

Index